Southwest Ireland

Getting Your Bearings
In Four Days
Don't Miss
- Cork City
- Kissing the Blarney Stone
- Ring of Kerry
- Dingle Peninsula (Corca Dhuibhne)

At Your Leisure: More places to explore
Where to... ■ Eat and Drink ■ Stay ■ Shop
■ Be Entertained

West and Northwest Ireland

Getting Your Bearings
In Four Days
Don't Miss
- The Burren and the Cliffs of Moher
- The Aran Islands (Oileáin Árann)
- Connemara
- West Mayo

At Your Leisure: More places to explore
Where to... ■ Eat and Drink ■ Stay ■ Shop
■ Be Entertained

Northern Ireland

Getting Your Bearings
In Three Days
Don't Miss
- Belfast
- The Antrim Coast
- Ulster-American Folk Park
- Lough Erne and Belleek Pottery

At Your Leisure: More places to explore
Where to... ■ Eat and Drink ■ Stay ■ Shop
■ Be Entertained

Walks & Tours

- 1 Hill of Howth
- 2 Blackwater Bog
- 3 Croagh Patrick
- 4 Yeats Country
- 5 Walls of Derry
- 6 Strangford Lough

Practicalities 187

- Before You Go
- When to Go
- When You Are There

Atlas 193

Index 203

Written by Christopher Somerville
Revised and updated by Christopher Somerville

Project Editor Claire Strange
Project Designer Alison Fenton
Series Editor Karen Rigden
Series Designer Catherine Murray

Published by AA Publishing, a trading name of Automobile Association
Developments Limited, whose registered office is Fanum House,
Basing View, Basingstoke, Hampshire, RG21 4EA. Registered number
1878835.

ISBN: 978-0-7495-5970-0

The contents of this publication are believed correct at the time
of printing. Nevertheless, AA Publishing accept no responsibility
for errors, omissions or changes in the details given, or for the
consequences of readers' reliance on this information. This does not
affect your statutory rights. Assessments of the attractions, hotels and
restaurants are based upon the author's own experience and contain
subjective opinions that may not reflect the publisher's opinion or
a reader's experience. We have tried to ensure accuracy, but things
do change, so please let us know if you have any comments or
corrections.

A CIP catalogue record for this book is available from the British
Library

New Edition 2009

Cover design and binding style by permission of AA Publishing
Colour separation by Keenes, Andover
Printed and bound in China by Leo Paper Products

Find out more about AA Publishing and the wide range of services
the AA provides by visiting our website at www.theAA.com/bookshop

IRELAND

SPIRALGUIDE

AA Publishing

Contents

The Magazine

A great holiday is more than just lying on a beach or shopping till you drop — to really get the most from your trip you need to know what makes the place tick. The Magazine provides an entertaining overview to some of the social, cultural and natural elements that make up Ireland's unique character.

MODERN IRELAND

If you're coming to Ireland expecting leprechauns round the corner and a wise old countryman ruminating over every gate, you're in for quite a surprise. Ireland has moved a long way from the old stereotypes in the past few years.

These days the likes of Dublin, Cork, Galway and Belfast are some of the most vibrant and forward-looking cities in Europe. That's not to say that the old, gentle-paced and charming rural life has vanished. Far from it: you only need to turn off the main road and travel five minutes up the country lane to find that much-loved Emerald Isle, still alive and in full vigour just behind the sleek and prosperous new face of Ireland.

CITY...

The economic boom of the 1990s and early 21st century – known as the "Celtic Tiger" – has injected money, energy and a brash confidence into what had become in many ways a stagnant society. The Tiger roared loudest in Dublin; the sleepy old city on the River Liffey has transformed itself into a go-getting modern city with an ever-rising skyline.

...AND COUNTRY

The landscape of Ireland is changing, too – more building, more development – some of it good, some not so good. But along with the action has come the reaction – a greatly increased concern about environmental degradation. A new gas pipeline in remote County Mayo, a motorway pushed through in the shadow of ancient Tara of the Kings, windfarms on the glorious coasts and hills of the West of Ireland: each has met with protest and debate, and a determination to preserve the incomparably beautiful, rain-softened landscapes of the island.

LOOKING FORWARD

Rather than youngsters having to emigrate to find work, they are staying in Ireland these days. There's a great new atmosphere in the North, too, where political stability has arrived and brought optimism and enthusiasm along with it.

Below: Pedestrians enjoying the Millennium Walk beside the Liffey
Bottom: Belfast is undergoing a rapid development into a bright, modern city

GO FOR GREEN

If it's true that you can tell all about a country by the way it plays its sports, then Ireland is romantic, whole-hearted, crazily optimistic and remarkably successful for its size.

WATCHING THE BEST

Sports are played professionally all over Ireland, many of them attracting top-class international competitors – golf, for example, with both the Ryder Cup and Solheim Cup competitions, can boast numerous courses across the island, many in fabulous coastal locations. The Republic's soccer team have reached the finals of three world cups (1990, 1994 and 2002), while Northern Ireland's adventure in the 1958 World Cup Finals (they reached the quarter-finals) is a much-told tale. The popularity of rugby union is on the rise as is the quality of the game itself and the sport is sure to go from strength to strength in the coming years.

> "The celebrated love affair between the Irish and their horses goes back thousands of years"

The celebrated love affair between the Irish and their horses goes back thousands of years, and Irish race meetings – especially at The Curragh in Co Kildare, one of the best-known tracks in the world – regularly gather huge and extremely knowledgeable crowds, who bet as if stones were sovereigns.

JOINING IN

Professionals may catch the headlines, but games are played among friends, hard and humorously, just for the fun of it (all right, and in a spirit of healthy competition too), throughout Ireland. Beach-based sports are becoming hugely popular: kitesurfing in Cork, kiteboarding in Clare, surfing in Donegal, kitebuggying and landboarding in Derry. Country walking and hill climbing have been greatly facilitated by the development of nearly 40 waymarked ways. Fishing remains one of the great visitor attractions, too. There are also a number of country sports such as informal trotting races, and the extraordinary road bowling of south Armagh and west Cork, which involves players propelling an iron ball along a couple of miles of back country lanes in as few throws as possible – a finely developed skill.

GAELIC GAMES

Of the sports played in Ireland, it is the traditional Gaelic games that bind the Irish most effectively together as a nation. The two most spectacular ancient traditional sports are Gaelic football (in which players can kick and hit the ball), and hurling. To be part of a shouting, partisan crowd at a hurling match, as the players race the length of the pitch and whack the *sliotar,* or leather ball, with their club-like hurleys, is to taste true passion both on and off the field – whether you are among 80,000 at Dublin's Croke Park for the All-Ireland Final, or at a local ground way out in the sticks.

Elation after winning at The Curragh

THE *CRAIC*
"A GOOD TIME"

The word sounds like "crack", and the English write it like that – short, sharp and brusque, a shape entirely at odds with the word's true meaning. The Irish do it better: they write it as *craic*, a gentler idea altogether.

THE MIGHTY *CRAIC*

You might discover it while lazing under a hedge in County Kerry in the company of travellers. You're certain to discover it in Kilkenny if you catch the Cat Laughs Comedy Festival. You could stumble across it bubbling away in the kitchen of some anonymous bungalow in a suburb of Belfast or Dublin. It's likely to come your way among the horse-racing gamblers at The Curragh of Kildare, or the yelling fans at a hurling match, or Trinity College students celebrating just about anything. And it's a guaranteed certainty that you'll find the *craic* wherever musicians or storytellers, country farmers or city youngsters meet round a few pints of stout.

A RICH STEW

The *craic* is a mood, something in the air that can blow in out of nowhere. It is a bottomless pot into which anyone may throw anything. But the rich stew of the *craic* generally contains one or more of the following ingredients: music, lively chat, a spice of argument, a pinch of nonsense, a drop of strong drink or a sup of tea, a bite of food, and laughter – a

Whether the music is planned (right) or spontaneous (above), everyone has a good time

Another excuse to get together and have fun

gallon of laughter. The *craic* wears a number of different guises, according to what's going on and who's taking part. It could be great *craic* just sitting and listening in a country pub where locals have gathered to sift through their well-worn stock of jokes, songs and tall tales; or huddled out of the rain in a tin hut with two blarneying roadmen; or being whirled round by a total stranger in some unfamiliar dance at a village *céilidh*. Or the *craic* might be mightier still in an overcrowded bar in city-centre Belfast where the jokes fly black and strong, or among a clutch of elegant girls with their heads together round a table in Dublin's trendy Temple Bar district.

> "something in the air that can blow in out of nowhere"

Sometimes you pass it by, grin and keep on going; sometimes it reaches out and sucks you in.

This has to do with the Irish way of viewing the stranger as a bundle of possibilities, the chance provider of a story, song or bit of chat, rather than as a potential threat or source of embarrassment. When you enter a bar or a shop, you can expect to be sized up, questioned and drawn into conversation. There's nothing rude or sinister in this; it's just a very friendly nosiness, a hospitable opening of the door.

CRAIC FOR ALL

People can get all snobbish about the *craic,* holding that it cannot possibly rear its head around manufactured tourist events such as medieval

Green is much in evidence at any St Patrick's Day parade

THE MIGHTY *CRAIC*

The *Craic* Excited

"…So then the door flies open and in comes a man fit for dancing and he gets up on the floor there and starts into the jig. By this time there's a fiddle going and the whole room dancing…Fierce nice! Ah, the *craic* was mighty, all right…"
Kerry musician in conversation

banquets at Bunratty Castle, or busloads of visitors kissing the Blarney Stone. But it can, and does. The *craic* operates its own set of checks and balances, teasing a song out of the woman who swears she can't sing a note to save her life, curbing an aggressive drunk by its good humour, putting wind under the wings of a yarn spinner.

JOIN IN AND ENJOY

Essentially the *craic* is about good manners, and having a decent regard for your neighbour, however wild the company and copious the flow of drink.

So don't be scared to join in the *craic*. Put a song or a story into the pot, and you'll give pleasure, and receive it, too. And though everyone hopes that you will contribute, no one expects or demands it. Just relax, hang loose, enjoy the moment…and that's exactly what the *craic* is all about.

Movers and
SHAKERS

...Ireland has seen her fair share of fireball personalities, from mythical heroes to real-life tyrants, political giants and singers with plenty to shout about.

ST PATRICK

The patron saint of Ireland was a lad of 16 when Irish pirates lifted him from his native Wales, around the time the Romans were beginning to leave Britain. After six years' enslavement as a shepherd, he escaped from Ireland, getting away to Britain on a ship loaded with a cargo of wolfhounds. Few details are known of the time Patrick spent wandering and studying in Gaul, on the Continent. He became a priest and was consecrated bishop in 432 in order to lead a mission to Ireland. Landing in County Down, he set about converting the island to Christianity. By the time he died, around 461, he had seen his message take root all across Ireland. A confrontational approach with the local chieftains and druid-priests would have achieved little except his own summary execution. But Patrick, a subtle man, preferred to work with existing sacred places and established customs, not abolishing them but changing their focus from pagan to Christian.

FIONN MACCUMHAILL (FINN MCCOOL)

Who dares say that Fionn MacCumhaill never existed? Evidence of the Irish hero's mighty deeds is littered all over Ireland, from the rock near Sligo that he split with an angry sword-stroke, to the quoit (the massive flat stone from a dolmen tomb) that he threw 100km (62 miles) from the Bog of Allen to Howth Head. Every one of his warrior band, the Fianna Éireann, could write a poem, catch a wild boar, fend off nine spears in one instant, and pick a thorn out of his foot while running at full speed. How many Irish youngsters have been inspired by these tales of the inextinguishable Fionn MacCumhaill, a very literal mover and shaker?

OLIVER CROMWELL

The Lord Protector of England made it his business to come to Ireland in 1649, when it looked as if Roman Catholic rebels were getting the upper hand over the Protestant incomers who had been granted Irish land since Tudor times. Cromwell landed in Dublin with his own dedicated army of 20,000 men and within three years of merciless campaigning the rebels had been crushed, and hundreds of thousands lay dead. The Catholic landed gentry had been forced west into the wastes of Connacht and stripped of their civil rights and property. This was a brutal slam of the door on Ireland's Catholic and Celtic heritage – but, as things turned out, not a final one.

MICHAEL COLLINS (1890–1922) AND ÉAMON DE VALERA (1882–1975)

Michael Collins and Éamon de Valera, who between them oversaw the birth of an independent Ireland, were magnets for polarised opinions, icons at whose shrines bitterly divided opponents still worship. Collins led the British by the nose throughout the War of Independence, but came to see how the cause of Irish nationalism could only move forward on the back of a compromise settlement with the old enemy. The foundations for an independent Ireland were dug

Top: St Patrick had the satisfaction of watching Christianity flourish in Ireland
Centre: Oliver Cromwell crushed 17th-century Catholic resistance with brutal authority
Bottom: Éamon de Valera rallied republican support at passionate public meetings

just as much by Collins as they were by Éamon de Valera, motivator of the hardline Irish Republican Army (IRA).

De Valera had to endure a period in the wilderness after the IRA's defeat in the Civil War (1922–23), but he came back to lead his country through its final severance with Britain.

DERMOT MACMURROUGH AND STRONGBOW

The course of Irish history was shaken forever by Dermot MacMurrough, king of Leinster, who had a year-long affair with Dervorgilla, the wife of his rival Sligo chieftain Tiernán O'Rourke of Breifne in 1152. Banished for this misconduct, MacMurrough appealed to the Norman Earl of Pembroke, Richard de Clare, aptly nicknamed Strongbow. The Normans had been waiting for an excuse to get a finger into the rich pie of Ireland, and in 1170 Strongbow came over to Ireland to help MacMurrough regain his titles, and to scoop the rewards – plenty of land, the hand of MacMurrough's daughter in marriage, and the promise of succeeding to all his father-in-law's wealth and estates. This was followed by a full-scale invasion by Norman knights, the start of centuries of Anglo-Irish friction.

ARTHUR GUINNESS

Ireland's international image owes much to Arthur Guinness, who in 1759 bought up little Rainsford's Brewery at St James's Gate in Dublin and started black-roasting his malt. His legacy persists in the heady malt and hop smells that waft across Dublin, and in 2.5 million white-froth moustaches gladly worn in more than 120 countries worldwide every day.

BONO AND BOB

In their very different personas and ways of getting their messages across, the Dublin-born singers Bob Geldof and Bono (né Paul Hewson) have the world beyond pop music listening to what they have to say. The abrasive and Geldof, former frontman with the Boomtown Rats, masterminded 1985's epic international Live Aid concerts to raise money for and focus attention on famine relief in Ethiopia, and was also the catalyst for 2005's international Live 8 concerts, designed to put the cancelling of Third World countries' debts at the top of the agenda. U2's singer Bono, meanwhile, has become rock music's more diplomatic voice of conscience regarding the economic plight of Africa and the catastrophes of AIDS and Third World debt, playing benefit concerts and regularly meeting world leaders. He has also founded many charities and marketing companies to encourage the world to replace humanitarian aid to the Third World by a "fair trade" policy. Both Bob Geldof and Bono have been awarded an honorary Knighthood of the British Empire in recognition of their humanitarian work.

THE TWO MARYS

Mary Robinson's election as president of the Republic of Ireland in 1990 was a symbol of the social change that was sweeping the country. During her seven years in office she captured the high ground, going out to meet the people, saying yes to interviews, listening sympathetically to the views of northern Unionists, and throwing her weight behind Ireland's drive to modernise and develop. By the time Mary Robinson relinquished the presidency of the Republic in 1997, it had been reinvented as a dynamic focus for change. Her successor Mary McAleese, a Roman Catholic barrister born in Belfast, has proved herself to be just as effective, in a different way. "Building bridges" has been her chosen theme, and in reaching out across the sectarian divides of her native Northern Ireland and of the wider world she has gained a very high approval rating for the way she represents their country.

Top: Bob Geldof receiving an Irish Recorded Music Association (IRMA) Award in 2006.

Centre: Mary McAleese is the first woman to succeed another woman as an elected head of state. **Bottom:** Arthur Guinness first sold his porter in 1778

HUNGER, HOME RULE AND HOPE

The 20th century brought Home Rule for the Republic, but in the North politicians quarrelled and sectarian paramilitaries murdered their opponents and civilians. Now, devolved government and new hope have arrived in Northern Ireland.

FAMINE

Hunger had always been a fact of life among Ireland's Roman Catholic poor. During the 18th century the population had quadrupled, and by the 1840s had reached 9 million – most of them living chiefly on potatoes. In 1845 the *Phytophthora infestans* fungus arrived in Ireland, and potato blight spread rapidly through the country.

At first the British government provided assistance directly, through food depots; then changed their policy, organising relief work projects on

The Great Famine led to mass emigration from Ireland

which men, women and children laboured at often futile tasks – building unwanted roads, for example – to earn money to pay for corn meal. People died of starvation and disease: cholera, typhus, relapsing fever, infantile diarrhoea. And the potato fungus disease kept returning, in 1845, 1846, 1848 and 1849, reducing the tubers to stinking black slime.

The Great Famine of 1845–50 was an unmitigated catastrophe. Historians tell us that perhaps a million people died. Another 1.5 million emigrated to the USA, Canada and the UK, the start of a mass exodus from underfunded rural areas which continued until very recently. The famine changed the face of Ireland; the country, particularly out west, is still feeling the impact. The Great Hunger had another effect, too: it heightened anti-English sentiments in Ireland and fanned anew the flames of nationalism.

REBELLION

Through the 19th century, uprisings against the British went on: Young Ireland in 1848, the Irish Republican Brotherhood (IRB) – formed simultaneously in Dublin and New York in 1858 and also known as the Fenians – in 1865 and 1867. But it wasn't until Charles Stewart Parnell rose to prominence as a reforming Irish Member of Parliament at Westminster in the 1870s and 1880s that the Home Rule movement, which called for the establishment of an Irish Parliament in Dublin, took top place on the political agenda. The Home Rule Act was passed in 1914 and was promptly suspended for the duration of World War I.

A house ruined during the Easter Rising in Dublin in 1916

THE EASTER RISING

This suspension was too much for the Irish Republican Brotherhood, which initiated the Easter Rising of 1916. The rebels, numbering fewer than 2,000, took over a number of public buildings in Dublin and from the steps of the General Post Office proclaimed Ireland's independence from Britain and the birth of the Republic. Within a week the Rising had been crushed. Public opinion began to turn against the English as, one by one, 15 leaders of the rising were shot in Dublin's Kilmainham Gaol (▶ 58–59) the following month. It sowed the seed for success at the ballot box in 1918 for the republican Sinn Féin political party, whose military wing, the Irish Republican Army (IRA), began to mobilise for war with Britain.

THE WAR OF INDEPENDENCE

In 1919 the savage War of Independence saw the IRA pitted in guerrilla warfare against the British army. The dust settled in 1921, when a truce was followed by the signing of the Anglo-Irish Treaty, which allowed for partition of the Six Counties of Ulster from the 26 counties of the newly born Irish Free State. Radical elements in the IRA could not accept the terms of the treaty, and a bloody civil war followed. It ended in 1923 with the defeat of the IRA, after which the 26-county Republic of Ireland settled down to govern herself as a modern independent state. Meanwhile, the six counties of Northern Ireland (Down, Derry, Armagh, Antrim, Tyrone and Fermanagh) remained part of the United Kingdom.

Kerry was one of the counties that formed the partitioned state in 1921

All through the last three decades of the 20th century, the Republican paramilitaries of the Provisional IRA waged guerrilla war in Northern Ireland with Loyalist paramilitaries and the British Army. Two high-profile Northern Ireland political opponents became the very face of sectarian division and intransigence: Gerry Adams, President of the Republican political party Sinn Féin, and Ian Paisley, leader of the Democratic Unionist Party.

Nowadays Paisley's successor, Peter Robinson of the

> "This hitherto unthinkable state of affairs has come about in the aftermath of the Good Friday Agreement"

Democratic Unionist Party, heads the devolved Government of Northern Ireland as First Minister, with Martin McGuinness, Adams's second-in-command, as his Deputy. This hitherto unthinkable state of affairs has come about since the Good Friday Agreement of 1998, which officially rescinded the Republic's territorial claims on the North, proposed an elected Northern Ireland Assembly, and occasioned the release of paramilitary prisoners, the decommissioning of the Provisional IRA and Loyalist groups, and – to general shock and rejoicing – the announcement in July 2005 that the IRA was permanently ending its armed campaign. There have been hiccups along the way, but it looks as if Northern Ireland is in line to enjoy peace and progress.

Ian Paisley (left) and Martin McGuinness (right) at Stormont in July 2007

LONELY
BUT LOVELY
THE CREAM OF THE CROP

While you're here, there are so many sights to see and things to do, don't miss out on some of the very best.

UNDISCOVERED PLACES

- The great Bog of Bellacorick in northwest County Mayo is lonely, silent country – 260sq km (100sq miles) of blanket bog, hemmed in by the Nephin Beg Mountains. Both can be stark, dour places in rain and low cloud; both sparkle magically when the sun shines.
- The Sperrin Mountains, County Tyrone – high and wild with beautiful valleys between the ridges.
- The Slieve Bloom Mountains in County Laois – a perfect ring of lonely hills in the centre of Ireland, with a walking trail encircling their heights.
- Gorumna (Garumna), Lettermore (Leitir Moir) and Lettermullan (Leitir Mealláin), County Galway – granite-scabbed islands connected by causeways, with thatched houses among tiny, stony fields.
- Sheep's Head Peninsula, County Cork – the least known of the south-western peninsulas; glorious coast, and sheep tracks through the hills.

TOP BUZZES

- Sunset over two island-studded bays: Clew Bay, County Mayo, and Roaringwater Bay, County Cork.
- Sunrise on 21 December in the inner chamber of the ancient Newgrange passage grave, County Meath (➤ 81–84) – but you'll have to reserve your place ten years ahead!
- The view from the Round Tower at Clonmacnoise, County Offaly.
- Reaching the chapel at the summit of Croagh Patrick, County Mayo.
- Midnight in McGann's in Doolin, County Clare (tel: 065 7074133), with a new fiddler just walked in.

THREE GREAT ISLANDS

- Clare Island, County Mayo, where the pub opens at midnight.
- Clear Island (Oileán Cléire), County Cork, where rare birds make landfall and the islanders treat their guests like friends.
- Inishmaan (Inis Meáin), County Galway, where they still speak Irish and weave their own clothes.

THREE MEMORABLE VIEWS

- Macgillycuddy's Reeks seen across Dingle Bay at low tide.
- Bogland of southern Connemara, framed by the Maumturk Mountains and the Twelve Bens.
- The great cliff of Slieve League (Sliabh Liag), southwest Donegal, from Carrigan Head.

The sun sets over the hills near Clew Bay

BEST FEST

What you need to know so you can decide when to go.

JANUARY

Leopardstown Races with top riders, top runners.

Connemara Four Seasons Walking Festival, Clifden, Co Galway: experience the interior of Ireland's most romantic landscape.

FEBRUARY

Jameson Dublin International Film Festival – the best of Irish and international films.

MARCH

St Patrick's Festival (17 March) – parades, music and fun.

MARCH / APRIL

World Championships in Irish Dancing – the very best of Riverdance-style jigs and reels from all over the world.

Irish Grand National Steeplechase, held on Easter Monday at Fairyhouse in Co Meath.

MAY

Belfast Civic Festival and Lord Mayor's Show – street shows, entertainments and parades.

Celt Festival – art and song in Cork.

Irish 2,000 and 1,000 Guineas races at The Curragh, Co Kildare.

Belfast Festival of Fools – clowns, magicians and yarn-spinners.

JUNE

Music in Great Irish Houses – superb mix of music and mansions countrywide.

Bloomsday (16 June): the classic Dublin pub crawl/re-enactment/celebration of events in James Joyce's *Ulysses*.

Irish Derby at The Curragh – wear your best frock and hat.

Les Doherty as Leopold Bloom at the Bloomsday festival

The Cat Laughs Festival in Kilkenny – belly laughs galore.

JUNE / JULY
Castlebar International Walks, Co Mayo – a four-day festival. Walking the Mayo hills by day, and partying in local bars by night.

JULY
Ballybunion International Bachelor Festival, Co Kerry – join the fun, and the poseurs!
Willie Clancy Week, Milltown Malbay, Co Clare – piping festival.
Orangeman's Day (12 July) in Northern Ireland – parades, music and Battle of the Boyne commemorations.
Punchestown Racecourse, Co Kildare hosts the Oxegen music festival – a tremendous weekend of rock.

JULY / AUGUST
Galway Races – attendance at horse-related events is optional.
Galway Arts Festival – books, music, films, plays.

AUGUST
Connemara Pony Show, Clifden, Co Galway – sales of "wild" ponies. An authentic, local West of Ireland occasion.
Puck Fair, Killorglin, Co Kerry – crown and enthrone a goat, then let things develop from there.
Rose of Tralee International Festival, Co Kerry – hyped and much televised, but still fun.

Dingle Regatta and Dingle Show, Dingle, Co Kerry.
All Ireland Fleadh Cheoil – mighty traditional music festival.
Oul' Lammas Fair, Ballycastle, Co Antrim (last Monday/Tuesday) – seafood and merrymaking.
Kilkenny Arts Festival – ten days of music, literature, visual art and street events.

SEPTEMBER
Matchmaking, Lisdoonvarna, Co Clare – fix yourself up with a partner, more in fun than earnest these days.
All-Ireland Finals of Hurling and Gaelic Football, Croke Park, Dublin – fiercely contested by players and fans.

SEPTEMBER / OCTOBER
Dublin Theatre Festival – the best of Irish and international drama.

OCTOBER
Gourmet Festival, Kinsale, Co Cork. Sample superb seafood, music and hospitality.
Guinness Jazz Festival, Cork, Co Cork. Ireland's biggest and most prestigious jazz event.

NOVEMBER
Belfast Festival, Queen's University – arts and pints.

DECEMBER
Dingle Wren, Co Kerry (26 December): midwinter madness celebrating St Stephen's Day.

THE PEN and the FLUTE

Ireland is famous for the *craic*, for Guinness, for horses, for soft rain and good times…but, above all, for the astonishing genius of her sons and daughters with words and music. That such a small population can produce so many world-beaters with the pen and the flute is a marvel.

THE PEN…

Even if you have never visited Ireland before, Ireland has almost certainly visited you through the written word. For such a small country, Ireland has produced an enormous number of wonderful writers, something that strikes everyone who loves a good tale or a well-turned phrase marinated in wit.

King of the walk is James Joyce (► 65), whose *Ulysses* (1922) is certainly one of the greatest novels – many say the greatest – ever written. It's huge (over 700 pages), heavy and rambling; reading it is like swimming in a salty sea of words and ideas. "The book to which we are all indebted," said T S Eliot, "and from which none of us can escape."

Poetic expressions flow through Irish writing and talk, and poets abound. Famous for polemic and satire was Jonathan Swift (1667–1745), Dean of St Patrick's Cathedral in Dublin and author of such works as *Gulliver's Travels* and *A Tale of a Tub* (► 57). W B Yeats (► 178) is still the best-known "old school" Irish poet, his work rooted in the folklore and landscape of Sligo. County Monaghan's Patrick Kavanagh is another renowned poet, with a fluid and beautiful touch. Derry-born Seamus Heaney, whose deceptively uncomplicated style has a penetrating and innovative quality, wears the crown today. And the short story – in the hands of masters such as Kerry's humorous celebrant of local heroes, the publican and author John B Keane, Cork's Frank O'Connor with his poignant fables of the War of Independence and Sean O'Faolain, or Clare's Edna O'Brien (also a celebrated novelist) – seems the ideal medium for that very Irish gift of telling a good story grippingly.

Of course the Irish have always been master storytellers. Their bards were spinning tales of the heroes Fionn MacCumhaill and Cuchulainn, and of scheming Queen Mebh and her lust for power that led to

> ## TWELVE GREAT IRISH READS
>
> *Last Night's Fun* by Ciaran Carson
> *Ulysses* by James Joyce
> *Resurrection Man* by Eoin McNamee
> *Twenty Years A-Growing* by Maurice O'Sullivan
> *The Country Girls, Girl with Green Eyes, Girls in their Married Bliss* by Edna O'Brien
> *Amongst Women* by John McGahern
> *Guests of the Nation* by Frank O'Connor
> *The Snapper, The Van, The Commitments* by Roddy Doyle

Seamus Heaney was awarded the Nobel Prize for Literature in 1995

the epic Cattle Raid of Cooley, long before anyone in Ireland had learned to put pen to paper. Given this heritage of fireside storytelling, perhaps it's not surprising that so many great playwrights originated here: think of Oscar Wilde and Richard Sheridan, J M Synge and Sean O'Casey, George Bernard Shaw and Samuel Beckett. The Abbey Theatre (► 30) founded in Dublin by Synge, Yeats and Lady Gregory is still active, and many other venues over Ireland showcase established and up-and-coming Irish playwrights.

...THE FLUTE

Irish traditional music is essentially music to accompany rural dancing. Jigs and reels predominate, along with the slower airs that were made to float a song on. A round goatskin drum called a *bodhrán* provides the beat and rhythm, along with guitar, bouzouki or banjo; accordion, melodeon, penny whistle and flute carry the melody, while on top skate the fiddle or uillean pipes. The Irish respect and cherish this music as vibrantly alive; but they are not afraid to experiment, even to the point of translating it altogether to jazz or rock genres, or to neo-classical arrangements for piano and orchestra. The music is tough enough to withstand these wrenchings, and versatile enough to flourish within them.

Irish traditional music has enjoyed a tremendous vogue in recent times, promulgated by stage shows such as *Riverdance*, and by the rediscovery of their traditional musical roots by rock acts such as U2 and Van Morrison, along with shock artists like The Pogues. In America the punky hardcore Dropkick Murphys pack their shows with Irish jigs and reels.

In fact this resilient music has never been away. Whatever the seesawing trends of popular music, the island's rich repertoire of traditional music has always been played with love and respect by local musicians all over Ireland.

Irish music is timeless, which is not to say it is stuck in a time warp. Turlough O'Carolan, the 18th-century blind harpist, is well respected; so are fiddler Michael Coleman and the melodeon player Joe Cooley, musicians of the early and middle 20th century who directly influenced today's generation of players. The tunes they handed down, many very old, receive new life each time they are played; each rendition is unique. And new tunes are constantly being made. As you listen – or maybe pluck up enough courage to join in – you will be launching yourself on a wonderful voyage of discovery which, if you are lucky, will go on for ever.

LIVE MUSIC

If you're in the vicinity, try these noted session pubs.
Furey's, Sligo, owned by traditional band Dervish (➤ 144).
Matt Molloy's, Westport, County Mayo, owned by Chieftains flute-player Molloy, who often plays (➤ 133).
O'Connor's, Doolin, County Clare. All the greats have played here.
O'Donoghue's, Dublin. And here too (➤ 70).

An ABC
of Icons and Touchstones

An alphabet of yardsticks by which the Irish measure today's proud nationhood against a strife-filled past and a treasury of ancient traditions.

Abbey Theatre in Dublin, opened in 1904 by Lady Augusta Gregory and her protégé, the poet W B Yeats. Relocated after a fire, it is still in use as Ireland's national theatre.
Bodhrán, a goatskin drum beaten with hellish enthusiasm by session musicians in pubs and clubs.
Croagh Patrick, County Mayo's Holy Mountain (➤ 176–177). When gold prospectors wanted to mine here in 1990, worldwide protests stopped them in their tracks.
Drumcree, Northern Irish town and symbol of Ulster intransigence. This is where Protestant Orangemen insist they have a right to march and Catholic nationalists insist they do not.
Ennistymon, County Clare's most brilliant town for traditional music.
Famine, the most disastrous event in Irish history. It emptied the west, and scarred the national psyche.
General Post Office (GPO) on O'Connell Street in Dublin. In 1916 it was the scene of the rebels' proclamation of the Republic of Ireland, and has acquired the status of a national monument.

Hill of Tara, the great mound rising out of the Meath Plain, from which the ancient High Kings of Ireland ruled for a thousand years (➤ 88).
Irish language, taught in schools, spoken in the Gaeltacht of the west, and heard around the world in the lyrics of traditional Irish songs.
July 12, Orangeman's Day in Northern Ireland, celebrating William of Orange's victory over James II at the Battle of the Boyne. Orangemen parade to martial music, and tensions rise.
Knock, a pilgrimage centre in County Mayo, and other places in Ireland where ordinary people have seen miraculous visions.
Lazybeds, cultivation ridges that define the former potato fields. Scars on the rural landscape, they are poignant reminders of hard times past.
Music, wild, sweet, infectious, angry, played and sung all over Ireland.
National anthem, "Amhrán na bhFíann" (The Soldier's Song), often sung in Irish at the end of a music session. Everyone stands up

The ancient royal fort of Tara has been an important site since the late Stone Age

for it, so don't be caught napping. Yes, it certainly does still happen!
Orange, William of. He's "King Billy", victor of the Battle of the Boyne in 1690, who can be seen riding his white horse on Unionist banners and gable ends.
Poteen, "mountain dew", "the pure drop", "the crater" – a colourless, illicitly distilled spirit, usually made from potatoes.
Queenstown, now called Cobh, the port south of Cork, from which countless thousands of Irish families sailed on their emigration journeys (➤ 98–99).
Reels, the unforgettable leaping dance tunes that lie at the heart of Ireland's traditional music.
Stout, a strong beer as black as night, as smooth as velvet. No visit to Ireland is complete without at least a sip.
Turf, not as sold wholesale by Bord na Móna (the Irish Peat Board), but as cut with the special turf

spade called a slane, and burned on a hearth for its slow heat and sweet smell. Perfectly acceptable in this small-scale, hand-cut way.
U2, Dublin's mega-successful rock-band-with-a-conscience, closely followed by…
Van Morrison, east Belfast singer of bluesy soul and soulful blues, one of contemporary music's most enduringly popular figures.
Wells – holy ones, blessed by saints, scattered over the land, whose water can cure your ills.
Xavier, Brigid, Patrick, Aloysius and dozens of other Christian names from the calendar of saints.
Yeats brothers, the poet William Butler and the painter Jack, whose love of County Sligo's flat-topped mountains and rugged shores is celebrated in their work.
Zip codes, absence of: a testament to the Republic's small population, and the in-depth local knowledge of Irish postmen.

SPEAKING OF IRELAND

From thundering pronouncements to wicked verbal darts, it seems that everyone has something to say about the place…

"Hey presto!
We have taken our eyes off them for one second and lo, both are gone! The Dublin Man and his pint have both vanished. The tumbler stands, a veritable monument, with delicate traceries of foam slowly sinking to the bottom.
Trace, explain, unmask this Man? It can't be done. I tell you."
Myles na Gopaleen (Brian O'Nolan)
The Dublin Man

"The Irish are a fair people; they never speak well of one another."
Dr Samuel Johnson,
18th-century essayist, journalist and lexicographer

"I particularly remember those stark murals, colourful and grotesque, which have come to be part of Belfast, and part of the historic expression of the people and their city."
Brian Keenan,
An Evil Cradling

"You can't get into the soup in Ireland, do what you like."
Evelyn Waugh, Decline and Fall

"Connemara – the name drifts across the mind like cloud shadows on a mountainside, or expands and fades like circles on a lake after a trout has risen…How can I indicate this Connemara, but as the edge of brightness that follows a cloud shadow across the mountainside, or the stillness of a lake before the trout rises?"
Tim Robinson, Connemara

"Ireland is an infernal country to manage…the graveyard of every reputation."
Benjamin Disraeli,
19th-century British politician

"For the great Gaels of Ireland
Are the men that God made mad,
For all their wars are merry,
And all their songs are sad."
G K Chesterton,
Ballad of the White Horse

Finding your feet

First Two Hours

Arriving: Republic of Ireland

Dublin and Shannon airports are the main points of entry for visitors arriving by air. Most arrivals by sea come through Dublin Port or Dun Laoghaire south of Dublin; Rosslare, County Wexford, has ferry links with the UK and France. All ports and airports have currency exchange bureaux, the major car-rental firms, and taxi ranks (fares are about five times the bus fare). Most journey times to city centres are between 30 and 60 minutes, depending on traffic.

Dublin Airport ✚ 201 D5
- To get to Dublin city centre from the airport by **car**, take M1 south.
- An **Airlink bus** leaves the airport at least every 20 minutes (moderate fare) taking passengers to the city centre via the central bus station (Busarus) and Connolly and Heuston railway stations.
- **Taxis** line up outside the Arrivals area. Fares can be expensive.

Dun Laoghaire ✚ 201 E5
- If travelling by **car** to Dublin, simply follow signs for the city centre.
- There is a frequent **Dublin Bus** service to Dublin city centre.
- **Taxi fares** range from moderate to expensive (depending on traffic).
- An inexpensive **DART** service (➤ 35) from Dun Laoghaire to Dublin runs every 30 minutes (sometimes more frequently).

Shannon Airport ✚ 199 D4
- To get to Limerick from Shannon Airport by **car,** take N18 east.
- **Bus Éireann** runs a frequent, inexpensive airport-to-Limerick/Ennis service.
- **Taxis** from Shannon Airport to Limerick are moderate to expensive.

Arriving: Northern Ireland

Visitors arriving by air will probably fly to either Belfast International or George Best Belfast City airport. Belfast and Larne ferryports are the main points of entry for arrivals by sea. All ports and airports have currency exchange bureaux, the major car-rental firms, and taxi ranks (fares are about five times the bus fare).

Belfast International Airport ✚ 197 E4
- The journey to central Belfast takes 30 to 60 minutes, depending on traffic.
- To get to Belfast city centre from the airport by **car**, follow M2 motorway.
- **Airport Express 300 service** (moderate fare, children free) runs to Belfast city centre every 30 minutes (sometimes hourly on Sundays).
- **Taxi fares** from the airport to central Belfast tend to be expensive.

George Best Belfast City Airport and Belfast Ferryport ✚ 197 E4
- The journey to Belfast takes 10 to 15 minutes, depending on traffic.
- **Taxi fares** to Belfast city centre are moderate.

Larne Ferryport ✚ 197 E4
- The journey to central Belfast takes 30 to 60 minutes, depending on traffic.
- To get to Belfast city centre from the ferryport by **car**, take A8 south.
- An **Ulsterbus** service runs frequently to the city centre.
- **Taxi fares** to central Belfast tend to be expensive.
- There is a frequent **rail service** to Belfast Central railway station.

Tourist Information Offices

The central Dublin and Belfast tourist offices provide an excellent service, giving assistance with reservations and information on what's on in each city.

- **Dublin Tourism** Suffolk Street, tel: 1850 230330 or 01 605 7700 (within Ireland); 0800 039 7000 (UK); 353 605 7700 (from all other countries); email: information@dublintourism.ie; www.visitdublin.com.
- **Belfast Welcome Centre** 47 Donegall Place, Belfast, tel: 028 9024 6609; fax: 028 9031 2424; email: info@belfastvisitor.com; www.discovernorthernireland.com or www.gotobelfast.com.

Admission Charges

Admission charges for museums and places of interest are indicated by price categories: pounds for Northern Ireland, Euros for the Republic (➤ 189).
Inexpensive: up to £4/€5 **Moderate**: £4–£8/€5–€10 **Expensive**: over £8/€10

Getting Around: Republic of Ireland

CIE runs bus and train services in the Republic of Ireland through its subsidiaries Irish Rail (Iarnród Éireann; www.irishrail.ie), Irish Bus (Bus Éireann; www.buseirann.ie) and Dublin Bus (Bus Átha Cliath; www.dublinbus.ie).

Dublin

LUAS, Dublin's light railway system, buzzes you round the inner city (tel: 1800 300 604; www.luas.ie). The **DART**, an efficient and moderately priced rail service, connects outer Dublin, north and south, with the city centre. **Dublin Bus** (tel: 01 873 4222) runs services in Greater Dublin, as far as the outskirts of counties Meath, Kildare and Wicklow.

Bus Services

- Tickets can be bought on the buses, but it is cheaper to buy them *en bloc* in advance from the CIE information desk in Dublin Airport, Dublin Bus (59 Upper O'Connell Street), or from one of the ticket outlets in the city.

DART (Dublin Area Rapid Transit)

- There are 30 DART stations altogether; the three most central are **Connolly** (north of the river, a ten-minute walk from O'Connell Street), **Tara Street**, and **Pearse Street** (both south of the river and five minutes from Trinity College).
- **Trains** run every 5 minutes in rush hours, every 10 to 15 minutes at other times of the day.
- **Tickets** are available singly from any DART station, but it is cheaper to buy them *en bloc* from Dublin Bus (59 Upper O'Connell Street), from some newsstands around the city or at the stations.

Taxis

- You cannot hail or stop Dublin taxis in the street: call them by telephone (numbers in the *Golden Pages*), or find a taxi rank.
- The main city centre **taxi ranks** are at St Stephen's Green, College Green, O'Connell Street, and Westland Row to the east of Trinity College grounds.
- Dublin taxis are mostly metered; agree fares in advance with others.

Public Transport

All the major towns and cities in the Republic are connected by rail. Bus services run to all towns and cities, and to many rural villages. Public transport in the Republic is more efficient than folklore would have you believe. Timetables, however, particularly on the railways, become subject to creative interpretation the further from Dublin that you travel.

Railway Services

- **Irish Rail** (tel: 01 836 6222) runs the Republic's railway services. These are efficient north and south of Dublin, but in need of investment further west.
- The **Dublin–Belfast express** (eight trains per day) takes two hours: book ahead in the high season, and for crowded last trains on Friday and Sunday evenings.

Bus Services

- **Bus Éireann** (tel: 01 836 6111), with its distinctive red-setter logo, runs services to all towns and cities, and to many rural villages.
- The daily **express coaches** between Dublin and Belfast are good value, and can beat the train for time if traffic conditions permit.

Tickets

- Tickets are available from any train or bus station or online (www.buseireann.ie).
- Under-16s and other concessionary fares can be as little as half-price of the adult fare.
- **Irish Explorer** passes are valid on Bus Éireann Expressway and Bus Éireann city services in Cork, Limerick, Galway and Waterford, and also on Iarnrod Éireann Intercity, DART and suburban rail. They are not valid for travel on cross border services.
- The **Emerald Card** is valid as the Irish Explorer pass and also on Ulsterbus and Northern Ireland Railways.
- The **Open-Road Pass** is a flexible pass valid for Bus Éireann Expressway, local, city and town services.

Student Discounts

- The **International Student Identity Card** gives good discounts on a number of fares including mainline rail, long-distance bus and ferry tickets – all for the price of a paperback novel. It's available from **USIT** (19–21 Aston Quay, O'Connell Bridge, Dublin 2, tel: 01 602 1904). You will need proof of your student status.

Internal Air Travel

Aer Lingus, the national airline (tel: UK 0870 876 5000; US 1-800 474 7424; Ireland 0818 365000; www.aerlingus.com), flies from Dublin to Shannon. **Aer Arann** (tel: 01 844 7700; www.aerarann.ie) flies from Dublin to Donegal, Sligo, Knock, Galway, Kerry and Cork.

Car Ferries

Two short car ferry trips that save hours on the road are:
- Across the Shannon (20-minute crossing, every hour every day except 25 Dec) between Killimer, County Clare, and Tarbert, County Kerry (tel: 065 9053124; www.shannonferries.com).
- Across Waterford Harbour (10-minute crossing, continuous operation) between Ballyhack, County Wexford, and Passage East, County Waterford (tel: 051 382480).

Driving

Driving in the Republic, generally speaking, is still a pleasure. Out of the big towns the roads are uncrowded and most drivers courteous. The further west you go, the more patience you need: roads are narrower, steeper and more twisty. Signposts take some getting used to, with distances shown in kilometres on green-and-white signs and in miles on black-and-white signs.

Driving Essentials
- Drive on the **left-hand side** of the road.
- Drivers and front seat passengers must wear **seat belts**.
- The **speed limit** in the Republic is: motorway (blue) 120kph/75mph; national roads (green) 100kph/62mph – in some areas 80kph/50mph; regional and local roads (white) 80kph/50mph; urban roads 50kph/31mph.
- The **legal alcohol limit** is 0.08 per cent (80mg) alcohol per 100ml blood.

Renting a Car
- **Fly-drive** or **rail/sail-drive** packages offer the best deals. Book ahead, mid-July to mid-August, or you may not get a car.
- **Prices** are half as much again during high season; they usually include Third Party, fire, theft and passenger indemnity insurance, as well as unlimited mileage and VAT (value added tax). You will have to pay a deposit.
- You will need a **full valid driving licence** of your country of residence, held for two years without endorsement. The age limit is generally 25–70.

Bringing Your Own Car
- You will need a **motor registration book** (with letter of authority if car is not registered in your name), a **full driving licence** or international permit and a Green Card or **insurance certificate**, valid for the Republic of Ireland.
- No Irish resident is allowed to drive your car, apart from garage employees.

Leaving Dublin
- M1/N1 to Dublin Airport, Drogheda, Dundalk and Belfast
- N2 to Ashbourne, Slane and Derry
- N3 to Navan, Cavan and Enniskillen and Sligo
- M4/N4 to Kinnegad (where N6 leaves for Galway), to Longford (where N5 leaves for Westport), and on to Sligo
- N7 towards Cork, Limerick and Killarney
- N11 to Bray, Wicklow, Wexford and Rosslare car ferry

Getting Around: Northern Ireland

Belfast
Bus Services
- **Metro** (tel: 028 9066 6630; www.translink.co.uk) operates buses within the city of Belfast.
- Buy tickets in **Europa Bus Centre** (Glengall Street) or **Laganside Bus Centre**, near Central railway station (Oxford Street) or on board buses. Multiple tickets/concessions are available.

■ A **free bus** connects Central railway station with the two bus stations and the International Youth Hostel (you must have a valid bus or train ticket to travel free); **Rail-link bus** connects Central and Yorkgate railway stations.

Taxis
Find taxi firm numbers in *Yellow Pages*. Black "London" cabs with yellow identifying discs are metered; others may not be. Taxi ranks are at Yorkgate and Central railway stations, at both bus stations and at City Hall.

Public Transport
Public transport in Northern Ireland is reasonably priced and well run. For information on ticket deals and student discounts ➤ 36.

Railway Services
■ **Northern Ireland Railways** (tel: 028 9066 6630; www.translink.co.uk) runs a service from Belfast to Larne (Yorkgate Station, tel: 028 9074 1700), and to Derry, Bangor and Dublin (Central Station, tel: 028 9089 9400).
■ Buy **tickets** at stations. For **discounts**, contact Northern Ireland Railways.

Bus Services
■ **Ulsterbus** (tel: 028 9066 6630; www.translink.co.uk) runs services to all towns and most villages across Northern Ireland.
■ Buy **tickets** at bus stations or on board buses. For cheap round-trip fares, unlimited travel tickets, bus/rail options, and concessionary fares, contact Ulsterbus.

Driving
Road surfaces tend to be better than in the Republic and signpost distances are given in miles only. The same rules and laws apply as in the Republic, with the legal alcohol limit at 80mg alcohol per 100ml blood.

Renting a Car
■ **Requirements** as for the Republic (➤ 37), except that you need only have held a driving licence for one year. If you plan to drive in both the Republic and Northern Ireland, check that your insurance covers you.

Bringing Your Own Car
■ No documents are needed, apart from a **driving licence**, by those arriving with a car by ferry from the UK or by road from the Republic of Ireland.

Leaving Belfast
■ A2 north up the coast to Antrim and the Giant's Causeway, east through Bangor and round the Ards Peninsula
■ M2/A6 to Derry
■ M1 to Dungannon/A4 to Enniskillen
■ M1 to Junction 7/A1 to Dundalk and Dublin

Accommodation

This guide recommends a carefully selected cross-section of places to stay, ranging from luxury hotels to farmhouses. Standards of accommodation are generally high in both the Republic and Northern Ireland and prices are similar. That said, the choice of well-run, interesting places to stay is more limited in Northern Ireland.

Guest-House and Bed-and-Breakfast Accommodation

Even inexpensive **bed-and-breakfasts** (B&Bs) usually have simple private bathroom facilities and, if you want to meet Irish people and go to the places the locals like, this can be the best option. Most (but not all) B&B and **guest-house** accommodation is in the **family home**, and hosts are usually pleased to help you plan itineraries in the locality and recommend places to go for food, shopping and entertainment.

Many **specially built guest houses**, with a standard of accommodation similar to a small hotel, have been built in the last few years. The level of comfort is high, but, as the **hosts usually live elsewhere**, visitors who had hoped to stay in a family home (and sample traditional Irish hospitality) can sometimes be disappointed. It's useful to know that **food** in smaller establishments is usually limited to **breakfast** and, in country areas, sometimes **high tea** is served in the evening instead of dinner. Many hosts take pride in providing a traditional breakfast, and the best B&B, guest house or farmhouse breakfasts can beat any hotel's. As well as the full **Irish breakfast** (bacon, egg, sausages, tomato, often black or white pudding, possibly also mushrooms and potato bread, served with soda bread), many places now offer a wider choice including **fresh fruits**, **fish** and **farmhouse cheeses**. **Freshly baked bread** or scones (biscuits) and specialities like potato bread are often served at breakfast and at high tea.

Hotels

As the best guest houses provide standards of comfort that compete with hotels', the cost of some hotels can seem hard to justify, until the **location**, the **facilities** and, particularly, the **service** are taken into consideration. Hotel amenities have improved dramatically and many now have excellent **leisure facilities**, often including fitness centres and golf. It's always worth asking at hotels about **special offers** or short breaks, especially off-season. If the price quoted is beyond your budget, never be afraid to see if the hotelier will bargain.

Booking Accommodation

Booking ahead is always a good idea. The **cities**, especially Dublin, are busy all year round. Except for the very remote scenic holiday areas, where most (but not all) accommodation closes for the winter, the **season** starts earlier and ends later than used to be the case. Summer does attract bumper crowds to seaside resorts, especially West Cork, Kerry and Galway, so an **off-season** visit can be more enjoyable. All-year pressure on accommodation in **Dublin** has made it very **expensive** and it's hard to find bargains. One solution is to use hotels such as the **Jurys Inns** (found both in the Republic and the North), which provide comfort without service and charge a **flat rate** for a room without breakfast. Further information on accommodation is available from tourist information offices everywhere or you can refer to these sources:

■ Full listings of the Irish hotels and B&Bs available can be found and booked at the **AA's internet site** (www.theAA.com).

■ The **Irish Hotels Federation** (13 Northbrook Road, Dublin 6, tel: 01 808 4419; www.irelandhotels.com) publication *Be Our Guest* lists hotel and guest-house accommodation (including Northern Ireland).

■ **Town & Country Homes Association** (Belleek Road, Ballyshannon, Co Donegal, tel: 071 9822222; www.townandcountry.ie) produces a B&B directory (€10).

■ **Tourist offices** also have a range of specialised directories for other types of places to stay, including ones that cover self-catering and farmhouse accommodation.

- The **Northern Ireland Tourist Board** (www.discovernorthernireland.com) publishes a series of free accommodation guides, including hotels and guest houses, bed-and-breakfasts, budget accommodation and self-catering.
- The **Irish Farmhouse Holiday Association** (tel: 061 400 700; www.irishfarmholidays.com) provide traditional hospitality and a taste of rural life.

Food and Drink

Eating well can be a highlight of a visit to Ireland. Good-quality local ingredients, such as Galway oysters, Dublin Bay prawns, Atlantic salmon, Connemara lamb and organically grown vegetables and herbs have become a point of pride, and there's no shortage of talent among Irish chefs. At its best, whether it's a special meal or simple pub food, eating out in Ireland is a satisfying combination of genuine hospitality, high standards and value for money.

International Cooking

International cooking styles tend to predominate over local tradition in a way that many visitors can find disappointing, and you are far more likely to find various world cuisines than traditional Irish food. When well produced this cosmopolitan food is fun, vibrant and tasty, but often it's just a muddle.

- **Hotel dining-rooms** are emerging as serious contenders in the restaurant stakes as they have taken on top-class chefs. The accommodation recommendations reflect this, including the Clarence and Merrion hotels in Dublin (➤ 68–69), and many examples around the country.
- There is a shift towards buzzy, informal **cafés and bars** serving colourful, cosmopolitan fare. Lively, efficiently run bistros and brasseries such as Isaacs in Cork (➤ 113) and Excise Bistro (➤ 66) provide value for money, as do café-bars like Dublin's Café en Seine, where drink (often coffee rather than alcohol) is the main attraction and food is the accompaniment.

Irish Cooking

Until the 1990s Irish dishes such as *colcannon* (mashed potatoes and green cabbage, seasoned with chives), *boxty* (filled potato pancakes), Dublin coddle (a stew made with sausages, bacon, onions and potato), Irish stew and corned beef with dumplings and cabbage were most likely to be found only in pubs. With a few notable exceptions, restaurant chefs felt that traditional Irish dishes were too plain, but this is changing. With the active support of the **Restaurant Association of Ireland** (11 Bridge Court, City Gate, St Augustine Street, Dublin 8, tel: 01 677 9901; www.rai.ie) and **Bord Bia** (the Irish Food Board), many of Ireland's top chefs are now working on the concept of a **New Irish Cuisine**. Though light and modern, it is based on traditional ingredients, including many **artisan Irish food products**, such as farmhouse cheeses and smoked Atlantic salmon.

- **Bord Bia** has produced a New Irish Cuisine **recipe booklet** (tel: 01 668 5155 for details).
- Much of the country's best food is produced by owner-chefs in **family-run restaurants** and country houses.
- **Kinsale** in County Cork started the first Good Food Circle in the early 1970s and, since then, many others have flourished. There is also an annual themed Kinsale Gourmet Festival.

- **Kenmare** (County Kerry) has two of the country's finest hotels – Sheen Falls Lodge (tel: 064 41600; www.sheenfallslodge.ie) and Park Hotel Kenmare (tel: 064 41200; www.parkkenmare.com) – and the most concentrated collection of fine restaurants, quality accommodation and good pubs.
- Other culinary hotspots around the country include **Dingle/An Daingean** (County Kerry), **Clifden** (on the Connemara coast), **Carlingford** (at the foot of the Mountains of Mourne), **Athlone** (right in the centre of the Republic) and **Moycullen** (just outside Galway), all of which have something exciting to offer.

A Practical Guide to Eating Out

The following tips give practical information to make eating out in Ireland an enjoyable and carefree experience.

- **Eating hours** are: breakfast from about 7:30 or 8am to 10 or 10:30am; lunch from noon or 12:30 to 2:15pm or 2:30pm; early dinner (often especially good value) from 5:30 or 6pm and main dinner from about 7:30 to 9:30pm or 10:30pm.
- There is no specific **service charge** – it can be anything from 10 to 15 per cent, or discretionary.
- Many restaurants offer **early evening menus** (usually up to 7pm), which are very good value. Where lunch is available at leading restaurants, it's usually a bargain.
- **Dress codes** are increasingly relaxed and very few restaurants will insist on male diners wearing a jacket and tie, although many people like to create a sense of occasion when dining out and feel more comfortable with a little formality.
- The key **language** on menus throughout the country is English, although some will include an Irish version. A few enterprising restaurants (especially near the Shannon, which attracts holidaymakers and fisherfolk from Europe) offer menus in several European languages.
- For further reference, Tourism Ireland produces a **restaurant directory**, *A Flavour of Ireland.* For Northern Ireland you can access the *Taste of Ulster* guide (www.tasteofulster.org).

Shopping

It would be hard to imagine a visit to Ireland that didn't include at least a little light shopping. The traditional goods for which the country is famous are in the main high-quality classics that will give years of pleasure. Much to the surprise of those who have been making and selling them for generations, many have recently become fashionable too.

Irish Classics

As natural fabrics and country looks become more desirable, Irish **tweeds**, **linen** and **hand-knitted sweaters** are suddenly "must-haves" for discerning shoppers from all over the world. This turn of events has resulted in a new generation of all kinds of goods with verve and style: for example, Irish **crystal** manufacturers have commissioned designers such as John Rocha to create high-fashion contemporary designs that appeal to a younger, more design-conscious shopper. The same applies in other areas: Louise Kennedy, for example, designs **clothes** for the international market but the roots of her inspiration are firmly Irish.

Where to Buy Irish Classics

Dublin has the biggest selection of shopping options anywhere in the country; notably, Irish fashions, antiques, books, handicrafts, food and drink. **Cork** is smaller and more selective, but is particularly enjoyable for shopping, or just browsing, and has a number of outlets selling outstanding food. **Galway** has a good range of small galleries, boutiques and specialist shops, and is renowned for books.

- **Crafts** of internationally high standard are widely available across the country and you can often find something special at one of the many craft workshops – a beautiful turned wooden bowl or one-of-a-kind item of jewellery perhaps.
- **Antiques** can still be a good buy in Ireland, although the days of easy-to-find bargains have gone. Belfast, Dublin, Cork, Galway and Limerick are all good browsing grounds, and it's worth checking the newspapers for auctions, which are often held outside the cities.
- **Jewellery** is worth considering. Check out the antiques shops, but also look at modern designer jewellery (see Kilkenny ► 92 and Belfast ► 170) and the traditional Irish wedding rings called Claddagh rings (see Galway ► 143).
- Irish cut **lead crystal** has been produced since the 18th century and is world famous. The best known manufacturer is Waterford Crystal, and its produce is available in department stores and gift shops all over the country as well as from the factory itself (► 79). Other hand-cut crystals, from Dublin, Cork, Kinsale, Tipperary, Galway and Tyrone, are less expensive, and there is also interesting contemporary uncut crystal, such as Jerpoint (► 92).
- **Traditional Irish foods** are much sought after. Foods that travel well include smoked salmon; make sure it's wild **Atlantic salmon**, not farmed, and buy it vacuum packed. The firmer, milder, whole handmade **farmhouse cheeses** such as Gubbeen, Durrus and Cashel Blue are also a good buy; they are widely available in delicatessens, specialist cheese shops and supermarkets, and at airports (where you pay much more).
- **Irish whiskey** has great cachet. A tour of one of the distilleries – Old Jameson Distillery, Dublin; Old Midleton Distillery, County Cork (► 108); and Old Bushmills Distillery, County Antrim (► 163) – will include a whiskey tasting, and you can buy some unusual blends on site. The well-known brands, like Jameson, Paddy, Powers and Bushmills, are widely available. **Baileys**, now one of the world's top-selling drinks, was created to make the best possible use of ingredients plentiful in Ireland – cream and whiskey. Along with **Irish Mist**, a sweetish liqueur made from whiskey and honey, it is widely available.
- **Knitwear** is highly popular and everything from chunky Aran sweaters to sophisticated fashion knits are on offer. Every craft shop in the country has something of interest.
- **Linen** is a great luxury, but worth the price, being wonderfully hardwearing. Most linen is made in Northern Ireland (► 170). As well as the classic table- and bed-linen, linen can also be high fashion, as reflected in designer clothes in shops such as Kilkenny in Dublin (► 69).
- **Tweeds**, too, never date.The best buys are classics such as men's jackets, although more contemporary-styled clothing is becoming increasingly popular. Many craft shops stock tweeds, and there are specialist shops around the country (see Magee's ► 144), as well as in the major cities.

Opening Times

Opening hours are usually 9am or 10am until 5 pm or 6:30pm Monday to Saturday for mainstream shopping, with limited Sunday hours and, in cities, late-night shopping until 8:30pm or 9pm on Thursday. In country areas, some shops still close for a half day (Wednesday and Saturday are most likely), and craft shops in holiday areas have variable hours. Browsing is quite acceptable: although assistance will usually be offered, pressure to buy is the exception.

Payment
Credit cards are widely accepted, except in small craft shops.

Entertainment

Irish entertainment most often takes the form of festivals (devoted to just about everything, ➤ 24–25), sporting events and music. Bord Fáilte (the Irish Tourist Board) and the Northern Ireland Tourist Board jointly produce a calendar of events, which is worth having if you're spending some time in Ireland. Bord Fáilte also produces booklets on golf, cycling, walking, hiking, fishing, sailing, tracing your ancestors, literary Ireland, wildlife and many more. These are available from larger tourist offices. There are similar publications relating to Northern Ireland. Detailed information on all aspects of Irish sport and entertainment is available daily in the local press and, for advance information, the Internet becomes more comprehensive all the time.

Spectator Sports
- **Horse racing** is central to Irish sporting life. There are 27 racecourses and races are held most days. Major events are well publicised; for information contact **Horse Racing Ireland** (tel: 045 455455; www.goracing.ie).
- **Greyhound racing**, held at night, is enjoying a revival, and Irish dogs are highly regarded internationally; ask locally about events.
- Ask about local venues for **Gaelic football** and **hurling**, both fast and exciting games.

Outdoor Activities
- **Golf** brings many visitors to Ireland. There are over 400 golf courses in the country, including many world-class championship courses. The Republic of Ireland's golfing association, the **Golfing Union of Ireland** (Unit 8, block G, Maynooth Business Campus, Maynooth, County Kildare; tel: 01 505 400; www.gui.ie) can supply information.
- **Hiking** is increasingly popular; long-distance paths are indicated by trail markers and signposts. The longest in the south is the Kerry Way (214km/133 miles); Northern Ireland's 800km (496-mile) Ulster Way, a circuit round Northern Ireland and County Donegal, is an even greater challenge, but splits into a number of shorter Waymarked Ways, ranging from 32km (20 miles) to 52km (32 miles).

Pubs and Clubs
- Increasingly strict drink-driving laws have forced pubs to diversify, and many now serve **food**, at least at lunch-time. A no smoking policy has been introduced in all enclosed places, including pubs and clubs.
- **Music in pubs** is usually free if it's in the main bar, but amplified music and/or dancing in a separate room usually has an entrance fee. Impromptu sessions are still widespread, but music is increasingly organised and, to the chagrin of many people, even small pubs are introducing amplification.

Festivals

Consult newspapers and check your hotel room and the Tourist Information Offices for local guides to what's on (➤ 24–25).

Dublin

- Dublin's festival season begins with the **Jameson Dublin International Film Festival** (mid-February) and the **St Patrick's Day Festival and Parade** (around 17 March), followed by **Bloomsday** (16 June), **Kerrygold Dublin Horse Show** (early August), **Dublin Theatre Festival** (early October) and **Dublin City Marathon** (late October).
- The **All-Ireland Finals of Hurling and Gaelic Football** are held at Croke Park in September.

Cork

- The **Cork Film Festival** (October) and the **Cork Jazz Festival** (late October) are major events.

Galway

- Kinvarra holds a traditional boat gathering, **Cruinniu na mBad** (Galway Tourist Office tel: 091 537 700), in early August, and also in Kinvarra you can attend **literary banquets** themed on local writers, including W B Yeats and Sean O'Casey, in the medieval Dunguaire Castle (tel: 061 360788; www.shannonheritage.com).
- Galway's festivals include **Galway Arts Festival** (tel: 091 509700) in mid- to late July, followed by **Galway Races** (Ballybrit, tel: 091 753870), then several September **oyster festivals**. August brings Clifden's **Connemara Pony Show**.

Belfast

- Belfast is really buzzing all the time these days, with events at the Waterfront Hall, the Grand Opera House, King's Hall, Ulster Hall and numerous theatres, as well as the Odyssey science centre and entertainment complex.
- Northern Ireland's cultural highlight is the **Belfast Festival** at Queen's University, a mixture of film, theatre, music and dance in late October to early November.

Gay Scene

Outhouse is Dublin's resource centre for gay issues (105 Capel Street, tel: 01 873 4932; email: info@outhouse.ie; www.outhouse.ie). **Queerspace** (64 Donegall Street, Belfast; www.queerspace.org.uk) has information for Northern Ireland.

Pronunciation Guide

á is an "aw" sound. So *bodhrán* is pronounced bow-r*aw*n
ane is a short "an" sound. So Cloghane is pronounced Clogh-*an*
bh is a "v" sound. So Cobh is pronounced Co*ve*
ch is pronounced in the same way as "ch" in the Scottish word loch
dh is silent in the middle of a word. See *bodhrán* above
eagh or **eigh** is an "ay" sound. So Glenveagh is pronounced Glen-*vay*
gh is silent at the end of a word and slightly softer than the "ch" sound in loch in the middle of a word
h is slightly throatier than "h", slightly less throaty than loch

Dublin

Getting Your Bearings

"In Dublin's fair city, where the girls are so pretty..." Is it that snatch of an old romantic song that attracts so many people to Dublin? Or is it Dublin's reputation as one of the most vibrant and fun capital cities in Europe where people still have time for the stranger? Whatever the cause, the effect has been spectacular. During the last couple of decades of the 20th century, Dublin broke free of a clinging image of shabbiness and quaintness, of being far behind the times, and emerged as a go-ahead city – loud, joyful, affluent, with a brashness that attracted more than it repelled.

Dublin lies low and beautiful. There are few high-rise blocks to overshadow the historic buildings – Trinity College, the Custom House, St Patrick's Cathedral. This compact city is easy to walk around in a day, with the Dublin Area Rapid Transit railway (DART) to get you out along the shores of Dublin Bay, and the new Luas light rail system to transport you out to the suburbs.

South of the river you'll find the chic pavement cafés and fashionable watering holes of Temple Bar, once a run-down area but now Dublin's snappiest spot that continues to grow around Cow's Lane. Only a stone's throw away is Ireland's best Georgian architecture in the streets and squares around St Stephen's Green. North of the Liffey, wide O'Connell Street and the area behind it in Henry Street has had a major

Page 45:
Looking across Dublin's skyline
Left: The Ha'penny Bridge

★ Don't Miss

At Your Leisure

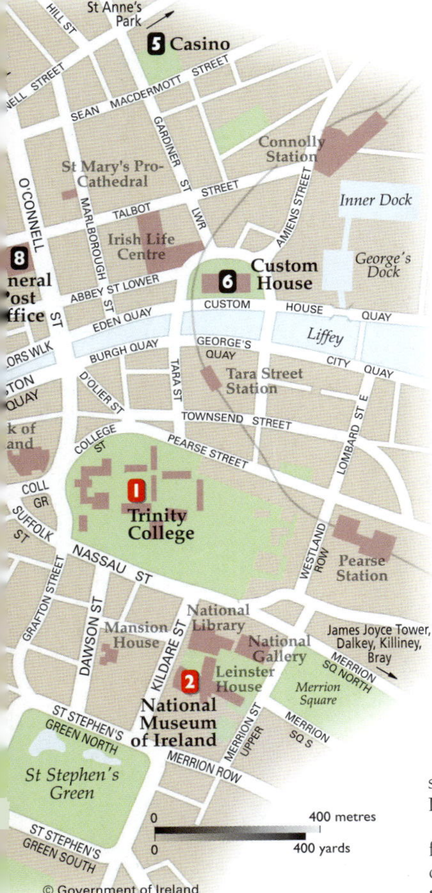

facelift, and Smithfield Village is taking shape as a cultural area. To the west there are street-market quarters and hidden pubs to discover. The further north and east you go, the greener, quieter and more respectable grow the neighbourhoods.

Dublin has so much going for it. There are literary connections in abundance – from old masters James Joyce and Sean O'Casey to young lions such as Emma Donoghue. Music flows through the heart of the city, from the stadium rock of U2 to the cheery good-time pub folk of bands such as The Dubliners and the energetic, sunny sound of youngsters The Delorentos.

This is a friendly city. And the friendliness is genuine, not part of some PR campaign. Enjoy it to the hilt, and then some...

In A Day

If you're not quite sure where to begin your travels, this itinerary recommends a practical and enjoyable day out in Dublin, taking in some of the best places to see using the Getting Your Bearings map on the previous page. For more information see the main entries.

9:30am

Be at **❶ Trinity College** (right, ➤ 50–53) bright and early, to avoid the crush in the "Turning Darkness into Light" exhibition and so get an uncluttered look at the glorious Book of Kells. Leave Trinity by the Nassau Street exit, and make your way down Kildare Street.

10:30am

Pop into the **❷ National Museum of Ireland** (➤ 54–56) to view the dazzling gold and jewels of ancient Ireland. Turn down Molesworth Street and cut through to reach Grafton Street, Dublin's shop-till-you-drop thoroughfare. Relax with a coffee and a sticky bun in Bewley's Café, and watch the buyers go by.

12:00 noon

Stroll down the west side of St Stephen's Green and take a look at Harcourt Street's superb Georgian houses with their characteristic doorways. Then follow Cuffe Street and Kevin Street to **3 St Patrick's Cathedral** (below opposite and left, ➤ 57), to pay your respects at the grave of Jonathan Swift, writer and dean of the cathedral. From here it's a 10-minute walk via Golden Lane to South Great George's Street.

1:30pm

Take the weight off your feet and enjoy the excellent soup and sandwiches in **The Globe** on South Great George's Street. After lunch, walk on north through trendy **9 Temple Bar** (➤ 61) until you meet the River Liffey, and turn right for Aston Quay.

3:00pm

Hop on a 79 bus at Aston Quay for the 10- to 15-minute ride out to **4 Kilmainham Gaol** (➤ 58–59), an icon of Irish history. After the tour of the gaol, make your way up the South Circular Road to the Islandbridge Gate into **14 Phoenix Park** (➤ 64–65).

5:00pm

Blow away the cobwebs with an hour's saunter through the wide open spaces of Phoenix Park. You might see anything from a herd of deer to a fast-paced hurling match. Then catch the 10 bus (from NCR Gate) back to the city centre.

6:30pm

The night is yours! Start in Temple Bar, maybe, with a drink in the St John Gogarty, followed by dinner at the lively Market Bar and Tapas, perhaps, or **The Mermaid Café** in Dame Street (➤ 67). Then on to the Brazen Head or the Long Hall or Doheny & Nesbitt's or…

ⓞ Trinity College and the Book of Kells

Renowned as the most beautiful book in the world, the glorious and priceless Book of Kells is the unchallenged star of the show at Trinity College. These 680 pages of monkish Latin script and painting present a virtuoso display of richness of imagination, breadth of humour and wit, and faithful observation of the world of nature, all executed with a breathtaking delicacy of touch. The monks who copied out and illustrated the four Gospels at the Monastery of Kells in County Meath around the year 800 may have learned their skill in St Columba's celebrated monastery on the Scottish island of Iona; they were certainly among the best illuminators at work in that area.

Trinity College

The Book of Kells is on display at Trinity College, an iconic Irish institution in itself. As you turn off College Street and pass through the low, unobtrusive doorway under the blue clock face, the roar of traffic fades and is overlain by the chatter of young voices and the clop and scuffle of shoes on the cobbled courtyards of Trinity College. In these peaceful quadrangles, surrounded by the mellow architecture of four centuries, you catch a sense of how Dublin must have been in a quieter age.

Not that Trinity, Ireland's premier university, is a stuffy or hidebound place these days. The college was founded in 1592 by Queen Elizabeth I "to civilise Ireland with both learning and the Protestant religion…for the reformation of the barbarism of this rude people." Up until 1966 Catholics were admitted only under special dispensation; today Trinity is completely mixed by both religion and sex (women were admitted to degrees as long ago as 1903).

The magnificently illustrated Greek letters Chi-Rho, formed from the first two letters of the Greek word for Christ, beginning a verse in Matthew's Gospel. The microscopic detail is characteristic of the Book of Kells

Emerging from the tunnel-like entrance into the cobbled enclosure of Parliament Square, you will find to your left the **university chapel**, built in 1798 to an elegant oval design. Inside, its walls are lined with rich dark wood, its ceiling stuccoed green, grey and peach. Ahead stands a tall Victorian **campanile**. In front of this bear right around the end of the **Old Library** (1733) to reach its entrance. Inside, the excellent **"Turning Darkness into Light" exhibition** places the 9th-century manuscript in its historical perspective and helpfully prepares you for your encounter with the Book of Kells.

Georgian grandeur in the peaceful heart of Trinity College

The Book of Kells

The book lies under glass and the pages on show are changed every three to four months. The monkish illustrators used chalk for white colour, lead for red, lapis lazuli for blue. Blue also came from woad, black from carbon and green from copper verdigris. Over the centuries, the colours on the much-admired principal pictorial pages have faded; the pages of less highly decorated script are remarkably white and well preserved. The more you look, the more you can see: sinners misbehaving, angels, ravening beasts and demons, floral tendrils, scenes wildly fantastic and touchingly domestic, conundrums of geometry that resolve, as you stare at them, into initial letters.

Trinity literary son, Oscar Wilde

Other precious manuscript gospels are displayed in rotation alongside the Book of Kells: the 8th-century **Book of Mulling** and **Book of Dimma**, the **Book of Armagh** from about 807, and the **Book of Durrow**, which probably dates back to around 675 and is the oldest surviving decorated gospel book.

SIGNIFICANT STUDENTS

Illustrious Trinity alumni include: Jonathan Swift, author of *Gulliver's Travels;* playwrights Oliver Goldsmith, Oscar Wilde and Samuel Beckett; patriots and politicians Robert Emmet, Edward Carson and Henry Grattan.

High book stacks and a vaulted roof give a tunnel effect to the Long Room

The Long Room

From the Book of Kells display room, climb the stairs to reach the cathedral-like Long Room. Well over 60m (200 feet) long, this superb old library room contains nearly a quarter of a million vintage books under its wooden barrel-vaulted roof. On display here is one of the precious dozen surviving copies of the original **Proclamation of the Republic of Ireland**, whose rolling phrases were read out by Pádraic Pearse from the steps of the General Post Office on Easter Monday 1916: "…we hereby proclaim the Irish Republic as a Sovereign Independent State, and we pledge our lives and the lives of our comrades-in-arms to the cause of its freedom, of its welfare, and of its exaltation among the nations."

Nearby, on the right as you walk through the Long Room, stands a **harp**, gnarled and shiny with age, beautifully carved out of dark willow wood. It can be hard to spot, its ancient brown wood camouflaged against the brown hues of the surrounding books. Unromantic carbon dating says the harp was made around 1400. But legend tells a better tale, insisting that it was once owned by Brian Boru, mightiest of the High Kings of Ireland, who fell on Good Friday 1014 at the moment of victory over the Danes at the Battle of Clontarf.

ALERT ATTENDANTS

Make time to chat to the attendants posted around the "Turning Darkness into Light" exhibition. Not only are they friendly, they are also knowledgeable, and will point out and explain tiny details tucked away in the intricate illustrations.

TAKING A BREAK

Meander from Trinity College into Temple Bar, a district packed with lively cafés and bars. The exuberant café-restaurant **Kilkenny** is a good choice for a light lunch.

✚ 202 C3 ✉ College Street, Dublin 2
☎ Book of Kells 01 896 2320; Library 01 896 1661;
www.tcd.ie/library/
🕐 Old Library and Book of Kells Exhibition: Oct–May Mon–Sat 9:30–5, Sun 12:30–4:30; Jun–Sep Mon–Sat 9:30–5, Sun 9:30–4:30; closed 10 days over Christmas and New Year.
🚌 All cross-city buses ✋ Moderate

THE BOOK OF KELLS: INSIDE INFO

Top tips On a summer holiday weekend it can get very crowded around the case containing the Book of Kells, and you may end up with a frustratingly brief glimpse before being ushered onwards. If possible, visit on an out-of-season weekday, when you will have time to let your eyes adjust and there will be plenty of space to stand and stare.

2 National Museum of Ireland

The National Museum of Ireland encompasses four museums, three in Dublin and one in County Mayo (➤ 133), but for many visitors the name is synonymous with the central Dublin branch, which houses the main historical collections. Officially the Museum of Archaeology and History, it preserves the historic heart and spirit of Ireland. This superb collection includes Europe's finest ancient gold items; richly ornamented early Christian crosses and cups; and Viking bows.

Most of this treasure – much of it dug up by chance from peat bog or potato field – is displayed in the **Treasury** in the museum's Great Hall. There is far too much fine artistry to take in during one visit, but try at least to see the Ardagh Chalice, the Cross of Cong and the "Ireland's Gold" exhibits.

The **Ardagh Chalice**, a heavily decorated two-handled 8th-century silver cup, was discovered by a labourer named Quinn while digging up potatoes he had planted in the ring fort of Reerasta, near Ardagh in County Limerick. Quinn, unaware of its true value, was delighted to sell his treasure trove – the chalice, some brooches, a cup and other items – for a few pounds to a local doctor. The **Cross of Cong** is a processional cross made in 1123 for Turlough O'Conor, King of Connacht, with decorative animal heads, beaded gold wire and inlaid enamel. The magnificent 8th-century **Tara Brooch**, gleaming with amber and coloured glass and covered in intricate interlacing patterns, is the finest piece of Irish jewellery in existence, and certainly the most copied by modern jewellers.

The **Broighter Hoard**, unearthed in County Derry in the 1890s, is the Treasury's biggest collection of gold objects. Made in the 1st century BC of sheet gold beaten to paper thinness, it includes a wonderful miniature boat, elaborate collars, and a string

The 8th-century Tara Brooch has provided inspiration for countless pieces of Irish jewellery

Victorian ironwork frames the roof of the National Museum of Ireland

of hollow gold balls forming a necklace. Remarkable, too, are the shrines made of worked metal and wood to hold sacred objects. Among them is the 12th-century shrine of **St Patrick's Bell**, complete with the big, iron bell itself, which is early 5th century and contemporary with the saint. Legend has it that St Patrick's Bell was used to good effect when its owner climbed the holy mountain of Croagh Patrick. Attacked by a black cloud of demons, St Patrick hurled his bell at them, and they promptly disappeared.

Other major attractions are the enormous **Lurgan log boat**, made around 2400 BC, which is long enough to transport the population of an entire village; the **Viking Gallery** with its swords, pins, brooches and splendid 10th-century yew longbow; and the three galleries of the **Medieval Ireland** exhibit, documenting rural life, the nobility and religious practice from 1150 to 1550.

TAKING A BREAK

Hang out with the fashionable crowd at nearby **Café en Seine**, a great place for coffee and a bite to eat. Alternatively, stop for a relaxed cup of coffee at a Dublin favourite, **Bewley's Café** (78 Grafton Street) and watch the shoppers as they pass by on the busy street outside.

National Museum of Ireland
✚ 202 C2
✉ Kildare Street, Dublin 2
☎ 01 677 7444; www.museum.ie
🕐 Tue–Sat 10–5, Sun 2–5; closed Mon, Good Fri and 25 Dec
🚌 7, 7A, 10, 11, 13; 172 Museum Link
🚆 Pearse Station, DART ✋ Free

W ✚ 202, off A3
✉ Benburb Street, Dublin 7
☎ 01 677 7444; www.museum.ie
🕐 Tue–Sat 10–5, Sun 2–5; closed Mon, Good Fri and 25 Dec
🚌 25, 25A, 66, 67, 90, 172; Museum Link
🚆 Heuston Station (main line); Museum (Luas) ✋ Free

The craftsmanship of the 8th-century Ardagh Chalice makes it one of Ireland's finest pieces of silverware

NATIONAL MUSEUM OF IRELAND: INSIDE INFO

Top tips If you have time, make the 2-km (1-mile) trip from the city centre to Collins Barracks, a handsome 18th-century building that was once used as a barracks but now houses the **Museum of Decorative Arts and History**. The collection details Ireland's social history with exhibits ranging from domestic furnishings to relics of Ireland's political martyrs, as well as paintings and sculpture.

Hidden gem Tucked away in the National Museum of Ireland is a collection of **sheela-na-gigs**, stone carvings of women uninhibitedly displaying their charms. To inspect them, you have to apply in advance to the curator.

One to miss You could afford to miss the **Egyptian exhibition** on the National Museum's upper floor; there is plenty in the Irish exhibits to keep you fascinated for hours on end.

3 St Patrick's Cathedral

St Patrick's Cathedral is a dignified church, large and handsome, dating back to 1190, with its tower and spire soaring to 68m (223 feet).

Inside you'll find the **memorials to Dean Jonathan Swift** (1667–1745), passionate social reformer and author of *Gulliver's Travels* (► 26), and his companion "Stella", whose real name was Esther Johnson (1681–1728), with whom he had a long relationship. They lie side by side under brass plaques set into the nave floor, beside the second pillar just beyond the entrance desk. On the aisle wall nearby is Swift's self-penned memorial: "Laid where fierce indignation can no longer rend the heart. Go travellers, and imitate, if you can, this earnest and dedicated Champion of Liberty."

The cathedral also contains some splendid tombs, notably the 17th-century monument to the Boyle family (of which the scientist Robert Boyle was a member), and a collection of memorials to Irish soldiers killed in British Empire wars. Often overlooked, in the aisle wall south of the choir, are four superb 16th-century brass memorial tablets, very rare in Ireland. In the north aisle is a rather uninspiring memorial to the revered blind harpist Turlough O'Carolan (1670–1738); he deserves something bigger and better.

St Patrick's is at its peaceful best early in the morning or late in the afternoon.

TAKING A BREAK

The Globe on South Great George's Street, a 10-minute walk from the cathedral, is a great place for a light snack.

✝ 202 A2
✉ St Patrick's Close, Dublin 8
☎ 01 475 4817; www.stpatrickscathedral.ie
🕐 Mar–Oct Mon–Sat 9–6, Sun 9–11, 12:45–3, 4:15–6; Nov–Feb Mon–Fri 9–6, Sat 9–5, Sun 10–11, 12:45–3
🚌 49, 49A, 50, 54A, 56A (Eden Quay), 65, 77, 77A
🚆 Pearse Station ✋ Moderate

SWIFT'S SKULL

One item in the Swift exhibition in the north transept is a plaster cast of his skull, a reminder of 19th-century fascination with the macabre. The skull was dug up in the 1830s and "passed around the drawing rooms of Dublin". It was reburied in 1920.

The high altar

4 Kilmainham Gaol

The grim but atmospheric prison of Kilmainham is a national monument that holds within its walls the key to much of Ireland's turbulent history. Here Home Rule rebels – Wolfe Tone's 1798 supporters, "Young Irishmen" of 50 years later, Fenians, and leaders of the Easter Rising – suffered imprisonment, punishment and death.

Kilmainham's entrance sets the tone, a thick door with a spyhatch in a massive stonework frame. The **guided tour** (which is obligatory) starts in the museum, introducing you to bygone Dublin and the slum conditions that bred the debt and petty crime for which most prisoners were incarcerated here. As the guide will tell you as you are taken into the great four-storey hall with its multiple floors of tiny, cold, stone cells, Kilmainham Gaol was considered a model prison when it opened in 1796. Dark corridors lead to granite stairs worn hollow by the tread of feet. Debtors, murderers, sheep stealers, rapists, prostitutes, all ended up here. Famine victims, too – during the 1840s and 1850s the gaol became overcrowded with people who had committed petty crimes in order to qualify for the thin but regularly served prison gruel.

You'll be shown the cells that held Pádraic Pearse, Thomas Clarke, Joseph Plunkett, James Connolly and the other leaders of the 1916 Easter Rising (► 20); the chapel where Plunkett and his fiancée, Grace Gifford, were married; and the high-walled yard where the leaders were shot for treason. The last prisoner to be released before Kilmainham closed in 1924 was the Republican leader Éamon de Valera (► 14) – later to become both head of government and president of Ireland.

Whatever your views, you can't fail to be moved by the stories you'll hear, or by the atmosphere in this cold, echoing, haunted place. It's essential viewing for any visitor who wants to understand Ireland's recent history.

The landings and cells in the gaol's grim interior

✚ 202, off A3

✉ Inchicore Road, Dublin 8

☎ 01 453 5984;

www.heritageireland.ie

🕐 Apr–Sep daily 9:30–6; Oct–Mar Mon–Sat 9:30–5:30 (last admission 4), Sun 10–6 (last admission 5)

🚌 51B, 78A, 79 (Aston Quay)

🚆 Heuston Station; Suir Road, Luas

✋ Moderate

KILMAINHAM GAOL: INSIDE INFO

Top tips Get the guide to shut you into one of the cells, to **taste the grim reality** of four narrow white walls.

Hidden gem Don't miss the **Five Devils of Kilmainham**, five snakes carved in stone above the entrance door. Chained by the neck and writhing helplessly, they symbolise the containment of evil.

One to miss The **audio-visual presentation** pales into insignificance in comparison to the rest of the tour. If pushed for time, give it a miss.

At Your Leisure

Dubliners opposed the construction of the 18th-century Custom House, fearing that it would be an eyesore

5 Casino at Marino

You can take a guided tour around Dublin's strangest building, a well-kept secret tucked away off a suburban road. Built between 1758 and 1776 by the Earl of Charlemont, it is a three-storey pleasure palace of cleverly designed, ingeniously lit rooms, all concealed in what looks from the outside to be a simple one-roomed temple. Despite its name, the Casino houses no roulette or blackjack tables, just some contemporary furniture. Bizarre!

202, off C5 Off Casino Park, Malahide Road 01 833 1618; www.heritageireland. ie Jun–Sep daily 10–6; Oct, May daily 10–5; Apr Sat, Sun noon–4; Feb, Mar noon–4; closed Dec, Jan 20, 20A, 27, 27B, 42C, 123 Clontarf, DART Inexpensive

6 Custom House

This is Dublin's grandest building, a great domed Georgian masterpiece started in 1781 by English architect James Gandon (1743–1823) to replace the old customs point further up the River Liffey. It stretches its portico and long arcaded wings along the north bank of the river, just east of O'Connell Bridge. Republicans torched it in 1921; restored, it houses a visitor centre. Much the best view of the Custom House is from George's Quay across the river.

202 C4 Custom House Quay, Dublin 2 01 888 2538 Mid-Mar to Oct Mon–Fri 10–5, Sat, Sun 2–5; Nov to mid-Mar Wed–Fri 10–5, Sat, Sun 2–5 Cross-city buses Tara Street Station, DART Inexpensive

7 Dublin Writers' Museum

A beautifully restored and refurbished house, 10 minutes' walk north of O'Connell Bridge, contains this excellent museum dedicated to some of Ireland's greatest writers. There are photographs, first editions, personal belongings, letters, rare books, and masses of memorabilia to satisfy your curiosity about Swift, Sheridan, Joyce, Shaw, Wilde, Yeats, Beckett, Brendan Behan and many others.

202 B5 18 Parnell Square North, Dublin 1 01 872 2077; www.writersmuseum. com Mon–Sat 10–5 (also Mon–Fri 10–6, Jun–Aug), Sun, public hols 11–5 10, 11, 11A, 11B, 13, 13A, 16, 16A, 19, 19A, 22, 22A, 36 Connolly Station, DART Moderate

8 General Post Office (GPO)

This splendid Palladian building (1814–18) is almost all that was left of Dublin's late Georgian architecture after the developers got their hands on the city centre in the 1960s and 1970s. The GPO was the headquarters of the Irish Volunteers during the Easter Rising of 1916 (➤ 20) and it was from its steps that Pádraic Pearse read out the Proclamation of the Irish Republic. In the intense shelling that followed (you can still see shrapnel scars on the columns), the GPO was gutted by fire. Reopened in 1929 after rebuilding, it became a potent symbol of Irish independence. Inside is a plaque recording the Proclamation, and a sculpture of the mythical hero Cuchulainn, a symbol of Irish heroism.

🕂 202 B4 ✉ O'Connell Street, Dublin 1 ☎ 01 705 7000 🕐 Mon–Sat 8–8 🚌 Cross-city buses 🚈 Tara Street Station, DART; Connolly, Luas ✋ Free

9 Temple Bar

In the 1980s Temple Bar was a run-down area, due for demolition to make way for a bus station. These days it's Dublin's trendiest, liveliest and most innovative quarter. This is definitely a place to stroll the cobbled streets without a time limit. Young Dublin architects have twisted roof levels, inserted metal panels, and used glass and ceramics freely as they have renovated the old buildings. Street eateries and serious restaurants rub shoulders; so do street musicians and artists.

The heart of Temple Bar is Meeting House Square, often the venue for open-air performances. Around the square cluster the **Irish Film Institute** (tel: 01 679 5744; www.irishfilm.ie) and **Film Archive**, an arts centre, the **Gallery of Photography** (tel: 01 671 4654; www.galleryofphotography.ie), and **the Ark**, with children's workshops and activities (tel: 01 670 7788; www.ark.ie; advance booking advisable). Wander around the Saturday morning food market while Dubliners breakfast in the open air.

If you're looking for live music gigs, try the Button Factory in Curved Street (tel: 01 670 9202; ww2.buttonfactory.ie). Cow's Lane Market is good for Irish-designed fashion and accessories from clothes to bags and jewellery to lingerie.

🕂 202 B3 ✉ Just outh of Wellington and Aston Quays, on the south bank of the Liffey. Temple Bar Cultural Information Centre is at 12 East Essex Street, Dublin 2 ☎ 01 677 2255; www.temple-bar.ie 🕐 Mon–Fri 9–5:30 🚌 Cross-city buses 🚈 Tara Street Station, DART

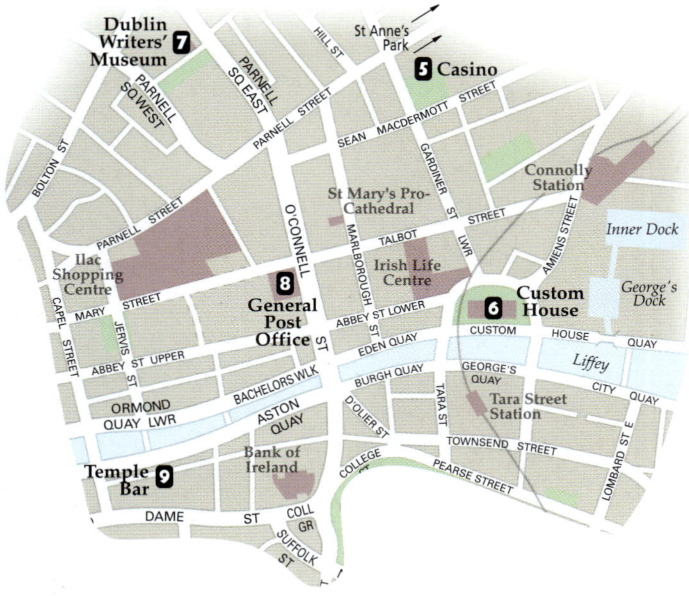

10 Dublin Castle

Grand occasions such as the inauguration of the president and European summit meetings take place in Dublin Castle's splendid State Apartments. Some of the original Norman castle still exists, but much is fine 18th-century rebuilding. You can examine all this along with the restored 19th-century Chapel Royal with its carved stone likenesses of British royalty outside and its elaborate woodwork and plaster-work within.

✚ 202 A3 ✉ Dame Street, Dublin 2 ☎ 01 677 7129; www.dublincastle.ie 🕓 Mon–Fri 10–4:45, Sat–Sun, public hols 2–4:45; closed 1 Jan, Good Fri and 25–26 Dec 🚌 49, 56A, 77, 77A, 77B, 123 🚆 Tara Street, DART ✋ Inexpensive

11 Chester Beatty Library and Gallery

This is one of the world's great private art collections, notable not for its size (though it contains more than 22,000 manuscripts, rare books and miniature paintings), but for its quality. Sir Alfred Chester Beatty (1875–1968), a Canadian millionaire who made his fortune through mining and came to live in Dublin

The sumptuously furnished State Drawing Room at Dublin Castle

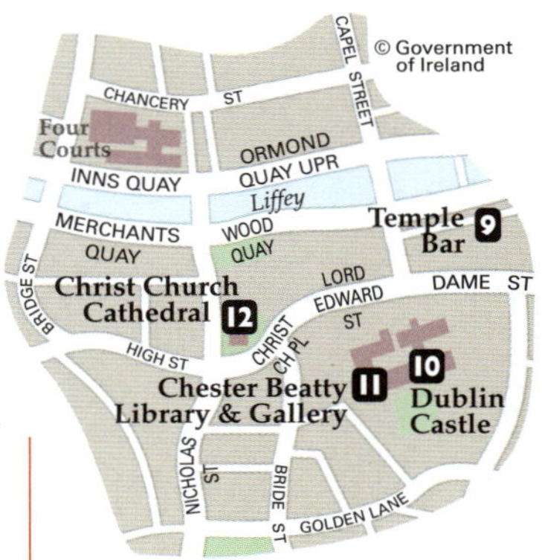

in 1953, put together his collection over most of his long lifetime. The Japanese scrolls are particularly fine, dating from the early 17th to the late 19th centuries. Religious legends, tales of romance and scenes of battle are painted in meticulous detail across rolls of paper or silk up to 25m (82 feet) long. There are Japanese prints of actors and tea drinkers and courtesans with oblique gazes and tiny mouths, and a whole clutch of delicately carved *netsuke*, or cord toggles. Other exotic curiosities include tiny snuff bottles in mother-of-pearl, jade and porcelain from China, and an Egyptian love poem written in 1160 BC, the world's most important surviving example of ancient Egyptian poetry.

Pride of place goes to the library's collection of manuscripts. Some of these are astonishingly old and rare, including ancient copies of the Koran, richly gilded and tooled, and a medieval Iraqi treatise on engineering, artillery and astronomy. There are also some very early biblical fragments, such as a Gospel of St Luke and a Book of Revelations, both dating from the 3rd century, and the Epistles of St Paul, written out in the 2nd century, and portions of the Books of Numbers and Deuteronomy dating back to about AD 150.

✚ 202 A3 ✉ The Clock Tower, Dublin Castle, Dublin 2 ☎ 01 407 0750; www.cbl.ie 🕓 May–Sep Mon–Fri 10–5, Sat 11–5, Sun 1–5; Oct–Apr Tue–Fri 10–5, Sat 11–5, Sun 1–5; closed 1 Jan, Good Fri, 24–26 Dec 🚌 49, 56A, 77, 77A, 77B, 123 🚆 Tara Street, DART ✋ Free

12 Christ Church Cathedral

The 11th-century king Sigtryggr Silkenbeard founded it in wood, then around 150 years later the Norman Earl Strongbow rebuilt it in stone; it is a splendid early Norman cathedral and the oldest stone building in Dublin. Despite an over-thorough restoration in the 19th century, plenty of that Norman stonework remains. "Strongbow's tomb" lies in the south aisle, but the Norman earl himself is probably buried elsewhere. The original crypt runs the length of the church; don't miss the gloomy statues, monarchical relics, and a celebrated showpiece, "the cat and the rat", whose mummified remains were found in an organ pipe.

✚ 202 A3 ✉ Christ Church Place, Dublin 8 ☎ 01 677 8099; www.cccdub.ie ◎ Jun–Aug daily 9–6; Sep–May 9:45–5 🚌 50 (Eden Quay); 78A (Aston Quay) 🚆 Tara Street, DART ✋ Moderate

The interior of Christ Church Cathedral

OFF THE BEATEN TRACK

St Stephen's Green, just south of Trinity College, is a popular place to hang out in the sunshine. If you walk on south down Harcourt Street, however, and turn left into Clonmel Street, you will discover the much more private, tranquil and uncrowded **Iveagh Gardens**. A beautiful green retreat among fountains and mature trees, the gardens are a great place to escape from the rigours of city life.

FOR KIDS

Dublin Zoo (tel: 01 474 8900; www.dublinzoo.ie, open: Mon–Sat 9:30–6, Sun 10:30–6, in summer; Mon–Sat 9:30–4, Sun 10:30–4, in winter; admission: expensive), surrounded by the wide open spaces of Phoenix Park, is good of its kind. At the time of going to press, **The National Wax Museum** is due to reopen at new premises in Smithfield (tel: 01 872 6340 for further information).

13 Guinness Storehouse

Ireland's favourite brew has travelled to more corners of the world than the Irish themselves, which is saying something, and the first thing many visitors to Ireland want to do is to taste it on its home soil. The next step is to visit this exhibition at the brewery itself, to discover just why the "black stuff" has such appeal. Housed in a former fermentation plant, the Storehouse tells the story of Arthur Guinness and his brewery, with displays about how Guinness is made, how it is transported worldwide, and its hugely popular and entertaining advertising campaigns. At the end of the tour you get a complimentary pint in the circular roof-top Gravity Bar, with floor-to-ceiling windows and spectacular views over Dublin.

✚ 202, off A3 ✉ St James's Gate, Dublin 8 ☎ 01 408 4800; www.guinness-storehouse. com ⏲ Daily 9:30–5 (till 7 pm Jul–Aug); closed Good Fri and 24–26 Dec 🚌 51B, 78A (Aston Quay), 90 (Connolly Station), 123 (O'Connell and Dame streets) 🚉 Heuston ✋ Expensive

14 Phoenix Park

Phoenix Park (main entrance about 1.5km/1 mile west of the city centre) is the largest walled city park in Europe, covering approximately 800 hectares (2,000 acres). This huge expanse of land, laid out in the mid-18th century, contains woods, lakes, hillocks, streams and gardens, set against the backdrop of the Wicklow Mountains. The Irish president lives here in a mansion, Áras an Uachtaráin. Here, too, are 17th-century Ashtown Castle, housing the Phoenix Park Visitor

Phoenix Park, west of central Dublin, is the perfect place to escape frenetic city life

Centre (tel: 01 677 0095), the American ambassador's residence, St Mary's Hospital, and Dublin Zoo – all swallowed up in the vastness of the park.

🕇 202, off A3 ✉ Main entrance on Parkgate Street, opposite Heuston Station; www.heritageireland.ie ☎ Visitor centre 01 677 0095 🕓 Visitor centre: daily 10–6. Last admission 5:15 🚌 37, 38, 39 to Ashdown Gate; 10 to NCR Gate, 70 🚆 Heuston, Luas ♿ Park: free. Visitor centre: inexpensive

Outer Dublin
Riding the DART (➤ 35) is by far the best way to taste the many delights of outer Dublin, and gain enjoyable views along the waterfronts, the Liffey and the city centre.

St Anne's Park
This quiet park, 8km (5 miles) from the centre, is little visited by non-Dubliners. It is crossed by a number of footpaths; the best runs down through the park's extensive woodland, past follies and temples hidden among the trees, to emerge beside the coast road with wide views out over North Bull Island to Howth Head.

🕇 201 E5 🚆 Killester or Harmonstown, DART

James Joyce Tower
The Martello Tower that overlooks the sea at Sandycove was featured by James Joyce in the opening sequence of *Ulysses*. Joyce lived in the tower for a month in 1904. Today it houses a collection of Joyce curios and memorabilia, along with photographs, books and a selection of letters. The oval tower itself, built early in the 19th century against the threat of a Napoleonic invasion, makes an atmospheric place to visit, and from the roof you can enjoy the same fine view as Buck Mulligan did in *Ulysses*.

🕇 201 E5 ✉ Sandycove Point, Sandycove ☎ 01 280 9265 🕓 Mar–Oct Mon–Sat 10–1, 2–5, Sun, public hols 2–6; closed Oct–Mar 🚆 Sandycove, DART ♿ Moderate

Dalkey
This quiet little seaside town 14.5km (9 miles) from central Dublin, immortalised with mordant humour by Flann O'Brien in *The Dalkey Archive*, is not so much a resort as a well-heeled commuter haven with a tangle of narrow lanes and a pleasant "out-of-it-all" feel.

🕇 201 E5 🚆 Dalkey, DART

Killiney
Killiney is a very exclusive place these days, the seaside refuge of rock stars, artists and other fashionable Dublin escapees. The best thing to do once you are tired of celebrity-spotting is to climb Killiney Hill and enjoy the splendid view out over Dublin Bay.

🕇 201 E5 🚆 Killiney, DART

Bray
Bray is a jaded seaside resort, 24km (15 miles) from the centre, with good sands and a plethora of cheap and cheerful amusements. Take a windswept walk around Bray Head.

🕇 201 E5 🚆 Bray, DART

Where to...
Eat and Drink

Prices
Expect to pay per person for a meal, excluding drinks and service
€ under €15   €€ €15 to €30   €€€ over €30

Il Baccaro €€

This intimate, informal restaurant has an interesting setting in a 17th-century cellar in the corner of Meeting House Square. Step down into a barrel-shaped room of open brickwork where the all-Italian staff rustle up some tempting regional dishes, including starters such as *bresaola Grana e rucola* (cured beef from Northern Italy with Grana cheese and rocket). Main courses feature meat, fish and vegetarian options. Good pasta, too.

✚ 202 B3 ✉ Diceman's Corner, Meeting House Square, Dublin 2 ☎ 01 671 4597
◉ Lunch Sun only from 12, dinner daily 6–11

Butler's Chocolate Café €

Chocoholics, chocolate junkies, lovers of a chocolate surprise with a great big choccie on the side – this is chocolate paradise. You can drink Butlers' heavenly chocolate, hot or as a whipped-cream milkshake, you can pop it under your tongue in the form of a melt-in-the-mouth fondant, or nibble it in dreamy cakes and croissants. To the devil with the measuring tape – Butler's is Chocolate Funky Town.

✚ 202 B2 ✉ Chatham Street, Dublin 2
☎ 01 672 6333; www.butlerschocolates.com
◉ Mon–Wed 9–6, Fri 8–7, Thu 8–9, Sat 9–7, Sun 11–7

Cornucopia €–€€

This long-established vegetarian restaurant off Grafton Street continues to be a favourite for its relaxed atmosphere and its excellent choice of delicious and imaginative dishes, such as Portobello mushrooms stuffed with walnuts and blue cheese; Moroccan carrot soup and roasted Mediterranean vegetable filo parcels. Breads and cakes are all home-baked too.

✚ 202 B3 ✉ 19 Wicklow Street, Dublin 2
☎ 01 677 7583; email: cornucopia@tinet.ie
◉ Mon–Sat 8:30–8 (till 9 Thu), Sun noon–6; closed 1 Jan, Easter Sun and 3 days Christmas

Excise Bistro €€

An exciting addition to Dublin's restaurants, situated in the heart of the financial district. Fortunately a drink is now easier to come by in a choice of two bars. The interior is a fusion of old and new and the ambience one of relaxed chic. A Mediterranean menu of fish, meat, pastas and risottos, served with flair.

✚ 202 C3 ✉ Lower Mayor Street, IFSC, Dublin 1 ☎ 01 672 1874; www.excisebar.ie
◉ Mon–Fri 12–2:30, 5–10, Sat–Sun 5–10

Jacobs Ladder €€€

Overlooking the playing fields of Trinity College, this cool, modern first-floor restaurant provides a lovely setting for the fine cooking. Well-balanced, hearty seasonal menus always include several imaginative vegetarian dishes. There's a good selection of local fish, shellfish and speciality Irish produce such as carrageen (edible seaweed) and farmhouse cheeses.

✚ 202 C2 ✉ 4 Nassau Street, Dublin 2
☎ 01 670 3865; www.jacobsladder.ie
◉ Lunch and dinner: Tue–Fri. Dinner: Sat; closed 3 weeks Christmas

Mao €€

Established in 1997, this café provided Dublin with a new kind of eating, in a minimalist setting with an upbeat atmosphere. The Asian fusion cooking is popular with dishes such as chilli squid, Thai fishcakes and mouth-watering stirfries. No reservations. Look out for two other sister restaurants in Dublin.

🚩 202 B2 ✉ 2–3 Chatham Row, Dublin 2 ☎ 01 670 4899; www.cafemao.com ⏰ Daily noon–11

The Mermaid Café €–€€

Near the edge of Temple Bar, the mood is modern, and the attention to detail touches everything. Imaginative France meets East Coast America: try braised mallard with juniper red wine onions and caramelised pears. Interesting Irish cheeses, excellent coffees and unusual wines add to the appeal.

🚩 202 A3 ✉ 69/70 Dame Street, Dublin 2 ☎ 01 670 8236; www.mermaid.ie ⏰ Lunch and dinner: Mon–Sat; Sun brunch noon–3:30; closed Christmas week

O'Connell's €€

If you are after fabulous food, cooked imaginatively and made from carefully sourced ingredients – here you are, and welcome. The menu lets you know where it all came from, and who produced it – a really nice intimate touch.

🚩 202, off C1 ✉ Bewley's Hotel, Merrion Road, Ballsbridge, Dublin 4 ☎ 01 668 1111; www.oconnellsballsbridge.com ⏰ Lunch Mon–Sat noon–2:40, dinner Mon–Fri 5:30–10, Sat, Sun 5:30–9:30

Old Jameson Distillery €

The restored Old Jameson Distillery is a great spot for a bite to eat. In the bright, contemporary café-style Still Room Restaurant the combination of self-service and table service hits just the right tone. Light food is available and locals eagerly join the line for lunch, which features well-made Irish comfort food.

🚩 202, off A3 ✉ Smithfield, Dublin 8 ☎ 01 807 2715 ⏰ Daily noon–5; closed Good Fri and 25 Dec

M J O'Neill's Public House €

An artsy-craftsy sort of a place with a famous clock-of-three-faces, O'Neill's is the sort of traditional corner pub that used to be styled an "emporium". The carvery is the thing here: piping hot roasts with "taters" (potatoes) and good veg, followed by a deliciously calorific pudding and one of the best pints of Guinness in Dublin.

✉ Suffolk Street, Dublin 2 ☎ 01 679 3656 ⏰ Mon–Sat noon–10:15, Sun 12:30–10:15

Queen of Tarts €

This is the ultimate little teashop with a big heart. Friendly owners will guarantee you a wholesome breakfast, welcome coffee break, scrumptious lunch or the most indulgent afternoon tea. Treats include savoury pies and mountainous sandwiches, healthy salads and yummy cakes and pastries, all home-made. Not many tables but do make the effort to squeeze in – it's worth it.

🚩 202 A3 ✉ 3 Cork Hill, Dame Street, Dublin 2 ☎ 01 670 7499 ⏰ Mon–Fri 7:30–7, Sat 9–6, Sun 10–6

23 €€€

The lastest addition to the Gresham's culinary selection provides a sophisticated, yet intimate, environment. With local produce the key element, the Irish cooking has a modern approach. Start with the likes of seared scallops, followed by grilled fillet of Doyle's Irish beef and finish with strawberry soup of passion fruit and white chocolate mousse.

🚩 202 B4 ✉ The Gresham, 23 Upper O'Connell Street, Dublin 1 ☎ 01 817 6116; www.gresham-hotels.com ⏰ Mon–Sat 5:30–10:30

Ukiyo Bar €€€

Dublin's first and only sake bar and karaoke booth venue also has a fine restaurant upstairs. Simplicity and quality combine with modern Asian cuisine influenced by the tastes of Japan and Korea. Diners eat on low tables and are encouraged to share dishes and experiment with flavours.

🚩 202 B4 ✉ 7–9 Exchequer Street, Dublin 2 ☎ 01 633 4071; www.ukiyobar.com ⏰ Lunch Mon–Sat noon–4, dinner daily 5pm–11pm

Where to... Stay

Prices
Expect to pay per night for a double room without tax
€ under €70 €€ €70 to €130 €€€ over €130

Aberdeen Lodge €€

This restored Edwardian house is a charming private hotel. Accommodation is charged by the room, with breakfast, providing good value for the location and high standard. Comfortably furnished rooms include two with four-poster beds; two suites have spa baths. Dinner is available and facilities include a garden and a gym close by.
202, off C3 53–55 Park Avenue, Ballsbridge, Dublin 4 01 283 8155; www.halpinsprivatehotels.com Open all year

The Clarence €€€

The rock group U2 bought this mid-19th-century Liffey-side hotel in the early 1990s and refurbished it in a contemporary style that is in sympathy with its Arts and Crafts origins. It offers the luxury and amenities expected by the stars who stay here. The hotel's fashionable restaurant, **The Tea Room**, is one of Dublin's favourite dining-rooms, and Temple Bar's top meeting place is the oak-panelled Octagon Bar.
202 A3 6–8 Wellington Quay, Dublin 2 01 407 0800; www.theclarence.ie Open all year

Harding €

This hotel is definitely a find in the lower price bracket. Overlooking Christ Church Cathedral, it is well placed for reaching all of Dublin's main sights. The purpose-built hotel, with 53 rooms, is attractively styled and pleasantly furnished. Darkey Kelley's bar and restaurant provides the venue with an excellent breakfast and the evening hosts contemporary and traditional music.
202 A3 Copper Alley, Fishamble, Dublin 2 01 679 6500; www.hardinghotel. ie Closed 3 days Christmas

Jurys Inn Christchurch €€

This modern hotel, in a central position near Temple Bar, offers a good standard of accommodation. You'll be pleasantly surprised by spacious, well-furnished rooms sleeping up to three adults (or two adults and two children), with well-lit desktops, tea/coffee facilities, TV, direct-dial phone and small, simple bathrooms with bath and shower. No room service, but there's a pub and restaurant on site. There are other Jurys Inns at Custom House Quay, Parnell Street and Ballsbridge.
202 A3 Christchurch Place, Dublin 8

01 454 0000; www.jurysdoyle.com
Closed 24–26 Dec

Kilronan House €€

This Georgian house is in a peaceful setting, within walking distance of St Stephen's Green and The National Concert Hall. It's stylish throughout, with original features and Waterford Crystal chandeliers. You'll find crisp linens and orthopaedic beds in the bedrooms, plus TV, beverages and baskets of quality toiletries. Breakfasts are definitely a highlight, with smoked salmon, pancakes, fresh fruit and the traditional Irish breakfast on the menu.
202 B1 70 Adelaide Road, Dublin 2 01 475 5266; www.dublinn.com Open all year

Merrion €€€

The epitome of relaxed grandeur, the Merrion comprises four gracious Georgian townhouses and has superb bedrooms and suites reflecting 18th-century architecture.

Opulent marble bathrooms complete the picture. Downstairs, turf fires greet you in winter, while the spa and pool facilities help you to relax. The excellent restaurants and bars include the acclaimed Patrick Guilbaud, considered one of the finest in Dublin.

🕂 202 C2 ⊠ Upper Merrion Street, Dublin 2 ☎ 01 603 0600; www.merrionhotel.com ⊚ Open all year

Raglan Lodge €€

In a peaceful position, only a short walk from the city centre, this elegant Victorian residence has exceptionally comfortable bedrooms with private bathrooms and all the usual amenities. Restored in 1987, it is now one of the city's most desirable guesthouses, for the comfort and service and also for outstanding breakfasts. Theatre reservations can be arranged and there's private parking.

🕂 202, off C1 ⊠ 10 Raglan Road, Dublin 4 ☎ 01 660 6697 ⊚ Closed 2 weeks over Christmas

Where to... Shop

Dublin's main shopping areas span the Liffey from the rejuvenated Henry Street and O'Connell Street area (on the north bank) to the more exclusive Grafton Street area (south bank), with a pedestrian link through Temple Bar and across the Ha'penny Bridge. Some of the top shops are unique to Dublin, including department stores such as Arnotts (Henry Street), Clery's (O'Connell Street) and the ultra-chic Brown Thomas (Grafton Street), and there are many specialist shops. International brands are everywhere, but it is owner-managed shops and boutiques that really make shopping here an enjoyable experience.

THINGS IRISH

South of the river, you'll find classy cosmopolitan shops in the Grafton Street area, notably on Hibernian Way, off Dawson Street. And there are outlets for quality Irish goods such as tweeds, woollens, pottery and crystal along **Nassau Street**. **Kilkenny** is the most interesting and stylish shop to browse, with a fine range of contemporary Irish fashions in natural fabrics, silver jewellery and pottery and crafts. Kilkenny is also a good choice for a meal, featuring its own food products. Nearby, **Blarney Woollen Mills** specialises in tweeds and sweaters, **Kevin & Howlin** is the place to go for men's traditional handwoven tweed jackets, suits and hats, while **House of Ireland** is an upmarket gift shop carrying a wide selection of typically Irish goods, including crystal, tweeds and woollens.

BOOKS AND ANTIQUES

Cathach Books (Duke Street) are second-hand book specialists; **Books Upstairs** (College Green) is small and excellent, while **Hodges Figgis**, the city's biggest bookshop, faces **Waterstones** across Dawson Street. Waterstones also has an outlet in the Jervis Centre.

Dublin's tradition of craftsmanship makes it a good browsing ground for antiques. Bargains are rare, but you'll have fun looking. The trade is centred in Dublin's oldest district, The Liberties. Francis Street especially is renowned. **The**

Powerscourt Townhouse Centre (South William Street) has an antiques gallery selling mainly silver and china. Here, too, is the Crafts Council of Ireland's HQ Gallery. There are many antiques and jewellery shops in the same neighbourhood. Beautiful shawls, scarves and woven goods from the **Avoca Handweavers Mill** (County Wicklow) are sold at their shop on Suffolk Street.

MARKETS

At **Temple Bar Market** (Meeting House Square), the best of artisan foods are sold every Saturday. **Mother Redcap's**, a covered market on Back Lane (Christchurch, open: Fri–Sun 11–6) has all sorts for sale, much of it second-hand. At the **Tower Design Centre** (Pearse Street, tel: 01 677 5655) you can watch craftspeople at work and buy silk painting, jewellery, designer knitwear, pewter, woodwork and such like.

Where to... Be Entertained

Listings covering theatre, cinema, live music, sporting events and festivals are carried in papers, *In Dublin* **magazine (published every two weeks) and** *Events of the Week***, a free sheet available from pubs and guesthouses. The** *Irish Times* **website (www.ireland.com) is a valuable source of information. Dublin Tourism Centre at St Andrew's Church, Suffolk Street, Dublin 2 (tel: 01 605 7700) can also help.**

FAMOUS PUBS

Spontaneous entertainment is provided by Dublin pubs: **Doheny and Nesbitt** (5 Lower Baggot Street, tel: 01 676 2945) is renowned for politician spotting, while **Toner's** (139 Lower Baggot Street) is a delight and is said to be the only pub W B Yeats ever entered. James Joyce is just one of the literary giants to have drunk at **The Duke** (9 Duke Street).

NIGHT-LIFE

Pub Music

O'Donoghue's (15 Merrion Row, tel: 01 661 4303) is renowned, and there's traditional music and good food in Dublin's oldest pub, **The Brazen Head** (20 Lower Bridge Street, tel: 01 679 5186). **Jurys** (Ballsbridge, tel: 01 660 5000) hotels offer regular cabaret. Outside the city, **Johnnie Fox's** (Glencullen, tel: 01 295 5647) is equally famous for its seafood menus and Irish "Hooley Nights", while **Howth's Abbey Tavern** (tel: 01 839 0307) offers traditional Irish music. **Taylors Three Rock Bar** in Rathfarnham (tel: 01 494 2999) has music and dancing. A young crowd heads for Temple Bar and other venues featuring Irish and international artists, such as **The Village Bar** (26 Wexford Street, tel: 01 475 8555) and **Whelan's** (25 Wexford Street, tel: 01 478 0766).

Nightclubs

Happening bands swagger at the **Sugar Club** (Lower Leeson Street, tel: 01 678 7188), while **Traffic** (Middle Abbey Street, tel: 01 873 4038) hosts Club Swirl and Acid Disco. The **Gaiety** (South King Street, tel: 01 677 1717) and **Olympia** (Dame Street) theatres have late-night music. For details of what's on at **The National Concert Hall** (Earlsfort Terrace) and **The Point**, see newspapers and listings. The **Comedy Cellar** (International Bar, Wicklow Street, tel: 01 677 9250) has Irish and international comedy upstairs every Wednesday.

Eastern Ireland

Getting Your Bearings

Eastern Ireland has subtle charms that well repay your time. The steep Wicklow Mountains – Dublin's own mini-mountains – rise right on the city's southern doorstep, and extend southwards with a fine coast of cliffs and long sandy beaches. South from here, big river estuaries (paradise for birdwatchers) cut into Ireland's southeastern foot around Wexford and Waterford. West of Dublin lie the great open spaces of The Curragh in County Kildare (prime horse country), while out to the north of the city the land smooths into green farming country.

Dotted throughout are the slow-paced small towns and villages so characteristic of rural Ireland. Life runs as easy here as it does in the west, and with half the tourist crowds, even though the chief attractions of eastern Ireland are among the best known in the country. Dubliners may venture south from the city to take a stroll in the Wicklow Hills or buy some knitwear from the weaving shops at Avoca, but many visitors look further west for their pleasures, hurrying through towards the dramatic scenery of Galway and Clare. All the more elbow room for those who allow themselves a few days to sample this overlooked corner of Ireland.

The hills of Wicklow offer superb walking and even better sightseeing, especially the monastic remains at Glendalough. Down in Waterford you can watch Waterford crystal being made, then buy a piece of this world-renowned glassware. Kilkenny is the most appealing medieval town in Ireland. There are equine eccentricities at the National Stud and Horse Museum near Kildare, and a chance to see thoroughbreds at full gallop on The Curragh. Relics of a

★ Don't Miss

1 **The Wicklow Mountains, Co Wicklow** ► 76
2 **Waterford Crystal, Co Waterford** ► 79
3 **Kilkenny, Co Kilkenny** ► 80
4 **Newgrange and Brú na Bóinne Irish Heritage Site, Co Meath** ► 81

At Your Leisure

5 The Wicklow Coast, Co Wicklow ► 85
6 Wexford Wildfowl Reserve, Co Wexford ► 85
7 Irish National Heritage Park, Co Wexford ► 85
8 Jerpoint Abbey, Co Kilkenny ► 86
9 Rock of Cashel, Co Tipperary ► 86
10 Dunmore Caves, Co Kilkenny ► 86
11 Moone and Castledermot High Crosses, Co Kildare ► 87
12 Irish National Stud, Irish Horse Museum and Japanese Gardens, Co Kildare ► 87
13 Hill of Tara, Co Meath ► 88
14 Monasterboice, Co Louth ► 88

Page 71: The ancient church and graveyard at Glendalough

glorious ecclesiastical past vary from the ancient churches and round towers of Monasterboice and the Rock of Cashel to the richly carved high crosses at Moone and Castledermot.

Pride of place, though, has to be given to the remarkable Stone Age passage grave north of Dublin at Newgrange, heavily decorated with enigmatic swirls of stone carving. One of Ireland's most memorable experiences is to creep along the ancient stone corridor to the chamber at the heart of the burial mound, where the sun still enters at the winter solstice to celebrate death and rebirth, as it has for 5,000 years.

In Three Days

If you're not quite sure where to begin your travels, this itinerary recommends a practical and enjoyable journey around Eastern Ireland, taking in some of the best places to see using the Getting Your Bearings map on the previous page. For more information see the main entries.

Day One

Morning
Leave Dublin (N81 or N11) in time to allow a morning's idling south through the **1 Wicklow Mountains** (left, ➤ 76–77), leaving at least an hour to explore **Glendalough** (above). Aim to reach Avoca in time for a dip into Avoca Handweavers (➤ 89–92) before lunch in Fitzgerald's Pub.

Afternoon
Continue south via Arklow to Enniscorthy. If you have some time to spare, turn south here for half an hour to reach **6 Wexford** and the **wildfowl** reserve on the mudflats of the North Slob (➤ 85). Otherwise, continue southwest to a night's stop in Waterford.

Day Two

Morning
Spend an hour or so in the **2 Waterford Crystal** factory and Visitor Centre
(➤ 79), then it's a 50km (30-mile) drive north to **3 Kilkenny** (High Street
above, ➤ 80), another place that's worth at least two hours' exploration
and is a good place for lunch.

Afternoon
Head north from Kilkenny to Portlaoise; then northeast via Portarlington
and Edenderry across the Bog of Allen, one of Ireland's most extensive
and evocative peat bogs. It's a vast expanse of wild country whose flatness
either repels or fascinates, depending on your mood. Continue to Trim,
beautifully placed with its Norman castle beside the River Boyne; then on
via the splendid ruins of Bective Abbey towards Navan.

Day Three

Morning
Continue northeast to **4 Brú na Bóinne** and **Newgrange** passage grave
(➤ 81–84) – the site deserves at least a morning's exploration.

Afternoon
Enjoy lunch in historic Drogheda. Afterwards follow N1, which saunters
to the coast at Balbriggan before setting its sights south for the capital; or
if you are in no hurry, idle back via the rural and delightful R108 through
Naul and Ballyboghil.

⓪ The Wicklow Mountains

The Wicklow Mountains beckon irresistibly on the Dublin skyline, enticing city-dwellers out at weekends in their thousands to enjoy the fresh air and freedom of the "Garden of Ireland".

Roads from Dublin into the Wicklow Mountains are all beautiful. You can ease yourself in from Bray on the northeast coast, ride in grandly from the west via the Sally Gap or the Wicklow Gap, or wriggle down from the north over Powerscourt Mountain. The real pleasure of these mountains is in taking a side turning and discovering the beautiful gorges, glens and remote pieces of wild country for yourself. But the main attraction is undoubtedly Glendalough, a scatter of monastic remains along an exceptionally lovely lake valley in the heart of the mountains.

Filling the country south of the capital, the Wicklow Mountains rise in peaks that are small in comparison to the world's great mountain ranges; the highest, Lugnaquilla, rises to just 925m (3,035 feet), and most of the other summits struggle to make 850m (2,790 feet). But they provide wonderful walking, through a network of footpaths and along the long-distance Wicklow Way footpath, which traverses

The open country of the Wicklow Mountains

the range from north to south. Wicklow is the most thickly forested county in Ireland. There are excellent forest trails in the Devil's Glen on the east of the mountains, at Djouce Woods near Powerscourt, at Ballinafunshoge in Glenmalure south of Glendalough, and around Glendalough itself.

Glendalough

The monastic site of Glendalough incorporates a 12th-century **Round Tower** (33m/108 feet high), the 11th-century **St Kevin's Kitchen** (a beautiful stone-built oratory), and a number of glorious views of the lake and its mountain backdrop. Founded possibly as early as the 6th century, the monastery gained a Europe-wide reputation for learning. Its most illustrious member (some say its founder) was St Kevin, who was of the royal house of Leinster in the 6th century.

It is best to avoid Glendalough in high season: on summer holiday weekends, it becomes something less than the tranquil paradise it can seem on a quiet spring or autumn evening.

TAKING A BREAK

Stop in the Wicklow Mountains at the renowned **Roundwood Inn** (➤ 89), where excellent bar food is served in an informal environment. In Avoca, try **Fitzgerald's Pub** or the **Avoca Handweavers** (➤ 89).

✚ 201 D4

✉ **Immediately south of Dublin, via N81, then R759 or R756. Alternatively, N11, then R755; or R115.**

Tourist information
County Wicklow Tourism, Rialto House, Fitzwilliam Square, Wicklow ☎ 0404 69117; www.wicklow.ie/tourism

AVOCA

The village of Avoca, in the southern part of the Wicklow Mountains region, has Ireland's oldest hand-weaving mill. To get there, go 21km (13 miles) south from Glendalough (R755 to Rathdrum; R752 to Avoca).

RESERVOIR ROAD

A scenic road curves around the shores of Poulaphouca Reservoir between Blessington and Hollywood – a good introduction to the Wicklow Mountains.

THE WICKLOW MOUNTAINS: INSIDE INFO

Top tips To get from **Dublin to Glendalough's** monuments and lakes, take the N81 Wexford road south from Dublin; at Hollywood (40km/25 miles), a left turn on to R756 takes you through the Wicklow Gap and on to Glendalough.
■ If you intend to go **walking in the Wicklow Mountains**, take a good map. The Irish OS 1:50,000 Sheets 56 and 62 maps cover the area in detail.

Hidden gem The **side road** that (almost) circumnavigates Trooperstown Hill, just east of Laragh and Glendalough, is a beautiful 14.5km (9-mile) meander.

WATERFORD CRYSTAL: INSIDE INFO

Top tips If you want to avoid uncomfortably crowded tours (and Waterford Crystal is one of Ireland's most popular tourist attractions), take the **early morning tour**. In the high holiday season, book ahead to make sure of a place.
■ Try the **quieter R733** as an alternative to the main N25 Wexford to Waterford road. It leads you into the Hook Head peninsula on the east side of Waterford Harbour. There are old castles here at Ballyhack and Slade, and coastal views.

Hidden gem Lucky Friday visitors may get to see workers in sinister face masks wilting as they withdraw **molten crystal** from the white-hot furnace.

2 Waterford Crystal

Watching a piece of Waterford Crystal slowly taking shape is like watching an expert magic trick: you can see every stage as it happens, but the end result still amazes.

Waterford Crystal is a commercial operation, well aware of its glamorous international reputation, and touring the glassworks, you can feel a bit like a sheep being herded along in a flock. But don't miss it.

The celebrated glassware is made in the same town on the south coast of Ireland, and by much the same method, as it was when the business was started up in 1783 by English brothers William and George Penrose. The expertise required, the instinct that tells a craftsperson when something is exactly right, and the long hours of practice that eventually make perfect – these remain timeless.

On your tour through the process you see how silica sand, litharge (lead monoxide) and potash – unprepossessing in themselves – are mixed in furnaces, then drawn out to be blown into glowing balls of molten crystal. Skilfully patted and smoothed in wooden and iron moulds, the crystal fades to pale yellow, then to a smoky transparency as it is shaped.

The next stage is the cutting, each craftsperson at a wheel carving the characteristic deep patterns of wedges and swirls into the cooled crystal. Then comes the engraving and sculpting workshop where master craftspeople cut delicate designs of faces, foliage, animals and birds. At all stages of the process the workers are happy to explain what they are doing and to answer questions.

Afterwards, you can buy some crystal from the showroom. However, bargain-hunters looking for a cheap "second" with some trifling flaw are wasting their time. To preserve the crystal's reputation, any imperfect glass is smashed into small pieces at the factory.

TAKING A BREAK

Enjoy an informal meal at **The Wine Vault**, a lively wine bar in the oldest part of Waterford.

Each piece of crystal is inspected carefully before it leaves the glassworks

✚ 200 C3
✉ Kilbarry, Cork Road, Waterford
☎ 051 332 500;
www.waterfordvisitorcentre.com
🕐 Tours Mar–Oct daily 9–6 (last tour 4:15); Nov–Feb Mon–Fri 9:30–5 (last tour 3:15). Visitor Centre Mar–Oct daily 9:30–6; Nov–Feb 9–5
🖐 Moderate

ANCIENT SKILL

The skilled craft of intaglio (engraving on glass with copper tools), which is still practised at Waterford Crystal, dates back to the Bronze Age, and has changed hardly at all since then.

3 Kilkenny

Kilkenny is a medieval gem, ideal for a leisurely exploration on foot. War and wild times have swept regularly through the little town, leaving it with an impressive castle, a fortress of a cathedral, and a maze of sloping side streets packed with ancient buildings. Ask at the tourist office about Pat Tynan's one-hour walking tours, a quick and amusing introduction to the historic town.

Kilkenny Castle is a fine Victorian remodelling of a 12th-century Norman fortress, superbly sited on a bend of the River Nore, with wide wooded parklands to stroll in. At the other end of the straggling High Street is **St Canice's Cathedral**, a squat 13th-century stronghold with a stubby tower like a head hunched between the high shoulders of the roofs. The nave is filled with beautifully carved old monuments and tomb slabs – a treasury of the stone-carver's art that shouldn't be missed.

The Long Gallery in Kilkenny Castle

Climb the cathedral's round tower for the best view over Kilkenny; then make for the little well house on Kenny's Well Road, just beyond the cathedral. **St Canice's Holy Well** here dates back to the 6th century AD – and probably much further.

Tourist Information

✚ 200 C4
✉ Shee Alms House, Rose Inn Street, Kilkenny
☎ 056 7751500; www.discoverireland.ie/southeast

St Canice's Cathedral

✉ Dean Street, Kilkenny
☎ 056 7764971
🕓 Jun–end Aug Mon–Sat 9–6, Sun 2–6; Apr, May, Sep Mon–Sat 10–1, 2–5, Sun 2–5; Oct–end Mar Mon–Sat 10–1, 2–4, Sun 2–4 ✋ Inexpensive

Kilkenny Castle

✉ The Parade, Kilkenny
☎ 056 7721450
🕓 Jun–Aug daily 9:30–7; Apr–May 10:30–5; Sep 10–6:30; Oct–Mar 10:30–12:45, 2–5. Guided tours only ✋ Moderate

KILKENNY'S WITCH

The oldest inscribed slab in Kilkenny Cathedral is to Jose de Keteller, who died in 1280. He was probably the father of Dame Alice Kyteler, who was accused of being a witch. She escaped, leaving her maid to be burned at the stake in her place.

4 Newgrange and Brú na Bóinne Irish Heritage Site

Brú na Bóinne ("Palace of the Boyne"), a curve of quiet green farmland along a 15km (9-mile) stretch of the River Boyne, is the site of Europe's richest concentration of ancient monuments – henges, forts, enclosures, standing stones and a superb collection of neolithic passage graves: Dowth, Knowth and Newgrange.

Newgrange had already been standing for 500 years when pyramid-building first started in Egypt and had been in use for a thousand years when work began on Stonehenge. As you explore this mighty tomb of beautifully crafted stone slabs incised with mysterious carved patterns and symbols, your imagination cannot fail to be stirred.

The circular kerbstone wall and grass-topped roof of Newgrange passage grave

The introductory **exhibition** gives a good idea of the little that is known about the period 4000 to 3000 BC, when enormous tombs like these were built all over Europe, and it provides an excellent introduction to the monuments of Brú na Bóinne, in particular the two great passage graves of Newgrange and Knowth.

The Building of Newgrange

Newgrange was built some time between 3300 and 2900 BC, a giant mound 85m (279 feet) across and 15m (49 feet) high, its perimeter defined by nearly a hundred huge kerbstones. At least 200,000 tonnes of stone went into its construction, a mind-numbing amount of material to transport and put into position.

A passage 19m (62 feet) long, walled and roofed with more huge slabs, was built into the heart of the mound, opening out there into three chambers, like a shamrock leaf. It is thought to have taken the neolithic farming community between 40 and 80 years to build Newgrange – twice the life span of an active male in that hard and dangerous era.

The tomb sits high above the road, a great mound bounded by its circular kerbstone wall and topped by a green grassy dome of a roof. Outside the entrance (rebuilt since it was first rediscovered in a collapsed state in 1699) lies the Threshold Stone, a big weathered slab lying on its side, covered in spiral and diamond carvings. Above the doorway is a slit in the stonework like a large letterbox. It is through this roof box that the dawn light enters at the winter solstice.

Once inside the tomb, the guide leads you by torchlight along the darkened passageway, sometimes stooping under the low stone slab roof. Spiral patterns are carved into the walls all around, well lit with electric light. At the end of the passage, you straighten up under a beehive domed roof to find yourself in the central burial chamber. The roof has rainproof qualities of which any modern builder would be proud. Vaulted with cleverly interlocked stone slabs, it has

The mighty, carved Threshold Stone and roof box at the entrance to Newgrange

The burial mound at Knowth is surrounded by other graves

kept the chamber perfectly dry for more than 5,000 years. The three recesses which open off this central area contain wide, shallow sandstone bowls, receptacles that once held the cremated remains of the dead.

Riddles of the Tomb

If you lie prone on the floor of the furthest recess from the entrance, you can squint along the passage to see the roof box slit outlined in light.

On 21 December, the shortest day of the year – and for a couple of days each side – the dawn light creeps in through the slit and advances along the roof and through the central chamber until it reaches halfway up the back wall. Here it lingers for a few minutes, and then withdraws. As it is such a rare event, people wanting to witness this phenomenon need to enter their names into a lottery.

When Newgrange was excavated, the remains of only half a dozen bodies were found. Though speculation is rife, it appears that funerary remains must have been regularly removed from the chamber. Why remove them? Why labour so long and hard to build a device for trapping a momentary ray of winter sun? Did the ancients have a yearly midwinter clear-out of cremated remains, in the belief that the

Right: Characteristic whorls of 5,000-year-old stone carving at Newgrange

retreating ray of light had taken the spirits of the dead with it, perhaps to ensure the return of next year's spring sunshine? Or is there another explanation? Stand at the mysterious heart of Newgrange and your guess is as good as anyone's.

Knowth

Knowth, Newgrange's neighbouring tomb, lies surrounded by at least 17 smaller passage graves, like a cluster of big green anthills. The tomb has two passages pushing in from east and west, and is rich in spiral and line carvings. Whorls, zigzags and parallel lines decorate the great stones, offering powerful evidence that, like Newgrange, the tomb had a significance beyond that of a simple burial place.

A carved mace head, one of the archaeological finds at Knowth

TAKING A BREAK

Daly's of Donore (in the village of Donore, tel: 041 982 3252) is within walking distance of Newgrange and is open for breakfast from 7am to 10am, and for lunch from 12:30pm to 3pm.

✚ 197 D1

✉ Brú na Bóinne Visitor Centre, 11km (7 miles) southwest of Drogheda, Co Meath

☎ 041 988 0300; www.heritageireland.ie

◉ Jun to mid-Sep daily 9–7; May and mid- to end Sep 9–6:30; Mar–Apr and Oct 9:30–5:30; Nov–Feb 9:30–5. Newgrange open all year round; Knowth open Easter–Oct (exterior only). Last tour of monuments 90 minutes before closing; last admission to visitor centre 45 minutes before closing

✋ Moderate

NEWGRANGE AND BRÚ NA BÓINNE: INSIDE INFO

Top tips Admission to Newgrange and Knowth is through the Visitor Centre; there is no direct access to the viewing areas. Visitors are taken to the monuments by shuttle bus. If you're visiting between June and September, it's advisable to arrive early in the morning and book your guided tour of Newgrange immediately. Better still, book well in advance. Those who turn up late in the day, unbooked, risk missing the tour.

Hidden gem When you are in the central chamber of Newgrange, inspect the **walls and roofs of the right-hand compartment**. They are richly carved with spirals and other motifs, well lit with electric light.

One to miss If hordes of visitors have descended on Newgrange, opt for the Knowth tomb visit – it's far less crowded, and the passage tomb art is better. But note that the tomb interior remains closed while excavations continue.

At Your Leisure

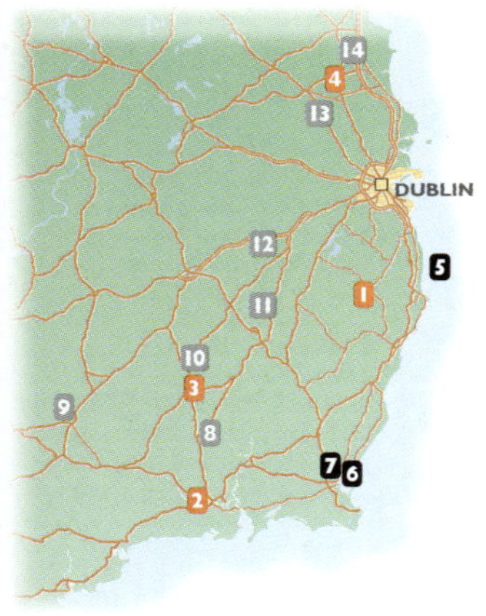

The reserve offers well-placed hides (blinds) and guided tours.

✚ 201 D3 ✉ North Slob, Wexford ☎ 091 912 3129 ◷ Daily 9–5 ✋ Free

7 Irish National Heritage Park

Allow a couple of hours for a stroll through Irish history beside the River Slaney, 5km (3 miles) north of Wexford. Reconstructed buildings range from pre-Christian round houses to a full-size *crannog* (stone-built defensive tower), a Viking shipyard with longboats under construction, and a Norman motte-and-bailey castle.

✚ 201 D3 ✉ Ferrycarrig, Co Wexford ☎ 053 912 0733; www.inhp.com ◷ Mar–Oct daily 9:30–6:30; Nov–Feb 9:30–5:30 ✋ Moderate

A reconstructed church at the Irish National Heritage Park

5 The Wicklow Coast

The Wicklow coast south of Bray and Greystones, the southern terminus of the DART (Dublin Area Rapid Transit) railway, is well worth exploring via R761, R750 and their side roads. Long sandy beaches fringe the coast as it approaches Wicklow on a long estuarine creek. South again are Wicklow Head, great for windy walks, and the Silver Strand around Brittas Bay, a fine strip of pale sand beaches. Arklow is an attractive little fishing town, noted for boat-building. The coast road makes an enjoyable return route to Dublin after a day in the Wicklow Hills.

✚ 201 E4

6 Wexford Wildfowl Reserve

Wexford is Ireland's prime bird-watching county, and the harbour of the North Slob – a tidal wetland just north of the town – is one of the best sites. About 10,000 Greenland white-fronted geese (one-third of the world population) overwinter here, along with many other goose and duck species. Swans, reed warblers, reed buntings, greenshank and redshank can be seen at other times of the year.

TONELAGEE

The mountain called Tonelagee, one of the highest in the Wicklow Mountains at 818m (2,684 feet), seems to be presenting its posterior to the prevailing wind. Hence its name – which in Irish literally means "arse-to-the-wind".

❽ Jerpoint Abbey

The ruins of Jerpoint Abbey are worth the short detour south from Kilkenny. These beautiful buildings show work from several centuries between the abbey's foundation in the late 12th century and its dissolution about 400 years later. Carved figures – one of a woman in a long pleated skirt, another of St Christopher with staff and upraised hand – stand between the double pillars of the fine cloister arches. A handsome pinnacled tower overlooks the roofless nave of the church. In the choir is the carved tomb of Abbot Felix O'Dulany, whose crosier is depicted being swallowed by a snake.

✚ 200 C3 ✉ Thomastown, Co Kilkenny ☎ 056 772 4623; www.heritageireland.ie ◷ Jun to mid-Sep daily 10–6; mid-Sep to Oct, Mar–May 10–5; Nov–Feb 10–4 ✋ Inexpensive

❾ Rock of Cashel

The Rock of Cashel astonishes at first sight. Perched spectacularly on a high rock outcrop is a walled cluster of historic ecclesiastical buildings, one of Ireland's most important centres in medieval times, from which powerful kings and churchmen ruled for nearly a thousand years.

The Rock of Cashel, perched atop a rocky outcrop, County Tipperary

On the rock you'll find a 12th-century round tower complete with conical cap, the lovely Cormac's Chapel (1127–34), and a roofless 13th-century cathedral. Take a torch (flashlight) with you so that you can enjoy the remarkable stone carving tucked away in the dark above the north door of Cormac's Chapel – a centaur in a Norman helmet, firing an arrow at a grinning lion which is trampling two smaller animals beneath its feet. This is a windswept spot in which to linger as you admire the brilliance and humour of the medieval master masons.

✚ 200 A3 ✉ Cashel, Co Tipperary ☎ 062 61437; www.heritageireland.ie ◷ Jun to mid-Sep daily 9–7; mid-Mar–May 9–5:30; mid-Sep to mid-Oct 9–5:30; mid-Oct to mid-Mar 9–4:40 ✋ Moderate

❿ Dunmore Caves

A guided tour takes you along walkways (with 106 steps) through this series of well-lit limestone caves. The caves are of sombre repute: legend says that the Lord of the Mice was slain here, while a more credible story tells of hundreds of locals slaughtered in the caves by Vikings in AD 928; skeletons of women and children have been found (though without signs of violence), along with Viking coins. You can see how the caves got their spooky reputation

The Japanese Gardens near Kildare

as you walk from one bizarre and freakish stalactite and stalagmite formation to the next.

✚ 200 C4 ✉ Mothel, near Castlecomer, Co Kilkenny ☎ 056 776 7726 ◷ Mid-Mar to mid-Jun daily 9:30–6; mid-Jun to mid-Sep 9:30–6:30, mid-Sept to Oct 10–5, Nov to mid-Mar Sat, Sun 10–4:30; last admission 45 minutes before closing; guided tours only ✋ Inexpensive

⓫ Moone and Castledermot High Crosses

The pre-Norman high crosses in the County Kildare villages of Moone and Castledermot are worth a detour. The cross at Moone is over 5m (16 feet) tall; the two at Castledermot stand near a beautiful little Romanesque doorway and a ruined round tower. All three crosses are made of granite and are carved with scenes from the Bible.

✚ 200 C4 ✉ Moone and Castledermot are on N9, south of Naas ✋ Free

⓬ Irish National Stud, Irish Horse Museum and Japanese Gardens

In 1902 rich and eccentric Scots brewery heir Colonel William Hall-Walker established the Irish National Stud on the southern outskirts of the town of Kildare. The colonel was fascinated by astrology and exotic religion. Stallions and mares were paired off according to the compatibility of their birth signs, their foals' progress was charted by horoscope, and the boxes in which they were accommodated had lantern skylights to allow entry of the influential rays of moon and stars.

The nearby grounds were laid out in 1906–10 as a Japanese garden, symbolising the life of a man through a journey to the Garden of Peace and Contentment by way of such obstacles and encouragements as the Hill of Learning, the Walk of Wisdom, the Hill of Ambition and the Bridge of Life.

Allow at least a couple of hours to visit the National Stud's stallions

in their stalls and paddocks, view the Irish Horse Museum (which displays the skeleton of champion steeplechaser Arkle) and stroll the subtle pathways of the Japanese Gardens.

✠ 200 C5 ✉ Tully, Co Kildare
☎ 045 522963/521617;
www.irish-national-stud.ie ⊕ Mid-Feb to Christmas daily 9:30–5 ✋ Expensive

⑬ Hill of Tara

This green hill, surrounded by earthworks, has been an important site since late Stone Age people built a passage tomb here. Its heyday of influence was during the first millennium AD as the main religious and political centre of Ireland, where kings and priests would gather every three years to make laws and settle quarrels. Tara features in many Irish myths and legends – and in more recent history too. Daniel O'Connell chose the Hill of Tara, symbol of Irish nationhood, as the venue for a "monster meeting" in 1843 to oppose the oppressive Corn Laws. And his instinct was justified when more than 100,000 people turned up (or maybe a million – estimates varied). This is a wonderful place to roam and enjoy the superb view.

✠ 197 D1 ✉ Off N3 south of Navan, Co Meath
☎ 046 9025903;
www.heritageireland.ie ⊕ Mid-May to mid-Sep daily 10–6, ✋ Inexpensive

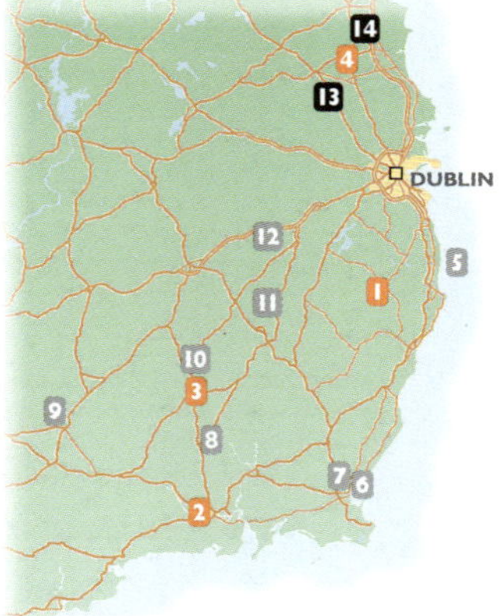

Heavenly vertical – the high cross at Monasterboice

⑭ Monasterboice

An astonishing variety of historic Christian monuments is crammed into this compact monastic site north of Drogheda: a leaning, 33m (108-foot) tall 10th-century round tower, ancient grave slabs, the ruined shells of two venerable churches, and – in pride of place – three wonderfully carved high crosses. Best of all is the South Cross or Cross of Muiredach, over 5m (16 feet) tall. Its carved panels include depictions of Eve tempting Adam, Cain murdering Abel, an Adoration of the Magi that seems to feature not three but four Wise Men, and a Judgement Day in which St Michael weighs the souls of the dead while the Devil tugs on the scales to gain more than his rightful share.

✠ 197 D1 ✉ Off N1, north of Drogheda, Co Louth ⊕ Daily ✋ Free

OFF THE BEATEN TRACK

Try the strand of Curracloe, not far north of Wexford, for a memorable sunrise walk along miles of empty sands with only seabirds for company.

Where to...
Eat and Drink

Prices
Expect to pay per person for a meal, excluding drinks and service
€ under €15   €€ €15 to €30   €€€ over €30

Avoca Handweavers €
You'll find delicious home-cooked food here, based on organic and locally produced ingredients. Delicatessen foods include farmhouse cheeses, home-baked breads and preserves, and vegetarians do especially well. There's a sister shop/restaurant at Powerscourt House, Enniskerry (tel: 01 204 6070).

✚ 201 E5 ✉ Kilmacanoge, Co Wicklow ☎ 01 286 7466; www.avoca.ie ⏰ Mon–Sat 9:30–5:30, Sun 10–6; closed 25–26 Dec

Roundwood Inn €–€€€
The perfect place to take a break in the Wicklow Mountains, this renowned inn has everything: roaring log fires, excellent bar food, and a formal restaurant too (requiring reservations), which serves a separate menu. Specialities include substantial soups, Galway oysters, smoked Wicklow trout and hearty hot meals including the house version of Irish stew.

✚ 201 D4 ✉ Roundwood, Co Wicklow ☎ 01 281 8107 ⏰ Bar meals: daily 12:30–9:30. Restaurant: Lunch: Sun 1 pm. Dinner: Fri–Sun 7:30–midnight. Inn: closed Good Fri and 25 Dec

Bodega! €€
What a relief to find a good place to eat where children are not just tolerated but are made very welcome. There's a nice bright feel to Bodega! In spite of its Spanish name, it has a South of France atmosphere. Spicy notes in the fish stews and meaty dishes betray that, too, and there's a great choice of puddings and ices to please the little ones and make them eat up their greens – not that they'll need much persuading here.

✚ 200 C3 ✉ John Street, Waterford ☎ 051 844177; www.bodegawaterford.com ⏰ Lunch Mon–Fri, noon–5; dinner Mon–Thu 5–10, Fri, Sat 5–10.30. Closed bank hol Mons, 1 Jan, Good Fri and 25–26 Dec

The Tannery €€€
This is a restaurant to treasure. The Tannery offers you bouillabaisse the way Maman used to make it, a lasagne of wild rabbit steaming with sage, or you can go for a steak and kidney pie rich in juices and delicate pie crust. Save space for a fantastic combination of sweet brie with truffle honey and candied almonds.

✚ 200 B2 ✉ 10, Quay Street, Dungarvan, Co Waterford ☎ 058 45420; www.tannery.ie ⏰ Lunch Fri 12:30–2:30, Sun 12:30–3; dinner Tue–Sat 6–9:30

Cashel Palace Hotel €€
Built in 1730 as a bishop's residence, Cashel Palace is a beautifully proportioned Queen Anne-style house. The informal Bishop's Buttery restaurant in the basement is open all day, and the Guinness Bar serves light snacks from 12 noon until late. Some of the reception rooms and bedrooms overlook the gardens and have views of the Rock of Cashel.

✚ 200 A3 ✉ Main Street, Cashel ☎ 062 62707; www.cashel-palace.ie ⏰ Closed 24–26 Dec

Chez Hans €€–€€€

Over 100 years old, this converted Wesleyan chapel under the Rock of Cashel has great atmosphere and food to match: seasonal menus offer a wide choice and put local ingredients to the best use in classic French cooking. Specialities include fresh fish and shellfish, roast duckling and rack of Tipperary lamb. There's always a good selection of farmhouse cheeses and an irresistible dessert tasting-plate.

✚ 200 A3 ✉ Moor Lane, Cashel, Co Tipperary ☎ 062 61177 🕐 Tue–Sat 6:30–10 pm; closed 3 weeks Jan, Good Fri and 25 Dec

KILKENNY

Lacken House €€–€€€

A husband-and-wife team runs the cellar restaurant of this Victorian house located on the edge of Kilkenny. You'll get to taste good local produce in a blend of traditional and New Irish recipes, featuring specialities such as Kilkenny lamb with basil and herb crust and a range of farmhouse cheeses. Overnight guests get delicious breakfasts.

✚ 200 C4 ✉ Dublin Road, Kilkenny ☎ 056 7761085; www.lackenhouse.ie 🕐 Jun–Sep Tue–Sat 6:30–10, Sun 7–10, Oct–May Tue–Sat 6:30–10. Restaurant: closed 2 weeks Christmas

New East Restaurant €€

In the Langton House Hotel, this is one of Kilkenny's better restaurants and a member of "the Kilkenny good food circle". The spacious dining room has a magnificent stained glass ceiling with huge lights suspended to create a bright and airy atmosphere; not the place for an intimate dining experience. Wholesome cooking, with many classic dishes such as steak, oven baked salmon and roast duckling, plus some oriental-style cuisine, is the attraction.

✚ 200 C4 ✉ Langton House Hotel, 69 John Street, Kilkenny ☎ 056 7765133; www. langtons.ie 🕐 Mon–Sat 6–10:30, Sun 6–9:30

MOONE AREA

Ballymore Inn €€

This charming country pub has a welcoming open fire, unusual furniture, interesting pictures and good food, too. Superb pizzas and hearty open sandwiches, salads and pasta dishes are served in the bar cum restaurant.

✚ 201 D5 ✉ Ballymore Eustace, Co Kildare ☎ 045 864585 🕐 Restaurant: Tue–Thu 12:30–3, 6–9, Fri–Sat 12:30–9:30, Sun 12:30–7, Mon 12:30–3. Pub closed Good Fri and 25 Dec; restaurant closed public hols

Moone High Cross Inn €

This 1870s country pub near Kilkea Castle (➤ 91) has open fires in both bars. The larger bar serves traditional dishes such as Irish stew and bacon and cabbage. There are eight bedrooms with bathrooms upstairs.

✚ 200 C4 ✉ Bolton Hill, Moone, Co Kildare ☎ 059 8624112 🕐 Mon–Thu 8am–11:30pm, Fri–Sat 8am–12:30am, Sun 8am–11pm; closed Good Fri and 25 Dec

NEWGRANGE AREA

Forge Gallery Restaurant €€–€€€

This two-storey restaurant is furnished and decorated with flair, making a fine setting for excellent food, hospitality and service. Menus combine country French, New Irish and world (notably Thai) cuisines, using seasonal and largely local ingredients with home-made breads.

✚ 197 D1 ✉ Collon, Co Louth ☎ 041 982 6272; www.forgegalleryrestaurant.ie 🕐 Dinner: Tue–Sat 7–9:30; closed 1 week Jan and over Christmas

Tides Bistro €€

This classy bistro, upstairs from its cool bar, serves interesting European cuisine with some Oriental touches, and traditional Irish staples smartened up with modern influences. Meat, fish and vegetarian options are available.

✚ 197 D1 ✉ Wellington Quay, Drogheda, Co Louth ☎ 041 9801942; www.tidesbistro.com 🕐 Daily 5:30–10:30

Where to... Stay

Prices

Expect to pay per night for a double room without tax

€ under €70   €€ €70 to €130   €€€ over €130

Ritz Carlton Powerscourt €€€

Recently built and splendidly arcaded in a modern twist on the Palladian style, the Ritz Carlton Powerscourt is sited in an estate whose centrepiece is one of the grandest 18th-century country houses and most superb gardens in the countryside around Dublin. If you are pushing the boat out for a special anniversary, this is absolutely the place to aim for. Service, setting and ambience are out of this world.

✚ 201 E5 ✉ Enniskerry, Co Wicklow ☎ 01 274 8888; www.ritzcarlton.com

Foxmount Country House €€

This 17th-century house is situated on a working dairy farm, just 15 minutes' drive from Waterford city centre. Yet it offers guests tranquillity, comfort and delicious home-cooked food. There's table tennis and a hard tennis court, and the accommodation includes a family room; all bedrooms have private bathrooms.

✚ 200 C3 ✉ Passage East Road, off Dunmore East Road, Waterford, Co Waterford ☎ 051 874308; www.foxmountcountryhouse.com 🌐 Closed Nov–Mar

Brown's Townhouse €€–€€€

A really friendly guesthouse not far from the waterfront in Waterford, where the hosts pride themselves on creating a relaxed family atmosphere. Breakfast features home-baked bread, with jams and other preserves produced in-house.

✚ 200 C3 ✉ South Parade, Waterford, Co Waterford ☎ 051 870594; www.brownstownhouse.com

Hanora's Cottage €€–€€€

Up in the mountains about an hour's drive from Waterford, this hospitable, but child-free, guesthouse makes a perfect base for bird-watching, walking or horseback riding. There is luxurious accommodation, legendary breakfasts and home-baked bread. The restaurant (open to non-residents for dinner) specialises in local produce.

✚ 200 B3 ✉ Nire Valley, Ballymacarbery, via Clonmel, Co Waterford ☎ 052 36134; www.hanorascottage.com 🌐 Restaurant closed Sun

Kilkea Castle & Golf Club €€€

This 12th-century castle is now a romantic hotel where many rooms have views over gardens, countryside and a golf course. The best bedrooms are in the castle; the rest surround an adjacent courtyard.

✚ 200 C4 ✉ Castledermot, Co Kildare ☎ 059 9145156; www.kilkeacastle.ie 🌐 Closed 24–26 Dec

Killyon Guesthouse €

Michael and Sheila Fogarty deservedly won two of the visitor industry's most prestigious awards in 2007 – Georgina Campbell's Bed & Breakfast of the Year, and Irish Breakfast Awards: Best B&B Breakfast. That tells you all you need to know about this delightful, warm and brilliantly run guesthouse.

✚ 197 D1 ✉ Dublin Road, Navan, Co Meath ☎ 046 907 1224; www.killyonguesthouse.ie

Where to...
Shop

See the mill in operation at **Avoca Handweavers** (Kilmacanogue, tel: 01 286 7466). They sell fabrics, clothing, crafts and specialist foods. For country clothing try **Fishers of Newtownmountkennedy** (tel: 01 281 9404). Roundwood village has gift shops and a Sunday afternoon market. Distinctive pots are hand-thrown at the **Kiltrea Bridge Pottery** (Enniscorthy, County Wexford, tel: 053 923 5107). At the **Waterford Crystal** Visitor Centre (Waterford City, tel: 051 332500) you can watch craftspeople at work, then buy from the display (➤ 79).

Kilkenny
At **Kilkenny Design Centre** (tel: 056 7722118), opposite the castle, there is the largest selection of crafts in Ireland including textiles, ceramics and jewellery. They are all brought together in a unique setting. Also look for the jewellery of family business **Murphy** (85 High Street, tel: 056 772 1127) and the books, toys and games at the child-friendly **Byrne's Kilkenny** book shop (82 High Street, tel: 056 7723400).

Bennettsbridge and Thomastown
Visit the **Stoneware Jackson Studio** (Ballyreddin, tel: 056 7727175), as well as the **Nicholas Mosse Pottery** (tel: 056 7727505), renowned for traditional spongeware. At nearby Thomastown, watch lead crystal being hand-blown at the **Jerpoint Glass Studio** (tel: 056 7724350).

Timolin
Allow time to stop at the **Irish Pewter Mill** (tel: 059 8624164) at Timolin, in County Kildare. It has a museum as well as the factory, and also a shop which sells traditional pewter items.

Where to...
Be Entertained

OUTDOOR ACTIVITIES

Activities in the Wicklow Mountains include walking, cycling, horseback riding, angling and golf. Local tourist information offices can provide details. There's an **Adventure Centre** (tel: 01 4582889) on the Blessington Lakes.

Horse Country
County Tipperary is home to three racecourses: Thurles, Clonmel and Tipperary. Kildare has three race-courses: The Curragh (tel: 045 441205), Punchestown (tel: 045 897704) and Naas (tel: 045 897391). Horseback-riding lessons are available at **Warrington Top Flight Equestrian Centre** (tel: 056 7722682).

Golf
The Arnold Palmer-designed **K Club** (Straffan, County Kildare, tel: 01 6017200) is challenging, and hosted the 2006 Ryder Cup. There's also **Kilkea Castle** (Castledermot, County Kildare, tel: 059 9145555), set in rolling parkland.

MUSIC

You will find live traditional music all over on various nights of the week. In Waterford, **T and H Doolans** (George's Street, tel: 051 84150), has music on summer nights and winter weekends. The **Wexford Opera Festival** (tel: 053 22144) from mid-October/early November stages a selection of rarely performed operas.

Southwest Ireland

Getting Your Bearings

The wild Atlantic blows up hundreds of storms a year along the coasts of counties Cork and Kerry, at the southwestern tip of Ireland. Here waves and wind have eaten away at the coast, creating big, ragged-edged peninsulas where the land faces directly into the Atlantic, and sheltered little coves between rocky headlands on the south-facing coast of Cork. You'll find literally hundreds of fine sandy beaches to enjoy along this, the most spectacular coastline in Ireland. But there are also plenty of attractive and enjoyable places inland, especially in the side valleys of the Shehy and Derrynasaggart mountains.

Sailing, diving, sea fishing and water sports of all kinds are big hereabouts. The climate, though often wet and windy, is notably mild and frost free, so there are a number of exotic gardens with plants and trees you would normally expect to find far nearer the equator. The Kerry Way offers superb long-distance walking through the hills, and there's good trout fishing in the lakes of the Iveragh Peninsula (whose circular Ring of Kerry must be Ireland's best-known scenic drive) and Killarney National Park, justly famed for its beauty. Inhabitants of Kerry and Cork are well known for their laid-back approach to life and for their elliptical wit.

⭐ Don't Miss

1 Cork City ➤ 98

2 Kissing the Blarney Stone, Co Cork ➤ 100

3 Ring of Kerry, Co Kerry ➤ 101

4 Dingle Peninsula (Corca Dhuibhne), Co Kerry ➤ 104

At Your Leisure

5 Old Midleton Distillery, Co Cork ➤ 108

6 Kinsale, Co Cork ➤ 108

7 The West Cork Coast ➤ 108

8 Mizen Head Signal Station, Co Cork ➤ 109

9 Muckross House, Abbey and Gardens, Co Kerry ➤ 110

10 Killarney National Park, Co Kerry ➤ 110

11 Adare, Co Limerick ➤ 111

12 Lough Gur, Co Limerick ➤ 112

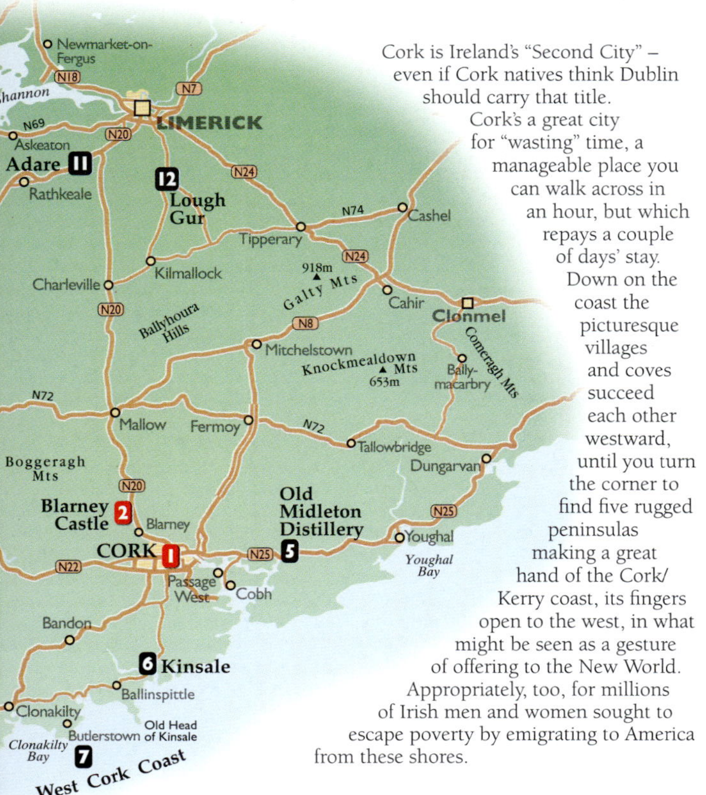

Cork is Ireland's "Second City" – even if Cork natives think Dublin should carry that title. Cork's a great city for "wasting" time, a manageable place you can walk across in an hour, but which repays a couple of days' stay. Down on the coast the picturesque villages and coves succeed each other westward, until you turn the corner to find five rugged peninsulas making a great hand of the Cork/Kerry coast, its fingers open to the west, in what might be seen as a gesture of offering to the New World. Appropriately, too, for millions of Irish men and women sought to escape poverty by emigrating to America from these shores.

Page 93: Fishermen untangle fish from the net at Kinsale

In Four Days

If you're not quite sure where to begin your travels, this itinerary recommends a practical and enjoyable journey around Southwest Ireland, taking in some of the best places to see using the Getting Your Bearings map on the previous page. For more information see the main entries.

Day One

Morning
Make sure to allow at least a morning for wandering around **1 Cork City** (a tribute to Rory Gallagher, left, ➤ 98–99), looking in at the art gallery, having a chat and a snack lunch in the English Market, maybe climbing the hill to ring the Bells of Shandon.

Afternoon
Go on, you have to do it… make the short trip out north to **2 Blarney Castle** (➤ 100), and kiss the Blarney Stone. Then it's back into Cork to try out your new gift of the gab in the **Hi-B** (➤ 99).

Day Two

Morning
Make an early start south to **6 Kinsale** (➤ 108–109) for breakfast or coffee. Then follow the rural road west to Clonakilty (R600). Continue to Rosscarbery, sidetracking from here via beautiful Glandore, Unionhall and Rineen to steep and attractive little Castletownshend. Then head west via Skibbereen to reach the one-time hippy hangout of Ballydehob in time for lunch.

Afternoon
Cruise two of the **7 Five Fingers** (➤ 109): go out to the cliffs of Mizen Head to visit the **8 Signal Station** (➤ 109–110) and back, then round the mountains and drink in the wonderful island views of the Beara Peninsula. You'll be tired, and satiated with beautiful landscapes, by the time you reach **Kenmare** for an overnight stop (➤ 116).

Day Three

Morning
From Kenmare you can enjoy a fairly late start to make up for yesterday. Drive at your ease over to **10 Killarney** (➤ 111), and stop for a quick cup of coffee; then set out on the wonderful circuit of the **3 Ring of Kerry** (➤ 101–103). Lunch in the Blind Piper at Caherdaniel (tel: 066 9475346).

Afternoon
Look around **Derrynane House** and grounds (➤ 101–102) – home of Daniel O'Connell, "The Liberator" – then complete your leisurely tour of the Ring of Kerry before pushing on from Killarney to stay overnight in Tralee.

Day Four

Morning
Take the whole day to explore the **4 Dingle Peninsula/Corca Dhuibhne** (Blasket Islands, below, ➤ 104–107). A ten o'clock start would put you in Dingle Town in time for a stroll before lunch.

Afternoon
Carry on around the peninsula via Dunquin (Dun Chaion) and Cloghane (An Clochán) – don't forget a windy saunter on the Magharees sandspit! Then return from Tralee to Cork.

① Cork City

Ireland's "second city" is a charming place that quickly slows you down to its easy pace. The River Lee divides into two channels as it flows through, forming an island of the city centre. Bridges are numerous, each with a fine riverfront view, making Cork an excellent place for a town stroll.

South of the South Channel, **St Fin Barre's Cathedral** on Bishop Street is worth a visit for its exterior statues, its fine collection of 19th-century stained glass, and the delicately coloured mosaic floor of the choir. Lift the choir seats to enjoy the handsome carvings of insects that decorate the misericords (and spare a thought for the weary choristers who perched on these ledges during long services).

In the city centre the covered **English Market** off Grand Parade is a lively mix of food, drink, book and craft stalls. Nearby in the Huguenot Quarter, an area of the city inhabited in the 18th century by French Protestant craftsmen fleeing religious persecution, you can stroll narrow pedestrian streets between small-scale old houses, shops, cafés and pubs, all chic and sleek. Head north towards the river to visit the excellent **Crawford Art Gallery** (tel: 021 4907855, open: Mon–Sat 10–5) on Paul Street.

Below: St Fin Barre's Cathedral and South Gate Bridge over the River Lee

Above: Organic fruit and vegetable stall on St Patrick's Street

The western entrance to St Fin Barre's Cathedral

North of the river, climb the steep streets of Shandon to reach **St Anne's Church** (➤ below) and take time to look around the craft workshops in the adjacent **Butter Exchange**. Half an hour's stroll west brings you to the Sunday's Well area, where you can learn all about the misery of 19th-century prison conditions at the old **Cork City Gaol** (tel: 021 4305022, open: Mar–Oct daily 9:30–6, Nov–Feb 10–5; admission moderate). Housed in the old railway station at Cobh, southeast of Cork, is **The Queenstown Story** (tel: 021 4813591; www.cobhheritage.com; open: May–Oct daily 9:30–6; Nov–Feb 9:30–5; closed 10 days over Christmas; admission moderate). Cobh, formerly known as Queenstown, was once a port of embarkation for the United States. This exhibition explores the pain of separation, hardship and danger suffered by the hundreds of thousands who, over the past two centuries, emigrated to America on the notorious "coffin ships". It is detailed, moving and inspiring.

TAKING A BREAK

Call in to the first-floor **Farmgate Restaurant** (➤ 114) for excellent pastries and a view of the market.

✚ 199 E2
✉ Tourist Information Office, Grand Parade
☎ 021 425 5100;
www.discoverireland.ie/southwest

ROCKIN' RORY

In the heart of the Huguenot Quarter is Rory Gallagher Square, named after the late rock musician, a sometime resident of Cork. He has a bold sculpture, a twisted Fender Stratocaster electric guitar entwined in flowing staves of music and lines from his songs.

CORK CITY: INSIDE INFO

Top tips Try **ringing the bells at St Anne's Church** on the Shandon side of town. You can "read" your tune off a crib card as you ring, or go at it freestyle.
■ At the Crawford Art Gallery, make straight for the **Gibson Galleries and the Irish Art Collection**, which is by far the most enjoyable part.

Hidden gem Tucked away above a chemist's shop opposite the General Post Office on Oliver Plunkett Street, the **Hi-B** (it stands for Hibernian Bar) is an entirely unspoiled pub, comfortable, a bit shabby and very friendly.

One to miss If you are short of time, give the rather threadbare **"Titanic" section** at The Queenstown Story a miss.

2 Kissing the Blarney Stone

Blarney Castle is a notably rugged and romantic-looking 15th-century tower in beautiful grounds full of pleasing grottoes and magic Druidic rocks half-hidden in greenery. None of this matters to the majority of visitors, who have come for one thing only: to kiss the Blarney Stone.

One legend says that the Blarney Stone was the pillow used by Jacob when he had his dream of angels in the desert. Another holds that the slab is only half of a much bigger stone, and that the other half is the Stone of Destiny on which Scottish (and then English) monarchs were crowned. The best-known legend, of course, says that anyone who can kiss the Blarney Stone will have the gift of eloquence magically bestowed on them.

Blarney Castle was once the stronghold of the MacCarthy chieftains, the former kings of Munster

The castle is extremely popular: come as early or late in the day as possible to avoid having to wait and head straight up the steps to the roof, where you will find the Blarney Stone built into the outer face of a gap in the battlements. You'll have to bend backwards and hang your head down (over a safety grille, and supported by one of the sturdy custodians) to kiss the stone. One word to the wise…empty your pockets before you kiss the Blarney Stone, or all your money will trickle out as you lean backwards.

✚ 199 D2
✉ Blarney Castle, Blarney, Co Cork
☎ 021 438 5252;
www.blarneycastle.ie
🕐 Jun–Aug daily 9–7; May and Sep 9–6:30; Oct–Apr 9–dusk; closed 24–25 Dec
♿ Moderate

3 Ring of Kerry

The Ring of Kerry scenic route around the Iveragh Peninsula is the most popular drive in Ireland, and certainly one of the most beautiful, with wild boglands, wonderful coastal views and fine hill scenery.

Lough Leane is on the eastern side of the Ring of Kerry

Starting in Killarney, you skirt the north side of mountain-framed Lough Leane on your way west to **Killorglin**. This atmospheric small town is best known for the three-day Puck Fair in August, where there's drinking, dancing, livestock buying and selling – and a goat on a podium presiding over the whole affair. From Killorglin take the side road to Lough Caragh – this route introduces you to the boglands and puts you in the right frame of mind for wilder country ahead.

Back on the main road (N70), Glenbeigh is the first village you come to. Below on the coast lies **Rossbeigh Strand**, a pebbly beach with a 3km (2-mile) spit of dunes and a wonderful view of the Iveragh and Dingle peninsulas. A steep hill road brings you circling back to the main road, on which you continue southwest in increasingly hilly and beautiful scenery. Steep hillsides, patched with small fields and farms, rise through bracken and heather to sharp peaks nearly 800m (2,625 feet) high.

Near **Cahersiveen** you pass the smoking chimney of a peat-fired power station. On your left just before the bridge into the village are the ivy-covered ruins of the house where Daniel O'Connell was born. O'Connell (1775–1847) was one of the most important political figures in 19th-century Ireland: he earned his nickname, "The Liberator", leading impoverished Roman Catholics towards emancipation. In the village a right turn past the eccentric castle-like "Barracks" (the 19th-century Royal Irish Constabulary barracks, now housing a heritage centre) takes you along side roads. Brown "Stone Houses" road signs lead to two remarkable stone forts: first **Cahergall**, then **Leacanabuaile** on its crag, with the remains of 9th-century beehive huts enclosed within an intact circular wall 25m (82 feet) in diameter.

Another worthwhile side-track from Cahersiveen takes you further west to Portmagee and the causeway to Valencia Island. This is a beautiful, quiet spot, with wonderful subtropical gardens laid out on the north side at Glanleam, and some spectacular cliff views on the north and west. Subject to weather conditions, boats leave **Portmagee** for trips to the **Skelligs**, craggy rocks several miles offshore with remarkable early Christian monastic remains.

There are glimpses of the Skelligs beyond Ballinskelligs Bay (Bá na Scealg) as you climb out of Waterville over Coomakista, and breathtaking views forward to the island-studded mouth of the Kenmare River. Down in Caherdaniel (Cathair Dónall) a side road leads to **Derrynane House** (tel: 066 9475113, open: May–Sep daily 10:30–5:15; Apr, Oct Wed–Sun 10:30–4:15; Nov–Mar Sat–Sun 1–5; admission inexpensive). The house was inherited by Daniel O'Connell in 1825 and is full of mementoes, from portraits and personal possessions to the bowl in which he was baptised and the bed in which he died. In the grounds are beautiful gardens, an ancient ring fort and a Mass rock, where Catholics would gather to hear Mass said during the 18th century, when the harsh Penal Laws forbade its observance.

At Castlecove a side track leads north to **Staigue Fort**, Ireland's best-preserved prehistoric fort, a round stone tower in a spectacular location up a lonely valley. After this the road

Above: The steep shapes of the Skelligs are framed by a cave on the shores of Valencia Island

View over the mountains and lakes near Killarney

reaches pretty little Sneem, and forks left at R568 for a wild mountain run back to Killarney.

TAKING A BREAK

Two excellent places to eat and drink in Caherdaniel are **The Blind Piper** and **Freddie's Bar**. They are just off the main Ring of Kerry road, on a side road to Derrynane.

✚ 198 C2
✉ Tourist Information Office, Beech Road, Killarney, Co Kerry
☎ 064 31633

RING OF KERRY: INSIDE INFO

Top tips If you have **limited time** and simply want to enjoy a four-hour drive amid beautiful scenery, stick to the main road circuit: N72 from Killarney to Killorglin, N70 from Killorglin to Kenmare, N71 from Kenmare to Killarney.

■ For **the best view of Lough Caragh**, fork left at O'Shea's shop in Caragh village ("Hotel Ard Na Sidhe" sign). In 1.5km (1 mile) turn left up a forestry track (wooden "Loch Cárthaí/Caragh Lake" sign) for 800m (875 yards) to reach a wide parking place with a wonderful high view over lake and mountains.

Hidden gem Anyone with an extra half-day to spare, and steady nerves on narrow hill roads, should try the side road that runs northeast up the **Inny Valley** from a turning 3km (2 miles) north of Waterville (An Coiréan). It climbs to the Ballaghisheen Pass (304m/997 feet) between the peaks of Knocknagapple and Knocknacusha, then dips over lonely bogland to Bealalaw Bridge, where you turn left for Lough Caragh and Killorglin.

4 Dingle Peninsula (Corca Dhuibhne)

This remote finger of unspoilt countryside, stretching 50km (31 miles) west of Tralee, is a magical place. It has mountains and a rugged coastline, sandy beaches, small towns of character and a remarkable concentration of prehistoric and early Christian monuments along with the Blasket Islands (Na Blascaodai) scattered in the sea. You leave Tralee along N86, passing the big white sails of the restored Blennerville windmill, and run west to the village of Camp with the indented wall of the Slieve Mish mountain range on your left. The waymarked Dingle Way long-distance footpath – a beautiful wild walk – runs on the slopes above the road.

High above Camp stands the 851m (2,792-foot) mountain of **Caherconree.** From below you can just make out a stone wall near the summit that marks an ancient fort. Legend says that King Cu Roi MacDaire abducted Blathnaid, sweetheart of the hero Cuchulainn, and held her there. But Blathnaid sent a signal to her lover, whitening the waters of the River Finglas by pouring milk into its spring. Cuchulainn attacked the fort, killed the king, and rescued his lady.

At Camp, take the mountain road over to **Inch** (Inse), on the peninsula's south coast. The view from here is one of Ireland's best; giant sandspits and whorled sandflats in

Boats in the harbour at Dingle

The tiny Gallarus Oratory dates from around 800 AD

HOG HOARD

Locals will tell you about the Spanish treasure ship that was wrecked in Tralee Bay. A golden pig was salvaged and buried in a triangular field nearby – so they say. It has never been unearthed.

Castlemaine Harbour, with Macgillycuddy's Reeks on the Iveragh Peninsula as a backdrop.

The south coast road goes on west, turning inland through **Anascaul** (Abhainn an Scáil). The South Pole Inn by the bridge was run during the early 1900s by Thomas Crean, one of Captain Scott's team on the ill-fated 1912 Antarctic expedition. Next along is **Dingle** (An Daingean), a small town on a circular bay where a playful dolphin is a frequent visitor. There's usually traditional music at The Small Bridge pub. Try Dingle pie: mutton pie with mutton broth poured over it, a local delicacy. Every year on 26 December the town goes mad, as fantastically dressed "Wren Boys" play rowdy tricks on each other and attempt to drink the pubs dry (➤ 25). In the past, participants in this event used to hunt and kill wrens (hence the name), which, custom held, had betrayed Christ.

Towards the western end of the peninsula are **Ventry** (Ceann Trá) on its perfect scythe-shaped bay, **Mount Eagle** (Sliabh an Iolair) whose slopes are covered with the *clochans* (beehive huts) of early Christian hermits, and, facing the open Atlantic, little **Dunquin** (Dún Chaoin), where the 1970 film *Ryan's Daughter* was filmed.

Out in the sea lie the **Blasket Islands**: Great Blasket, Inishvickillaun, Inishnabro and Inishtooskert. Between

THE SLOW TRAIN

Along the road between Tralee and Dingle (An Daingean) you may spot portions of trackbed and rusty old bridges. This is all that's left of the Tralee & Dingle Light Railway, one of the slowest and sleepiest rural branch railways in the world. Its working life lasted from 1891 to 1953. A short section between Tralee and Blennerville runs restored steam trains in the summer months.

1928 and 1939, islanders Tomás O'Crohan, Peig Sayers and Maurice O'Sullivan produced literary masterpieces about life on Great Blasket, whose population of 120 spoke little or no English and lived simple, remote lives. You can buy copies locally of their books (respectively *The Islandman*, *Peig* and *Twenty Years A-Growing*). A fisherman will probably run you out to Great Blasket if you want to wander through the writers' ruined village; the island was evacuated in 1953 when life became too hard. The sense of place and isolation can be overwhelming; it's an experience not to be missed, if you have the chance. If not, console yourself by reading about it in Dunquin's Blasket Centre on the mainland.

Start your journey back through Ballyferriter (Baile an Fheirtéaraigh), stopping to admire the tiny **Gallarus Oratory**. Just 1.5km (1 mile) away is **Kilmalkedar Church**, a very fine 12th-century ruin with some notable stone carving. Side roads lead to **Ballydavid Head** (Ceann Baile Dháith) and some headspinning cliffs. On a clear day you can walk the waymarked **Saints' Road** over to little Cloghane (An Clochán) on the north coast; from here determined walkers can ascend the 953m (3,127-foot) **Mount Brandon** (Cnoc Bréanainn) to

There are 3 miles (5km) of sandy beach near Inch

The colourful streets of Dingle are busier in August

St Brendan's Oratory at the peak. Before setting course back to Tralee, do make sure to take a detour up the sandspit of the **Magharees**. The beaches here are just about the best you'll find anywhere.

TAKING A BREAK

In Dingle, try **Lord Baker's pub** (➤ 115), probably the town's oldest bar. At **The Tankard** (➤ 115), west of Tralee, sample some excellent seafood and enjoy unbeatable sea views.

✉ **Tourist Information Offices:**
Ashe Memorial Hall, Tralee ✚ 198 C3 ◉ All year
Strand Street, Dingle ✚ 198 A3 ◉ All year
☎ Tralee 066 7121288; Dingle 066 9151188

DINGLE PENINSULA (CORCA DHUIBHNE): INSIDE INFO

Top tips If all you are looking for is a wonderful bathing beach and endless clean sand to run or walk on, look no further than the **sandy spit of the Magharees** that separates Brandon Bay and Tralee Bay on the north of the Dingle Peninsula, 24km (15 miles) west of Tralee.

■ In spite of the crowds, **August is a great month to be in Dingle (An Daingean)**. You can enjoy the Dingle Races, the Dingle Regatta and, best of all, the idiosyncratic Dingle Show, where locals gather to enjoy home-grown fun.

Hidden gem On a side road above N86, 3km (2 miles) east of Camp, is the ivy-smothered ruins of the village of **Killelton**, abandoned because of famine and emigration. Just off the path is a solid stone box with walls a metre thick, the remains of an ancient church built in the 7th century by St Elton himself.

At Your Leisure

5 Old Midleton Distillery

Jameson's old whiskey distillery, in the market town of Midleton 16km (10 miles) east of Cork, has been converted into a visitor centre. In the original distillery buildings you can see the biggest copper still in the world, a great groaning waterwheel, enormous iron-bound vats to hold the mash, and a display of barrel-making in the cooperage, before enjoying a tot of hot or cold whiskey. On the far side of the yard wall the New Distillery steams away, producing 23 million bottles of the golden stuff each year and filling the air with the sweet, pervasive smell of malt and spirit.

✚ 199 E2 ✉ Midleton, Co Cork ☎ 021 4613594; www.jamesonwhiskey.com/omd 🕒 Frequent tours Apr–Oct daily 10–5; Nov–Mar 11:30, 1, 2:30, 4 ✋ Expensive

6 Kinsale

A snug little fishing town with narrow, twisting streets and old stone houses, Kinsale, due south of Cork, is incredibly popular

Explore Kinsale on foot and then relax at one of its excellent fish restaurants

with visitors both for its charming appearance and for its position at the head of a narrow rocky harbour, the estuary of the Bandon River. The town bears the rather commercial title of "Gourmet Capital of Ireland", but it does have some excellent fish restaurants and an annual Gourmet Festival in October that draws the crowds.

Climb Compass Hill to the south of Kinsale to enjoy a panoramic view over the town and the estuary.

✚ 199 E1 ✉ Tourist Information Office, Pier Road, Kinsale, Co Cork ☎ 021 4772234; www.discoverireland.ie/southwest 🕒 Seasonal

7 The West Cork Coast

The Cork coast is spectacularly beautiful all the way west from Kinsale. The cliffs of the Old Head of Kinsale are followed by a succession of sandy coves, rocky bays and headlands, with villages such as Courtmacsherry and Rosscarbery tucked in picturesquely at their heads. **Castletownshend**, with a waterfront castle at the foot of the steep village street, is particularly attractive. Under a big chunk of sandstone in the graveyard of St Barrahane's Church at Castletownshend lies Edith Somerville; alongside is the grave of her cousin Violet Martin. Under the joint *nom-de-plume* of Somerville & Ross, the cousins wrote several best sellers around the turn of the 20th century, including the hilarious and (later) successfully televised *Some Experiences of an Irish RM*.

At the fishing village of **Baltimore** is a pub named "The Algerian". Its name is a reminder of a disastrous day in June 1631, when Barbary pirates raided the town and took scores of locals off into slavery. From Baltimore you can ride ferries out to Sherkin Island and Clear Island (Oilean Cléire), Ireland's southernmost point, in the aptly

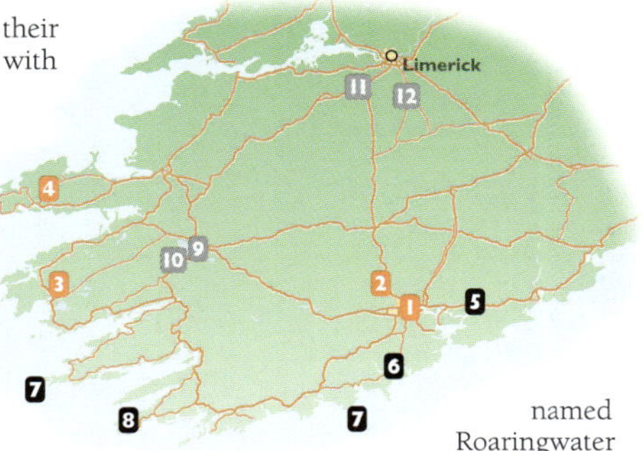

The medieval beacon, Lot's Wife, overlooks the bay near the village of Baltimore facing towards Sherkin Island

named Roaringwater Bay. On the north side of the bay start the **"Five Fingers"**, rugged peninsulas cut by the Atlantic out of the coastline. From Schull you drive down to the great cliffs of Mizen Head (➤ below), as far south as you can get on mainland Ireland; from Durrus you can reach the tip of the Sheep's Head peninsula, returning by a challengingly steep and twisty mountain road called the Goat's Path, with great views over Bantry Bay and its islands.

The **Ring of Beara** is a road circuit around the mountainous Beara Peninsula. Three island detours are worth making here: to see the subtropical gardens nurtured in the mild climate of **Garinish Island** off Glengarriff; to hilly **Bere Island** a little further west (both accessible by boat); and by an exhilarating cable-car crossing over a wild tide race to rocky and dramatic **Dursey Island**, off the very tip of the peninsula. (For more information on Iveragh and Dingle peninsulas ➤ 101 and 104.)
✚ 199 D1

8 Mizen Head Signal Station

Mizen Head is Ireland's most southwesterly point, on a spectacular stretch of rocky coastline with wonderful views. A short walk leads from the car park (but there are 99 steps to climb on the way back), and you'll see seabirds, wild flowers and seals – even whales occasionally surface offshore. On the headland, you can visit the signal station, established in 1931, see the various interesting displays about safety at sea, including a navigational aids' simulator and an automatic weather station, and tour the former light-keepers' quarters.

✚ 198 B1 ✉ West of Goleen ☎ 028 35115; www.mizenhead.net
◷ Jun–Sep daily 10–6; mid-Mar to May and Oct 10:30–5; Nov to mid-Mar Sat–Sun 11–4 ✋ Moderate

9 Muckross House, Abbey and Gardens

Muckross House is a handsome Victorian mansion built in Elizabethan style with high-pointed gables and tall chimneys; it contains an appealing folk museum of bygones. Nearby are three farms worked by traditional methods (great fun for children). The formal gardens are full of exotic trees and shrubs; rhododendrons and azaleas are a speciality, and there's a fine rock garden. The wider grounds of the park give plenty of scope for lakeside rambles or jaunting-car (two-wheeled carriage) rides. North of the house, in a beautiful position, stand the impressive ruins of Muckross Abbey, established in 1340 but mostly dating to the mid-15th century. The best features are the cloisters and the big skeletal east window under the huge square tower.

At the heart of Killarney National Park, this is a very popular and often crowded destination.

✚ 198 C2 ✉ Muckross, near Killarney, Co Kerry ☎ 064 31440; www.muckross-house.ie
◷ House and gardens: Jul, Aug 9–7; Mar–Nov daily 9–5:30. Farms: Jun–Sep daily 10–7; May 1–6; mid-Mar to Apr and Oct Sat–Sun, bank hols 1–6 ✋ House/gardens: moderate. House/gardens/farm: expensive

Muckross House, at the heart of Killarney National Park, has magnificent gardens all year round

10 Killarney National Park

While Killarney's lakes and mountains are famous for their

Pretty as a picture – thatched cottage at the neat estate village of Adare

beauty, Killarney town is infamous for its commercialisation. On the whole, it's best to get straight out into the hills. Sightseers, walkers and adventurers have been coming to the area for nearly 200 years, and things are well organised. You might consider paying the fairly high fee for a trip in a horse-drawn jaunting-car; the drivers, a smooth-talking breed known as "jarveys", know every nook and cranny. Otherwise, aim south of Killarney along the roads around **Lough Leane**, the centrepiece lake of the 10,125-hectare (25,008-acre) **Killarney National Park**. You can rent a boat to get to Innisfallen Island, or venture into the hills to view the Torc Cascade and ascend from the Middle to the Upper Lake.

The area around the lakes can become uncomfortably crowded in holiday season. That's the time to put on your walking boots and follow the trails into the mountains – the well-marked Kerry Way, perhaps, or the high and lonely Old Road to Kenmare, an adventurous 16km (10-mile) route among scenes of wild beauty.

🔶 198 C2 ✉ **Tourist Information Office, Beech Road, Killarney, Co Kerry** ☎ 064 31633

🔟 Adare

Adare, 19km (12 miles) south of Limerick City, is one of Ireland's prettiest villages, with thatched stone cottages and a charming riverside position. It was laid out as an estate village during the 19th century by the lords of the manor, the Earls of Dunraven, and everything here is kept neat, tidy and easy on the eye.

Monastic communities settled around Adare, and their work can still be seen in several spots: the many-arched bridge, built in about 1400; the parish church, a former 13th-century friary church; an Austin friary of about 1315, with a Dunraven mausoleum in the cloisters; and in the grounds of Adare

FOR KIDS

At West Cork Model Railway Village on Clonakilty Bay (open: daily 11–5; moderate) you can play among miniature houses and a railway.

OFF THE BEATEN TRACK

An hour's ride from Baltimore by ferry, Clear Island (Oilean Cléire) is Ireland's southernmost point. In spring and autumn the island becomes a birdwatcher's paradise with spectacular landfalls of migrating birds.

Manor, now a luxury hotel, the very evocative ruins of a 15th-century Franciscan friary.

The manor parklands stretch for miles; there is a medieval castle, rare trees and woodland walks. **Adare Castle** is accessible only on guided tours, which must be booked in advance at Adare Heritage Centre.

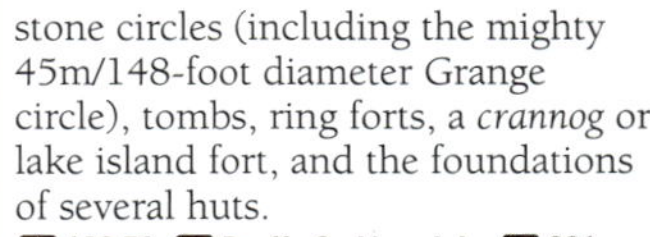

🕇 199 D3 ✉ Tourist Information Office, Adare Heritage Centre, Main Street, Limerick; www.adareheritagecentre.ie ☎ 061 396666 ☎ Adare Castle: 061 396566 ⏱ Adare Castle: Jul–Sep daily 10–5 ✋ Adare Castle: inexpensive

12 Lough Gur

In quiet countryside 27km (17 miles) south of Limerick, this is one of Ireland's most extensive and best-displayed archaeological sites. An informative Interpretative Centre, built and thatched to look like neolithic huts, takes you through the 5,000 years that humans have been established here. There are guided tours, or you can stroll at will around the site. There are stone circles (including the mighty 45m/148-foot diameter Grange circle), tombs, ring forts, a *crannog* or lake island fort, and the foundations of several huts.

🕇 199 E3 ✉ Bruff, Co Limerick ☎ 061 360788; www.ballyhouracountry.com/loughgur ⏱ May–Sep daily 10:30–6 ✋ Moderate

The scenery is just as impressive as the archaeology at Lough Gur

FIVE GLORIOUS WEST CORK VILLAGES

■ Courtmacsherry
■ Rosscarbery
■ Glandore
■ Castletownshend
■ Ballydehob

Where to...
Eat and Drink

Prices
Expect to pay per person for a meal, excluding drinks and service
€ under €15   €€ €15 to €30   €€€ over €30

Fenns Quay Restaurant
€€–€€€
Right in the heart of the city, next to the Courthouse, this popular restaurant has recently been extended and refurbished to provide bright, modern surroundings. Roast chump of Irish lamb with zingy Moroccan spices and tzatziki is a dinner menu favourite, and there's a wide choice of equally interesting meat, fish and vegetarian dishes, plus daytime snacks, sandwiches and breakfast items.
199 E2 Sheares Street, Cork 021 4279527; www.fennsquay.ie Mon–Sat 10am–late

Isaacs €€
Great flavour and attention to detail are the hallmarks at this modern restaurant in a large 18th-century warehouse. Menus have Mediterranean influences alongside Irish traditions. Stylish and relaxed, with coloured tables and fresh flowers to complement the zesty cooking, the restaurant's ambience appeals to all ages.
199 E2 48 MacCurtain Street, Cork 021 4503805; www.isaacsrestaurant.ie Mon–Sat 12–2:30, 6–10, Sun 6–9

Jacques Restaurant €–€€
This popular restaurant is a dashing Mediterranean-toned bistro serving good, zesty international cooking. You might find risotto cakes with field mushrooms, Gubbeen pork with apple sauce, or herb crusted rack of lamb. Set menus change daily and the à la carte menu is seasonal. Early dinner (6–7pm) is good value.
199 E2 9 Phoenix Street, Cork 021 4277387; www.jacquesrestaurant.ie Mon–Sat 6–10, closed Sun, public hols and 25–29 Dec

Little India €
Indian restaurants come and go, but Little India has maintained its traditions of efficient service and excellent cooking since opening in 1999. There's a nice feel to the place with its ornate plush chairs and golden statuettes of auspicious gods. Lady's fingers with mango, and king prawns with pickle and yoghurt are two specialities among many.
199 E2 Washington Street, Cork 021 427 9587; www.littleindia.ie Daily 5–11:30

Ballymaloe House €€€
Since 1964 Myrtle Allen and her family have led the movement for good regional and artisan foods that brought about the current culinary revival in Ireland. The atmosphere of this comfortable house remains unspoiled and, although the food reflects current trends towards global influences, it is not over-sophisticated. A food philosophy based on allowing finest quality ingredients to take centre stage is still crucial. Reservations are essential.
199 E2 Shanagarry, Midleton, Co Cork 021 4652531; www.ballymaloe.ie Daily 12–1:30, 7–9.30; Sun lunch only; closed 24–26 Dec

Blairs Inn €–€€
In a quiet, wooded setting just five minutes' drive from Blarney, this delightful pub has a riverside garden

for fine weather, and roaring open fires in winter. Good traditional food, based on local produce such as Kerry oak-smoked salmon or Dingle crab, is served in the bar and in the restaurant. There's live music, too, on Sunday nights all year and Mondays from May to October.

✚ 199 E2 ✉ Cloghroe, Blarney, Co Cork ☎ 021 4381470; www.blairsinn.ie ◷ Daily noon–midnight. Bar menu: 12:30–9:30; closed Good Fri and 25 Dec

Farmgate €–€€

The shop at the front of this establishment is a showcase for local organic produce and home baking. Behind, in an imaginative restaurant, is an irresistible display of freshly baked savouries, cakes and pastries. Later, this bustling daytime café becomes a sophisticated restaurant. A daytime sister restaurant, Farmgate Café (tel: 021 4278134), is at the English Market in Cork.

✚ 199 E2 ✉ The Coolbawn, Midleton, Co Cork ☎ 021 4632771 ◷ Mon–Wed 9–5, Thu–Sat 9–5, 6:45–9:30; closed 25 Dec–3 Jan

Longueville House and Presidents' Restaurant €€€

This elegant, supremely comfortable Georgian mansion is set on a hill overlooking the River Blackwater. The river, farm and garden supply fresh salmon, Longueville lamb, fresh fruit and vegetables. The cooking is among the finest in Ireland, inspired by the quality of seasonal local produce.

✚ 199 D2 ✉ Mallow, Co Cork ☎ 022 47156; email: info@longuevillehouse.ie; www.longuevillehouse.ie ◷ Bar lunch: 12:30–5. Restaurant: 6:30–9pm; closed Mon and Tue Nov–early Dec and 25–28 Dec

WEST CORK COAST

Annie's Restaurant €€

This intimate and informal restaurant is well known for its wholesome food. Fresh, local fish, local duck, West Cork farmhouse cheeses and smoked foods feature on the simple but tasty menu. Breads, ice creams and desserts are all home-made, too.

✚ 198 C1 ✉ Main Street, Ballydehob, Co Cork ☎ 028 37292 ◷ Tue–Sat 6:30–10:30; closed 14 Oct–1 Dec

Crackpots Restaurant & Pottery €–€€

A good reputation with both locals and visitors, Crackpots offers (at very reasonable prices) unusual and beautifully cooked meals, with ethnic and European influences brought to bear on modern Irish and International cuisine. The menus vary according to season, and cater for all tastes with plenty of seafoood. And if you like the tableware, you can buy that too, because it is made on the premises.

✚ 199 E1 ✉ 3 Cork Street, Kinsale, Co Cork ☎ 021 4772847; www.crackpots.ie ◷ Mon–Sat 6:30–10, Sun 12:30–3

La Jolie Brise €

Overlooking the harbour, this cheerful continental-style café serves good, inexpensive meals and moderately priced wines. Menus offer continental and full Irish breakfast, hot smoked salmon, fresh seafood, well-made pizzas (also to take out) and pastas, traditional mussels and chips, and chargrilled sirloin steaks. There's also spacious accommodation.

✚ 198 C1 ✉ The Square, Baltimore, Co Cork ☎ 028 20600 ◷ Daily 8am–11pm

Mary Ann's Bar and Restaurant €–€€

This delightful pub dates back to 1846, and renovations carried out by its current owners have respected its character. The highly regarded food includes specialities such as the platter of Castlehaven Bay shellfish and seafood and delicious home-baked brown bread, as well as steaks and roasts. Portions are generous, and local west Cork cheeses should not be missed.

✚ 198 C1 ✉ Castletownshend, near Skibbereen, Co Cork ☎ 028 36146 ◷ Bar meals: daily noon–2:30, 6–9. Restaurant meals: Tue–Sun 6–9; bar and restaurant closed Mon Nov–Mar, 3 weeks Jan, Good Fri and 25 Dec

Sea View House Hotel and Restaurant €€€

Set in lovely gardens, this country house hotel has elegant public rooms, with family furniture lending character. Enjoy the views over Bantry Bay while tucking into dishes based on local produce, especially seafood, and have coffee outside on fine summer evenings.

♦ 198 C1 ✉ Ballylickey, Bantry, Co Cork ☎ 027 50073/50462; www.seaviewhousehotel. com ⌚ Restaurant: daily 7–9pm. Lunch: Sun only; closed mid-Nov to mid-Mar

KENMARE

Packie's €€€

This stylish but unpretentious restaurant has flowers on the bar, small tables and generosity of spirit. Well known for intuitive creative cooking, Packie's produces intensely flavoured Irish-Mediterranean food, often involving local seafood. Many familiar dishes are given an original twist and there's always local cheese to finish. The proprietors, the Foleys, also own Shelburne Lodge (➤ 116–117).

♦ 198 C2 ✉ Henry Street, Kenmare, Co Kerry ☎ 064 41508 ⌚ Mon–Sat 6–10; closed mid-Jan to end Feb

The Purple Heather €€

Daytime sister restaurant to Packie's, this bar and informal restaurant serves good, simple, hearrty food. Soups are home-made; bread is freshly baked; orange juice is freshly squeezed; and organic salads, omelettes and sandwiches are followed by comforting puddings. Choice is good, but nothing fancy.

♦ 198 C2 ✉ Henry Street, Kenmare, Co Kerry ☎ 064 41016 ⌚ Mon–Sat 10:45–6; closed Good Fri and Christmas week

KILLARNEY AND THE RING OF KERRY

Aghadoe Heights Hotel & Spa €€€

Many are the awards and accolades earned by this superb hotel and spa, set in breathtaking scenery overlooking lakes and mountains. The dining room looks out on this stunning vista as well, providing a piquant sauce for fine dining in the classic style.

♦ 198 C2 ✉ Lakes of Killarney, Killarney ☎ 06431766; www.aghadoeheights.com ⌚ Restaurant: Daily 6:30–9:30. Lounge and Bistro: summer only 10–9:30. Restaurant closed end Dec to mid-Feb

Lord Kenmare's Restaurant €€

If you like duck you'll think you've gone quackers, in a good way – duck is the speciality at Lord Kenmare's, and lovers of the delicate dark meat come here to sample it. The seafood is excellent, too, with the emphasis on a Mediterranean twist to the dishes – peppers, olives and fresh herbs all playing a part.

♦ 198 C2 ✉ College Street, Killarney, Co Kerry ☎ 06431294; www.ireland-guide. com/establishment/lord_kenmares_ restaurant.6164.html ⌚ Daily 6–10; closed 2 days over Christmas

DINGLE PENINSULA (CORCA DHUIBHNE)

Lord Baker's €–€€

"Lord Baker" was the original owner of what is probably the oldest bar in the area. Bar food (maybe crab claws in garlic butter or chowder and home-baked bread) is served in front of the turf fire. A restaurant with a garden serves good food.

♦ 198 A3 ✉ Dingle, Co Kerry ☎ 066 9151277; www.lordbakers.ie ⌚ Daily 12:30–2, 6–10; closed Thu, Good Fri and 24–25 Dec

The Tankard €–€€€

This pub and restaurant is noted for its seafood. Dishes on the imaginative bar menu are available from lunch onward. The seafood cooking in the restaurant is particularly good, but there is plenty more to choose from, including steaks and Kerry lamb.

♦ 198 C3 ✉ Kilfenora Fenit, Tralee, Co Kerry ☎ 066 7136164; email: tankard@eircom.net ⌚ Bar: daily 12:30–10pm. Restaurant: daily noon–4, 6–10

Where to... Stay

Prices
Expect to pay per night for a double room without tax
€ under €70   €€ €70 to €130   €€€ over €130

BANTRY

Mossie's €€
This delightful country house is on the south side of the Beara Peninsula overlooking Bantry Bay. A former Presbytery, it now offers luxurious rooms, paying great attention to style and comfort. There is a choice between the elegant French Room, the charming Annie's Room or the luxurious Russian Room. Light lunches and teas are served on the lawns during the day and Mossie's Restaurant serves a fine dinner.
199 C1 Uluskel House, Adrigole, Beara, Co Cork 027 60606; www.mossiesrestaurant.com Open all year

CORK CITY

Garnish House €€
Decked with colourful windowboxes, this nice little guest-house is only five minutes' walk from the city centre. It's also handy for the port and airport, and offers 24-hour reception facilities. Some rooms have a Jacuzzi, and there's an extensive breakfast menu to set you up for the day.
199 E2 1 Aldergrove, Western Road, Cork 021 4275111; www.garnish.ie Open all year

Hayfield Manor Hotel €€€
Although built in the mid-1990s, this attractive hotel in the university area, less than 2km (1 mile) from the city centre, has the feel of a large period house. It's set in large gardens, and amenities include a bar, an elegant restaurant and drawing room, both overlooking the garden, and a leisure centre for residents only. Spacious bedrooms are furnished to a high standard and have marbled bathrooms.
199 E2 Perrott Avenue, College Road, Cork 021 4315900; www.hayfieldmanor.ie Open all year

Jurys Inn Cork €–€€
Like other Jurys Inns (➤ 39), this central, riverside hotel is conveniently located and provides comfort for a moderate price. There's no room service, but prices include accommodation for up to four. Rooms are well designed with good-quality furnishings and have phone, TV, tea and coffee facilities and full bathrooms.
199 E2 Western Road, Cork 021 425 2700; www.corkhotels.jurysdoyle.com Open all year

KINSALE

Trident Hotel €€–€€€
This 1960s waterfront building enjoys one of Kinsale's best locations. It's well run, hospitable and comfortable; bedrooms all have full bathrooms, and there are two suites with private balconies, directly overlooking the harbour. The food, in both the first-floor restaurant and the Wharf Tavern underneath it, is well above average hotel fare.
199 E1 World's End, Kinsale, Co Cork 021 4774173; www.tridenthotel.com Closed 25–26 Dec

KENMARE

Shelburne Lodge €€–€€€
This fine old stone house on the edge of Kenmare has been stylishly restored. There's an elegant drawing room and well-appointed dining room where delicious breakfasts with home-baked bread and hot dishes are served. Comfortable bedrooms with bathrooms are

decorated to a high standard. Guests can eat at Packie's (➤ 115).

✚ 198 C2 ✉ Killowen, Cork Road, Kenmare, Co Kerry ☎ 064 41013; www.shelburnelodge.com ◉ Closed 1 Dec to mid-Mar

Killarney Park Hotel €€€

This luxurious modern hotel has a country-house look and an elegant atmosphere. Spacious bedrooms, decorated in countryside colours, have large beds and lovely bathrooms. The modern, international food served is above average.

✚ 198 C2 ✉ Town Centre, Killarney, Co Kerry ☎ 064 35555; www.killarneyparkhotel.ie ◉ Closed 24–27 Dec

The Brandon Hotel €€–€€€

Tralee's largest hotel has spacious public areas, and the bedrooms are well equipped with direct-dial phone, radio and TV. Some bedrooms are small, but all have well-designed bathrooms. The hotel has a swimming pool and leisure centre.

✚ 198 C3 ✉ Princes Street, Tralee, Co Kerry ☎ 066 7123333 ; www.brandonhotel.ie ◉ Closed 23–28 Dec

Harbour View €

From here there are fabulous views over Kenmare Harbour, its islands and surrounding hills, first-class comfort and general standards are the keynotes of this wonderful guesthouse. There is plenty of variety at breakfast time, including fresh fruit and home-made muesli. Harbour View is a few minutes' drive out of the lively town of Kenmare, and makes a great place to base yourself if you are exploring the Beara or Iveragh peninsulas.

✚ 198 C2 ✉ Castletownbere Road, Dauros, Kenmare, Co Kerry ☎ 064 41755

Heaton's €–€€

This guesthouse has a lovely location, right by the water with spectacular views across Dingle Bay. Cameron and Nuala Heaton are welcoming hosts, and the accommodation is exceptionally good – all rooms have bathrooms with power showers, and the mini-suites have Jacuzzis. Daughter Jackie has attracted some renown for her excellent à la carte breakfast menu, a long list which includes local smoked salmon, Irish cheeses, Dingle kippers, porridge with a topping of Drambuie, brown sugar and cream, as well as the usual breakfast fare. Bread, scones and preserves are all home-made.

✚ 198 A3 ✉ The Wood, Dingle, Co Kerry ☎ 066 9152288; www.heatonsdingle.com ◉ Closed 9–27 Dec

Dunraven Arms Hotel €€€

Although it is now a large hotel, this 18th-century inn still has a relaxed country ambience. Bedrooms are beautifully furnished with antiques, and have dressing rooms and luxurious bathrooms. Amenities include a new leisure centre, and the hotel is a popular base for sporting holidays. The food is good in both the bar and the two restaurants.

✚ 199 D3 ✉ Adare, Co Limerick ☎ 061 396633; www.dunravenhotel.com

Glin Castle €€€

The Fitzgeralds, the hereditary Knights of Glin, have lived here for 700 years (though the current house is a mere 200 years old) and now welcome guests to share their home. There are 15 bedrooms; dinner is served in the beautiful dining room, which can seat up to 30 people. The castle's garden is open to the public (as is the house at certain times of the year).

✚ 198 C3 ✉ Glin, Co Limerick ☎ 068 34173; www.glincastle.com ◉ Closed mid-Nov to Mar

Where to...
Shop

CORK

Find local produce at the **English Market**, off Patrick Street. Antiques are best around **Paul Street**. Shanagarry is home to **Ballymaloe Cooking School** (tel: 021 464 6785), and **Stephen Pearce Pottery and Emporium** (tel: 021 4646807).

BLARNEY

Blarney Woollen Mills (tel: 021 4516111) sells a range of goods.

KINSALE

Visit **Kinsale Bookshop** (8 Main Street, tel: 021 4774244), for good literature, **Kinsale Crystal** (Market Street, tel: 021 477 4493) for sparkling crystal, and **Kinsale Art Gallery** (Pier Head, tel: 021 4773622) for superb art and crafts.

KENMARE

Kenmare lace is famous (Heritage Centre, tel: 064 41491); buy antique lace at **The White Room** (Henry Street, tel: 064 40600), rugs at **Avoca Handweavers** (Moll's Gap, tel: 064 34720) and clothing at **Cleo** (Shelbourne Street, tel: 064 41410).

KILLARNEY

Mucros Crafts & Gifts (National Park, tel: 064 31440) and **Bricin Craft Shop** (High Street, tel: 064 34902) both sell quality gifts.

DINGLE (AN DAINGEAN)

An Gailearai Beag (18 Main Street, tel: 066 9152976) is a showcase craft gallery. **Louis Mulcahy**'s sells his pottery at a factory shop near Dingle (tel: 066 9156229).

Where to...
Be Entertained

OUTDOOR ACTIVITIES

Activities include sailing (Castlepark Marina, Kinsale, tel: 021 4774959), sea angling, cycling, horseback riding and golf; information from tourist offices. Kenmare's **Seafari** (The Pier, tel: 064 42059; www.seafariireland.com) makes an entertaining wildlife cruise on Kenmare Bay. Dingle is a base for dolphin-watching (boats depart regularly from the harbour).

SPECTATOR SPORTS

Greyhound racing (Kingdom Stadium, tel: 066 7180008) and horse racing (Mallow, tel: 022 21592) are popular. Also look out for the local sport of road bowling.

MUSIC

Pubs in every town have live music most nights in summer. Good venues include: in Kinsale, **The Spaniard** (Scilly, tel: 021 4772436); in Bantry, **The Anchor Tavern** (tel: 027 50012); in Kenmare, the **Lansdowne Arms** (tel: 064 41368); and in Killarney, **Buckley's** (Arbutus Hotel, College Street, tel: 064 31037). Dingle is *the* place for live music, especially **An Droichead Beag** (tel: 066 9151723) – but almost any bar will be humming. Contrasting musical treats are the **Guinness Cork Jazz Festival**, late October (tel: 021 4278977) and the **West Cork Chamber Music Festival** (Bantry House, tel: 027 52788) late June to July.

West and Northwest Ireland

Getting Your Bearings

The west of Ireland may not have as dense a profusion of dramatic mountains and wild peninsulas as the southwest, but it has something else – sheer magic.

A succession of remarkable landscapes blends one into another, each entirely distinctive but only a part of the whole captivating jigsaw. They include the naked grey limestone hills of the Burren in County Clare, beautiful with carpets of wild flowers in spring and summer; the Connemara district of County Galway, with its remote mountainous heart and harshly lonely coasts; and the three windswept Aran Islands (Oileáin Árann) in Galway Bay, where life and work go

★ Don't Miss

At Your Leisure

Further Afield

High cross at Clonmacnoise, County Offaly, displays fine Celtic carving

on at an unhurried pace among the tiny, rocky fields and innumerable stone walls. The countryside round Clew Bay in County Mayo combines gentle green hills and forbidding mountains with ancient field monuments. Dominating the whole area is Croagh Patrick, the Holy Mountain. Then there's County Sligo – "Yeats Country" – and Donegal, a ragged-edged sea county with truly wild hills and cliffs, where people are few and far between.

This is the land that inspired playwright J M Synge and novelist Liam O'Flaherty, painter Jack Yeats and his brother, the poet W B Yeats. The landscape still inspires musicians; some of the best traditional music is played in the West of Ireland, from Clare's gently flowing tunes to the spiky reels of Donegal. Here in the West you can play the tourist – for instance at County Clare's Bunratty Folk Park; or you can take the other road and savour the lonely silences of the Nephin Beg Mountains. Whatever you do, be sure to climb Croagh Patrick: you will never forget the view from the summit.

Right: Fishing boats moored at Leenane, County Galway, on the deep water of Killary Harbour

Page 119: The view across Galway Bay

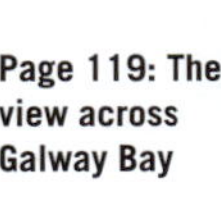

In Four Days

If you're not quite sure where to begin your travels, this itinerary recommends a practical and enjoyable four days in West and Northwest Ireland, taking in some of the best places to see using the Getting Your Bearings map on the previous page. For more information see the main entries.

Day One

Morning
Spend the day exploring the ❶ **Burren** (➤ 124–127). Travel the slow coast road from Ballyvaughan down to **Doolin**, stopping at one of its famous pubs for lunch (➤ 127).

Afternoon
Carry on a few miles down the coast to the spectacular ❶ **Cliffs of Moher**. Then take your time circling back inland by way of the great ancient monuments

of **Poulnabrone portal dolmen** (above) and **Gleninsheen wedge tomb**, making time for a stroll on the Burren's naked limestone hills. An hour's drive in the early evening will land you in Galway for the night.

Day Two

Morning
Take the ferry from the city quays and cruise down Galway Bay to ❷ **Inishmore/Inis Móir** (left, ➤ 129), the biggest of the Aran Islands (Oileáin Árann). Stop for lunch at Joe Watty's friendly pub in the small port of Kilronan.

Afternoon
Make your way up to the ancient fort of ❷ **Dún Aengus** (➤ 129) on the cliffs, preferably on foot or by rented bicycle. Be sure to be back in Kilronan in good time for the last ferry back to Galway!

Day Three

Morning
You'll have plenty of time for coffee, a stroll and a look around **9 Galway City** (► 135) before moving on in the early afternoon.

Afternoon
Take the **3 Connemara** coast road west, at first along the smooth upper shore of Galway Bay, then winding in and out around a succession of small, craggy bays. After a cup of tea in **Clifden** (► 130), push on 65km (40 miles) by way of dramatic Killary Harbour to **4 Westport** (► 132). Stay overnight here, and look for a great music session in Molloy's (► 133), Hoban's or McHale's.

Day Four

Morning
Set off bright and early for the hour's run (via the bridge) out to **4 Achill Island** (coast at Dooagh above, ► 133). Back on the mainland, continue north on the wild coastal road to Bangor Erris, then turn east across the bleakly impressive Bellacorick bog to reach civilisation and a late lunch at Ballina, perhaps at The Broken Jug pub in the centre of the town (tel: 096 72379).

Afternoon
Push on to **13 Sligo** (► 137; a pint in Hargadon's bar is obligatory here), and drive north towards W B Yeats's favourite mountains to pay your respects at his grave in **Drumcliff churchyard** (► 179). Then return through Sligo and drive on south for Galway.

Further Afield
If you have a day for a bleakly beautiful corner of Ireland (right), stay overnight in Ballybofey and spend the next day driving the spectacular circuit of southwest Donegal's coast, out by Glencolumbkille (Gleann Cholm Cille) and the Slieve League (Sliabh Liag) cliffs.

❶ The Burren and the Cliffs of Moher

The Burren is 1,300sq km (507sq miles) of hilly ground in the northwest corner of Clare, almost waterless, all but deserted, and largely made up of naked grey limestone. Yet in this bleak setting you'll find superb wild flowers, marvellous music, hundreds of ancient monuments and a beautiful coastline, culminating in the mighty Cliffs of Moher. And with it all comes that special laid-back County Clare atmosphere. The place is a paradox, but one you'll have unbeatable pleasure in exploring.

A Snapshot Tour

Start in **Ballyvaughan**, following the coast road down to **Doolin**, noted for its traditional music pubs, and on to the **Cliffs of Moher** for some spectacular views. Then take the road for **Lisdoonvarna** and **Kilfenora**, and on by **Corofin**, to enjoy some typical laid-back Burren villages. There are carved high crosses at Kilfenora, and the excellent **Burren Display Centre** there fills you in on the geology and flora of the region. See more early Christian remains at **Dysert O'Dea** south of Corofin, then meander north through the heart of the Burren to find the magical landscape of **Mullaghmore**, the great portal dolmen of **Poulnabrone**, and, in spring and summer, the carpets of wild flowers.

You could see the "Best of the Burren" in a long day like this. But you won't begin to see the place itself until you leave the car and walk out into the wilderness.

Floral Present and Stony Past

You don't have to be a botanist to see the beauty of the flowers of the Burren. The limestone pavements carry deep cracks, known as "grykes" to geologists. These trap water, sun and soil fragments, making them ideal hothouses for plants. The warm Gulf Stream moves offshore; sunlight bounces off the naked stone into the grykes. Whatever combination of factors makes it happen, the Burren bursts open each spring with an astonishing array of wild flowers: orchids, spring gentians, mountain avens, eyebright, bloody cranesbill. Plants that wouldn't normally be found anywhere near each other grow side by side – acid-loving and lime-loving, arctic, mountain, coastal, Mediterranean. The ferns, mosses and lichens are spectacular. Springtime and summer in the Burren are a botanist's dream, and beautiful for anyone who loves colour and variety in the landscape.

Scattered across this landscape are monuments bearing witness to five millennia of human habitation. Around 5,000 years ago, a forgotten people built the **Poulnabrone portal dolmen** – the stone uprights and cap stone of which would once have been covered with earth to form a tomb chamber. **Gleninsheen**, near Caherconnell, and other wedge-shaped tombs nearby date from about 1500 BC. With the introduction of Christianity came the wonderfully carved high crosses at **Kilfenora**, and in the 12th and 13th centuries respectively the monastic site of **Dysert O'Dea** in the south and the rich stonework at **Corcomroe Abbey** in the north. Round stone forts and enclosures with jaw-breaking names dot the hills: Cahermacnaghten, Caherballykinvarga, Cahercommaun. Under the hills stand fortified towers like the gaunt 16th-century **Newtown Castle** near Ballyvaughan, and imposing houses such as the picturesquely ruined 17th-century **Leamaneh Castle** outside Corofin. There are also the shells of ancient churches abandoned after Oliver Cromwell's troops invaded and subdued the Burren in the 1650s.

Fine Scenery and a Good Time

A great way to see the Burren is to spend a couple of days walking the **Burren Way**, a 42km (26-mile) footpath from Ballyvaughan to Liscannor. The most spectacular part is undoubtedly along the edges of the **Cliffs of Moher** at the southwestern extremity of the Burren. At their highest point these giant flagstone cliffs fall sheer into the sea: a great tourist attraction, and often a crowded one. There are more tremendous views from **Corkscrew Hill**, a section of N67 south of Ballyvaughan that snakes back and forth as

ARCHAEOLOGY

Five of the Burren's great archaeological delights:
- Poulnabrone portal dolmen
- High crosses at Kilfenora Cathedral
- Newtown Castle tower house
- Dysert O'Dea's church doorway with its carved saints and beasts
- Corcomroe Abbey

it climbs, and the whole of the steep, craggy coastline around Black Head.

You can tour the underground **showcaves at Aillwee** near Ballyvaughan, and escape other tourists at **Mullaghmore**, a magical hill reached by a country road north of Corofin, to enjoy strange land formations and delicious solitude.

TAKING A BREAK

In Kilfenora, try **Vaughan's** or **Linnane's**, and in Lisdoonvarna, the **Roadside Tavern**: you're guaranteed conversation and laughter. If you fancy a singalong in Doolin, **O'Connor's** is a good bet. If your taste is for traditional tunes and you're staying in Doolin overnight, try **McGann's** at around 10pm.

✉ Tourist information centres: Arthur's Row, Ennis and Cliffs of Moher; www.discoverireland.ie/shannon
☎ Ennis: 065 6828366. Cliffs of Moher: www.discoverireland.ie/shannon

Burren Display Centre
✠ 199 D5
☎ 065 7088030; www.theburrencentre.ie
🕐 Jun–Aug daily 9:30–6; mid-Mar to May 10–5:30; Sep–end Oct 10–5 ✋ Moderate

Aillwee Caves
✠ 199 D5
☎ 065 7077036
🕐 Tours only daily from 10am; last tour 5:30 (Jul, Aug 6pm); Dec by appointment only ✋ Expensive

Left: The Poulnabrone portal dolmen is impressive when you get up close
Right: Spring gentian in flower near the Burren

FLOWERS

Don't forget your flower book! Mary Angela Keane's *The Burren* (an Irish Heritage Series paperback that is widely available locally) gives an excellent introduction to the Burren flora. Real enthusiasts should bring a hand lens with them; this will give wonderful close-ups of the flowers. But remember – don't pick them!

THE BURREN: INSIDE INFO

Top tips Five of the **Burren's chief tourist attractions** lie on or very near N67: Ballyvaughan, Newtown Castle, Aillwee Caves, Corkscrew Hill, and the spa town of Lisdoonvarna. The Cliffs of Moher are 10km (6 miles) along R478.
■ Anyone with enough skill not to spoil the tune is welcome to join a pub **music session**. Don't be shy, ask if you can join in!

Hidden gems Holy wells, rock chairs that cure backache, Mass rocks and forgotten church ruins: the Burren is packed with them, and you can find them all (or almost all) with the help of **Tim Robinson's wonderful Folding Landscape** (► 128).

One to miss Don't bother with the **Cliffs of Moher on a high-season weekend** – the clifftops will be crowded, and all sense of awe will be on hold.

2 The Aran Islands (Oileáin Árann)

Seeming to float in the mouth of Galway Bay like three low grey boats in line astern, the Aran Islands (Oileáin Árann) resemble no other part of Ireland. Here Irish is still spoken everyday, the traditional black hide-covered boats called currachs are used for fishing (though now they're canvas covered and often motorised), transport is mostly on foot or bicycle, homespun clothing is still worn by some of the older folk, and the pace of life is driven not so much by the clock as by the tides and winds, and by tasks done and not done.

The islands are made not of Galway granite but of Clare limestone, which means that their spring and summer flower displays are glorious. Countless thousands of stone walls march in parallel lines across the bare grey and black rock, squaring off the islands into hundreds of tiny fields. Partly these walls show ownership; partly they are built of necessity, as handy repositories for stones picked laboriously from the fields by hand. The soil of the islands has been created by hand, a precious mixture of sand, seaweed and dung that grows the best potatoes in Ireland. Life out here on these windswept, barren rocks has always been hard, and still is.

Inisheer (Inis Óirr), nearest to County Clare (reached from Doolin), is the smallest of the Aran Islands at just over 3km (2 miles)

Left: Aran Island houses are built low to give maximum protection from bad weather

Right: Seaweed is gathered to be used as fertiliser on the rocky fields

GREAT ARAN READING

- *Skerrett* by Liam O'Flaherty – titanic, tragic struggle between Inishmore's priest and schoolmaster, written by a native and based on a true story.
- *The Aran Islanders* by J M Synge – classic account of the islands and their people at the turn of the 20th century, garnered during the playwright's sojourns on Inishmaan, 1898–1902.

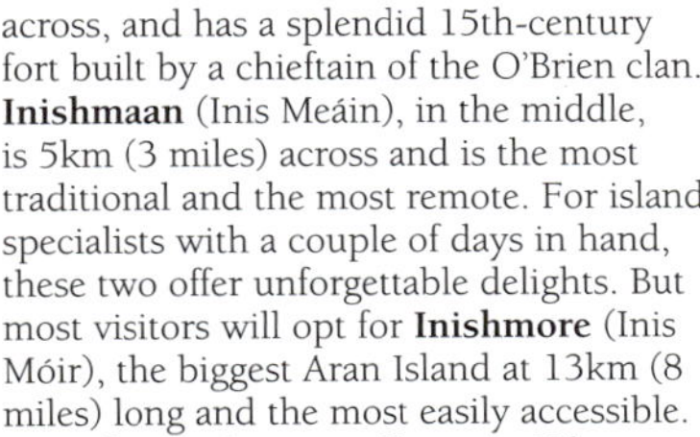

across, and has a splendid 15th-century fort built by a chieftain of the O'Brien clan. **Inishmaan** (Inis Meáin), in the middle, is 5km (3 miles) across and is the most traditional and the most remote. For island specialists with a couple of days in hand, these two offer unforgettable delights. But most visitors will opt for **Inishmore** (Inis Móir), the biggest Aran Island at 13km (8 miles) long and the most easily accessible.

Inishmore has a small port at Kilronan, and a tiny airstrip. You could drive from Galway to Rossaveal for a 40-minute ferry crossing, or fly over from Connemara Airport, just outside Galway City, and be in Inishmore in six minutes. There is a heritage centre at Kilronan with exhibitions to introduce you to the Aran Islands.

The island's chief attraction is the clifftop fort of **Dún Aengus** with its three giant rings of battlements; but the island is covered in pre-Christian and early Christian remains. Take time to walk, talk, listen, sit and stare. Even in Ireland, you won't find a more peaceful spot.

TAKING A BREAK

Stop for lunch in **Joe Watty's** friendly pub in Inishmore's tiny port of Kilronan.

Dún Aengus
☎ 099 61088
🕓 Mar–Oct daily 10–6; Nov–Feb 10–4
✋ Free
✚ 198 C5 ✉ Tourist information offices: Kilronan, Inishmore ☎ 099 61263; www.visitaranislands.com
Aras Fáilte, Forster Street, Galway ☎ 091 537700; www.discoverireland.ie/west
🕓 All year round (both)

THE ARAN ISLANDS (OILEÁIN ÁRANN): INSIDE INFO

Top tips Tours include Dún Aengus and Seven Churches. A bus leaves for Dún Aengus Mon–Sat at 10am, 1pm and 4pm in summer (last bus 2:30 in winter).
- If you are planning to visit Inishmaan, **check the weather forecast first**. Fog, mist or very high winds can suspend all travel between island and mainland.
- Note that there is only one ATM on Inis Móir, in the Spar Supermarket.

Hidden gem On Inishmore, about 6km (4 miles) east of Dún Aengus, is the less visited stronghold of **Dún Dúchathair** in a spectacular setting on the cliff edge.

3 Connemara

Connemara in northwest County Galway is the romantic heart of the west, a harsh land of boggy fields, knobbly mountains and savage sea coasts. Dublin schoolkids come here to learn Irish; the rest of us visit for the wild and beautiful scenery. But make no mistake, this is a tough place to live, with poor soil stretched thinly over beds of unyielding granite. As the locals say: "You can't eat scenery."

North of Galway stretches the immense inland sea of **Lough Corrib**. Here angling-oriented Oughterard is a pretty spot to base yourself for good trout fishing, while **Cong Abbey** on the north shore is worth the detour – a glorious little 12th-century building.

West of here is Joyce Country, so named because much of the population were of the Joyce clan, where the sister ranges of the **Maumturk Mountains** and the magnificent **Twelve Bens** (or Twelve Pins) pierce the sky with quartzite peaks. This is a cruelly beautiful landscape, and wonderful walking country, bounded on the north by mountains sweeping down to the narrow inlet of Killary Harbour.

Going west again, you are confronted by classic Connemara landscapes, a hard land of wide bog vistas, rugged brown hills and innumerable little lakes. **Clifden**, a Victorian holiday resort, sits out west in the centre of a wheel of craggy coastline, where a coast road crawls and climbs around the indentations. Follow it east, stopping at **Roundstone** to visit

The Twelve Bens rise above the Connemara National Park

A lonely cottage within the Connemara National Park

the workshop at Roundstone Musical Instruments, where Malachy Kearns makes the world's best *bodhráns* (goatskin drums). Then carry on in increasingly desolate scenery towards Galway City. Before getting there, spare a couple of hours to turn right at Casla/Costelloe, where a causeway road takes you through the Irish-speaking islands of **Lettermore** (Leitir Moir), **Gorumna** (Garumna) and **Lettermullan** (Leitir Mealláin). This wild, lonely back country gives a flavour of Connemara.

TAKING A BREAK

The Steam Coffee Shop in Clifden is a lively, inexpensive place to eat. In Roundstone, **Brown's** restaurant in the Alcock & Brown Hotel serves a high standard of freshly prepared cuisine.

✚ 194 B1   ✉ Tourist Information Office, Aras Fáilte, Forster Street, Galway City   ☎ 091 537700; www.discoverireland.ie/west

CONNEMARA: INSIDE INFO

Top tips To get straight from Galway City to Clifden, the "capital" of West Connemara, take N59. This road whisks you straight there on an 80km (50-mile) run through the heart of the region.

■ Bring your fly and coarse rods if you are an angler; the **coastal rivers of Connemara are some of the best in Ireland** for salmon, and the loughs provide excellent trout fishing.

■ If you are visiting in August, try to get to the **Clifden Show**, where appealing, long-haired Connemara ponies are brought for sale.

Hidden gem The **6th-century oratory on St Macdara's Island (Oileán Mhic Dara)**, 9.5km (6 miles) south of Roundstone (where you charter boats to the island).

One to miss Avoid **Salt Hill in holiday season**, when it becomes a crowded, very average seaside resort. There are better, quieter beaches a little further west.

④ West Mayo

West Mayo is one of Ireland's most atmospheric corners. While not exactly undiscovered, it is far enough distant from Dublin and walled in by serious enough mountains and boglands to retain (and flaunt) its own character.

Centrepiece of the region is broad **Clew Bay**, reputed to have 365 islands. Certainly there are several dozen of them, little drumlins (heaps of Ice Age rubble) with grassy backs turned to the land and yellow clay teeth bared to the west. At the mouth of Clew Bay is **Clare Island**, humpbacked and greenly beautiful, a great place to spend a few days away from it all; a boat service from Roonagh Quay on the southwestern extremity of the bay takes, depending on the weather, between 30 minutes to an hour to reach the island.

On Clew Bay's south shore stands the 765m (2,510-foot) cone-shaped mountain of **Croagh Patrick** (known locally as "The Reek"), Ireland's Holy Mountain, focus of a massed annual pilgrimage and one of Ireland's classic hill hikes (► 176–177). The top of The Reek is the best vantage point to view Clew Bay.

At the southeastern corner of Clew Bay lies **Westport**, a small town of great charm and character, planned in the latter part of the 18th century by celebrated Georgian architect James Wyatt at the request of the Marquess of Sligo, on whose estate it was built. **Westport House** (1730–34), beautifully furnished and with a fine collection of paintings, is worth a

White-washed cottages sit on a slope on Achill Island

look around, and its grounds are lovely. A zoo and atmospheric dungeons are a bonus for visitors with children. But the great attraction of Westport is its town life – gossip, storytelling, music-making. It is one of the best towns in Ireland for traditional music and each year, in late September/early October, hosts an excellent arts festival, showcasing home-grown and invited talent.

Over near Castlebar is the only national museum outside Dublin, the **National Museum of Ireland – Country Life**, appropriately located in one of Ireland's most rural counties. It contains the national Folklore Collection, comprising around 50,000 objects, and the displays reflect traditional rural life in Ireland between 1850 and 1950. The specially built museum is in the grounds of Turlough Park House, which is itself open to the public to show how the landowners lived.

A road bridge links Achill Island to the mainland

Out at the northwest corner of Clew Bay is **Achill Island**, a big ragged outline attached to the mainland by a road bridge across Achill Sound (Gob an Choire). This Irish-speaking island, superbly mountainous, is Ireland's largest. You can climb 672m (2,205-foot) Slieve More, Achill's highest peak, from Doogort (Dumha Goirt) on the north coast, or join a boat-rental party for a jaw-dropping inspection of some of Ireland's highest cliffs at the island's northwestern tip. Boats can be rented from Doogort Pier; for information contact Alice's Harbour Inn tourist office (tel: 098 45384).

TAKING A BREAK

Stop for a drink at **Molloy's** pub in Westport, in the High Street. Matt Molloy, flute-player with the celebrated Chieftains band, often sits in with the musicians when he's at home. Alternatively try **Quay Cottage** (➤ 140), a waterside restaurant on Westport's harbour.

✚ 194 C2
✉ Tourist Information Office, The Mall, Westport, Co Mayo
☎ 098 25711; www.irelandwest.ie

Westport House
✚ 194 C2
☎ 098 25430/27766; www.westporthouse.ie
◉ House and gardens: Easter–Oct daily 11:30–5:30. House, gardens and attractions: Jun–Aug daily 11:30–5:30, Easter–May and Sep–Oct 11:30–5
✋ Expensive

National Museum of Ireland – Country Life
✚ 195 D2
✉ Turlough Park, Castlebar, Co Mayo
☎ 094 903 1773; www.museum.ie
◉ Tue–Sat 10–5, Sun 2–5; closed Good Fri and 25 Dec
✋ Free

At Your Leisure

5 Bunratty Castle and Folk Park

Conveniently near to Shannon Airport (west of Limerick City), this complex is aimed squarely at a tourist market. There are nightly mead'n'minstrels medieval banquets in the castle (reservations are essential) – great fun if you're in a jolly mood, and a crowded "19th-century Irish village" in the grounds with costumed guides and demonstrations of traditional skills. Come here well out of season, however, and you can appreciate the atmosphere and the authentic touches without having your toes trodden on. The castle itself, built in about 1425, is a very fine restoration, with plenty of good tapestries and beautiful furniture, some dating back as far as the building.

✚ 199 D4 ✉ Bunratty, Co Clare ☎ 061 711200; www.shannonheritage.com ◉ Daily 9:30–5:30 (Folk Park also Jun–Aug 9–6) ✋ Expensive

Bunratty Castle was restored during the 1950s

6 Craggaunowen

At Craggaunowen, by a lake 21km (13 miles) north of Bunratty, the story of the Celts in Ireland is told by costumed guides amid clever reconstructions of Celtic buildings that include a *crannóg* or lake dwelling, a stone ring fort, round thatched huts and burial places. The leather-hulled boat *Brendan*, built by

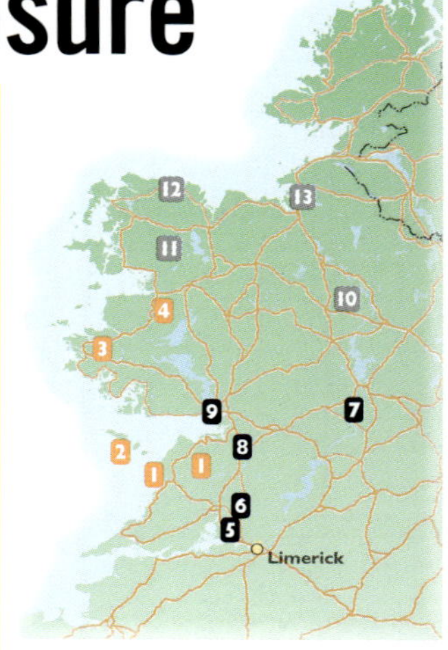

adventurer Tim Severin and sailed by him from the Dingle Peninsula to Newfoundland in 1976–77, is on display: it was this voyage that showed how St Brendan might have discovered America back in the 6th century AD.

✚ 199 D4 ✉ Quin, Co Clare ☎ 061 360788; www.shannonheritage.com 🕓 Mid-Apr to Sep daily 10–6 ✋ Moderate

7 Clonmacnoise

Clonmacnoise is one of Ireland's finest and most interesting ecclesiastical sites. It was the most influential centre in pre-Norman Europe in its day. Several Irish kings are buried here. Within the site are two Round Towers (the lightning-blasted 10th-century O'Rourke's Tower and the almost perfect MacCarthy Tower of 1124), eight ancient churches and a largely 14th-century cathedral. Of three notable high crosses, the best is the richly carved Cross of the Scriptures, also known as the Great Cross, which dates from the early 10th century and stands over 4m (13 feet) tall.

✚ 199 F5 ✉ On R444, north of Shannonbridge, Co Offaly ☎ 090 967 4195; www.heritageireland.ie 🕓 Mid May to mid-Sep 9–7; mid-Mar to mid-May and mid-Sep to Oct 10–6; Nov to mid-Mar 10-5:30 ✋ Moderate

8 Thoor Ballylee

I the poet William Yeats,
With old millboards and sea-green slates
And smithy work from the Gort forge
Restored this tower for my wife George.
And may these characters remain
When all is ruin once again.

This inscription at Thoor Ballylee tells the story of the medieval stone tower house bought by W B Yeats in 1916 for £35, and intermittently inhabited (and written about) by him. It is now a beautifully restored museum housing Yeats memorabilia and first editions.

✚ 199 D5 ✉ Gort, Co Galway ☎ 091 631436 (winter 091 537700) 🕓 Jun–Sep Mon–Sat 9:30–5 ✋ Moderate

The door of one of the eight ruined churches at Clonmacnoise

9 Galway City

Galway is one of the fastest growing cities in Europe and it is a thriving place with a lively atmosphere thanks to its university and the large number of job-providing industries that have sprung up around the town. During Galway Arts Festival late in July, and the Races that follow it, is a good time to visit. Everything centres on Eyre Square, which is undergoing a makeover; in the streets to the south and west you'll find most of the bars, and some good restaurants and shops. Further developments include a brand new Galway City Museum.

✚ 199 D5 ✉ Galway City Museum, Spanish Arch, Galway ☎ 091 532460; www.discoverireland.ie/west 🕓 Jun–Sep daily 10–7; Oct–May Tue–Sat 10–5 ✋ Free

FOR KIDS

Leisureland, a modern pool complex in Salt Hill, has a waterslide, Treasure Cove complete with pirate ship, a tropical beach pool and playground.

✉ Salt Hill, Galway ☎ 091 521455 🕓 Public opening times vary throughout the year. To avoid disappointment ring first ✋ Moderate

10 Strokestown Park House, Garden & Famine Museum

Allow a good half-day to explore this fascinating place. The big, white-fronted Palladian mansion, approached through a grand arch, dates back to the 1660s, though it was remodelled in the 1730s. The original 18th-century furnishings are still in place. Tunnels concealed the movement of servants from the patrician gaze of the Mahon family, owners of Strokestown. There was even a gallery constructed around the kitchen so that the lady of the house could observe what went on without being seen herself.

Money and privilege did not save Major Denis Mahon. He was murdered on his estate during the Great Famine of 1845–50 after he had tried to evict most of his starving tenants and ship them off to America. An excellent, if harrowing, Famine Museum, in the old stable yard, tells of the tragic events. Outside in the grounds is a fine garden with a stunning herbaceous border.

✠ 195 F2 ✉ Strokestown, Co Roscommon
☎ 071 9633013; www.strokestownpark.ie
◷ Mid-Mar to Oct daily 10:30–5:30; Nov to mid-Mar by appointment ✋ Expensive

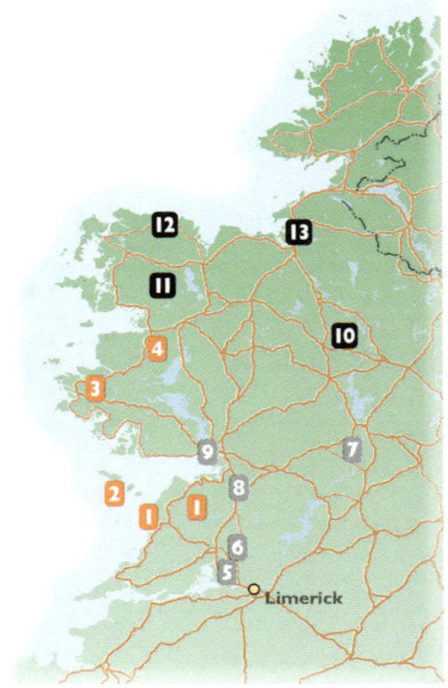

11 Nephin Beg Mountains

These roadless mountains in north-west Mayo fill a triangle of 200sq km (78sq miles) north of Westport, flanked by the wild Atlantic coast on the west and the great bog of

Strokesdown Park House is home to the Famine Museum

FOUR LONELY HEADLANDS WITH WONDERFUL VIEWS
- Malin Head, Donegal
- Achill Head, Achill Island, Mayo
- Mace Head, Connemara, Galway
- Hags Head, Clare

ALCOCK AND BROWN

Just off R341 coast road south of Clifden in western Connemara, a cairn stands in Derrigimlagh bog as a monument to Sir John Alcock and Sir Arthur Whitten Brown. It was here that their Vickers-Vimy biplane came to rest on its nose on 15 June, 1919, having completed the first non-stop flight across the Atlantic.

Bellacorick on the east. It is the remotest range in Ireland, crossed by one dramatic and demanding footpath, the 48km (30-mile) Bangor Trail from Newport to Bangor Erris. The path can be followed at any time of year, but only by experienced walkers with plenty of stamina. Don't attempt it on your own or in bad weather. For more information, contact the tourist office in Westport, tel: 098 25711.

🕇 194 C2

🔢 Céide Fields

A pyramidal eyesore of a visitor centre, housing a surprisingly good exhibition, is the focal point of the world's largest Stone Age site – 1,500 hectares (3,705 acres) of stone-walled fields, enclosures, dwelling areas and megalithic tombs dating back approximately 5,000 years. All have been painstakingly unearthed by archaeologists since the 1970s from the blanket bog that swallowed them.

🕇 194 C3 ✉ Ballycastle, Co Mayo
☎ 096 43325; www.heritageireland.ie
🕐 Jun–Sep daily 10–6; mid-Mar to May and Oct–Nov 10–5 💷 Inexpensive

Read the runes on Sligo's monument to W B Yeats

🔢 Sligo

Sligo is a delightful town, full of history and well supplied with restaurants and pubs. The small library, museum and art gallery contain paintings by Jack Yeats and manuscripts of poems by his brother, William; the brothers spent many of their holidays with cousins in Sligo, a place they loved (➤ 178–180 for a tour of Yeats Country). An annual Yeats Summer School fills the town with fans of the poet each August. There's superb medieval stonework in the ruined **Dominican Friary** church of **Sligo Abbey**.

Among the town's other attractions are Hargadon's – a classic pub where chat is firmly on the agenda – and **Sheela-na-gig**, where there are excellent sessions of traditional music; and opposite the Court House in Teeling Street the much-photographed window of solicitors Argue and Phibbs.

🕇 195 E3 ✉ Tourist Information Centre, Aras Reddan, Temple Street ☎ 07191 61201; www.discoverireland.ie/northwest

OFF THE BEATEN TRACK

Out beyond Clifden in westernmost Connemara lies the village of Claddaghduff. You can cross the sands here at low tide, with the aid of markers, to Omey Island, a secluded place where you'll find a hidden church, a holy well, ancient burial grounds and a beautiful circular walk. Keep an eye on the time – and tide – for getting back. For tide information contact the Connemara Walking Centre in Clifden, tel: 095 21379.

Further Afield

Donegal

Donegal forms the northwestern corner of Ireland, almost cut off from the Republic to which it belongs by the thrusting heel of Fermanagh in Northern Ireland. Of all the counties of western Ireland, it is probably the least explored, but if you enjoy rugged and lonely country and have time to spare, it shouldn't be missed.

Two parts of the county are particularly striking: the southwest coast, famous for its majestic cliffs, and the Inishowen Peninsula, whose flattened spear-blade shape forms the northernmost tip of Ireland.

The Southwest Coast

A 120km (75-mile) drive will show you the best of southwest Donegal, starting west from Donegal town to reach the village of **Killybegs**. This is a big fishing port where fish-processing factories line the roads and sturdy red-and-blue trawlers ride side by side in the harbour. A tumbled landscape follows – heathery hillsides, cragged headlands and pine forests – through which side roads take you around coastal inlets. In Carrick (An Charraiag) a left turn (signed "Teelin Pier") takes you via "Bunglass: The Cliffs" signs to a steep gated lane. This climbs to a thrilling viewpoint high above the cliffs of Slieve League (Sliabh Liag), rearing some 600m (1,970 feet) out of the sea in a blotched wall of yellow, black, orange and brown.

Now the main road swoops across wild bogland to **Glencolumbkille** (Gleann Cholm Cille), huddled in a long green valley under rugged headlands. St Columba of Iona established a monastery here, and the secluded valley is full of monuments that attest to its Christian heritage: stone slabs and pillars incised with crosses, cairns, early Christian chapels. Annually on 9 June pilgrims walk a 15-part Stations of the Cross route that links up several of these monuments. Glencolumbkille is an exceptionally peaceful and haunting place. Return via Ardara, and the mountain road back to Donegal town.

Inishowen Peninsula

Inishowen is even more isolated than Donegal's southwestern coast. Northeast of Letterkenny you pass **Grianan of Aileach** in the neck of the peninsula, a circular stone fort 6m (20 feet) high, perched high on a hill overlooking Lough Swilly. Grianan of Aileach was sacked in 1101 by Murtagh O'Brien, King of Munster, who ensured its demolition by ordering his soldiers to remove a stone for every sack of provisions they carried. From here the road runs north past the beach at Buncrana into the bog and hills of northern Inishowen. Up at the peak of the peninsula you climb to the old signal-tower on **Malin Head** where there is nothing between you and the Scottish islands of the Outer Hebrides 160km (100 miles) to the north.

The Donegal coastline is one of the quieter corners of Ireland

Where to...
Eat and Drink

Prices
Expect to pay per person for a meal, excluding drinks and service
€ under €15   €€ €15 to €30   €€€ over €30

Aillwee Cave Café €

Everything is fresh and home-made at this friendly eatery in one of Ireland's premiere attractions. After visiting the 2 million-year-old cave have a tasty snack or lunch. Pick from a long list: soup, sandwiches, rolls, salads, cakes and biscuits. Or check out the potato bar, where Ireland's staple comes with a choice of scrumptious fillings. Ice cream, popcorn and more to takeout, too.
✚ 199 D5   ✉ Ballyvaughan, Co Clare
☎ 065 7077036; www.aillweecave.ie
◷ Daily in peak season from 10am

Hylands Burren Hotel €–€€

This delightful old family-run establishment close to Ballyvaughan harbour has open fires, well-crafted furniture and a welcoming atmosphere. Their reputation for good food is growing – specialities include freshly caught seafood, Burren lamb, organic vegetables and herbs, and local farmhouse cheeses. Caring service and a genuine sense of hospitality add to the enjoyment.
✚ 199 D5   ✉ Ballyvaughan, Co Clare
☎ 065 7077037; www.hylandsburren.com
◷ Bar food: daily 12:30–9; closed 2 Jan–2 Feb. Restaurant: 7–9 ; closed Christmas

Sheedy's Country House Hotel €€

The hotel has been run by the Sheedy family for generations, and their hands-on approach shows in attractive furnishings, open fires and well-equipped bedrooms with bathrooms. However, good food is perhaps the major draw, with dishes such as traditional chowders and crab salads in the Seafood Bar, and more formal dining in the Sheedy's Restaurant. Exacting standards of produce and cooking apply to both, including fresh fish from the Burren Smokehouse nearby.
✚ 198 C5   ✉ Lisdoonvarna, Co Clare
☎ 065 7074026; email: info@sheedys.com; www.sheedys.com   ◷ Restaurant/Seafood bar: daily 6:45–8:45; closed mid-Oct to Easter

Kirbys of Cross Street €–€€

This dashingly informal restaurant/bar/café is next door to one of Galway's leading pubs, Busker Browne's and The Slate House. Lots of light wood, bare tables, and cheerful young staff give it a youthful atmosphere. The attractively presented contemporary cuisine is based on Irish themes, seasoned with influences from further afield. Cooking is sound and prices reasonable.
✚ 199 D5   ✉ Cross Street, Galway   ☎ 091 569404; www.kirbysrestaurant.com   ◷ Daily 12:30–2:30, 5.30–10:30; closed 25 Dec

Kirwan's Lane Restaurant €€€

This stylish modern restaurant in the Spanish Arch area of Galway City opened in 1966 and has since moved away from more refined dining to a relaxed bistro-style. Grills and Asian influenced dishes dominate the menu, but with some good fish cooking retained. The service and surroundings match the smart food and reservations are advised.
✚ 199 D5   ✉ Kirwan's Lane, Galway
☎ 091 568266   ◷ Daily 12:30–2:30, 6–10:30; closed 25 Dec

Moran's Oyster Cottage €–€€€

An idyllic thatched pub on Galway Bay, with its own oyster beds, Moran's attracts a loyal following from all over Ireland and beyond. The seafood is wonderful; the native oysters – in season from September to April – are a treat. You can have the farmed Gigas oysters all year, however, along with other specialities like chowder, smoked salmon and delicious crab sandwiches and salads.

199 D5 The Weir, Kilcolgan, Co Galway 091 796113; www.moransoystercottage.com Bar food: noon–10 pm; closed Good Fri and 25 Dec

White Gables Restaurant €€€

Open stonework and soft lighting create a soothing atmosphere in this attractive restaurant on the main street of Moycullen, 8km (5 miles) north of Galway City. The hearty cooking is always good, with freshly made soups, specialities such as black and white pudding with wholegrain mustard sauce, and a choice of seafood, including lobster fresh from the tank. The set Sunday lunch is particularly popular with locals and visitors.

199 D5 Moycullen, Co Galway 091 555744; www.whitegables.com Lunch: Sun 12:30–2:30; dinner: Mon–Sat 7–10; closed Dec 23–Feb 14, Mon (except mid-Jul to mid-Aug)

ATHLONE

Wineport Lodge Restaurant €€€

Attractions are the ten luxury guestrooms, the location on Lough Ree, the hospitality, and the seasonal menus. These are based on such local delicacies as Irish Angus beef, game, eels, home-grown herbs and wild mushrooms. The style of cooking is International and Modern Irish, some creative vegetarian cooking and an Irish farmhouse cheeseboard. Bar food is available 1–5 pm in summer.

195 F1 Glasson, Nr Athlone, Co Westmeath 090 439010; www.wineport.ie Mon–Sat 6–10; Sun 3–5, 6–10; closed 24–26 Dec

CONNEMARA

O'Dowd's Seafood Bar and Restaurant €–€€

This traditional bar serves a good pint; the bar menu is reasonably priced. The restaurant serves more substantial meals. There is also a coffee shop serving Irish breakfast and speciality teas and coffee.

194 B1 Roundstone, Co Galway 095 35809; www.odowdsrestaurant.com Bar food: noon–9.30. Restaurant: Apr–Sep noon–10; Oct–Mar noon–3, 6–9.30; closed Good Fri, 25 Dec

Steam Coffee House €

Steam Coffee House is a very welcome, child-friendly offshoot of the award-winning "High Moors" restaurant, which enjoys a fine reputation. This is the place to come for soup and a sandwich, puddings, ice-creams or just a cup of coffee.

194 B1 Courtyard Shopping Centre, Clifden 095 21526 Late openings Thu and Fri 6–8

WESTPORT

Quay Cottage €€

This stone waterside restaurant never fails to delight. Its maritime theme is strongly reinforced by the imaginative menu, with such items as chowder and seafood platter. There is much else of interest, including mountain lamb and innovative and creative vegetarian options. Tempting desserts or a farmhouse cheese selection, and freshly brewed coffee by the cup, make a fitting finale.

194 C2 The Harbour, Westport, Co Mayo 098 26412; www.quaycottage.com Daily 6pm till late; closed 24–26 Dec and mid-Jan to mid-Feb

CAVAN

MacNean House and Restaurant €€€

Known all over Ireland for its superb food when it was a laid-back bistro,

Where to... Stay

MacNean's is unlikely to go all wobbly and throw out excellence in pursuit of the uncritical tourist dollar now that it has had an extensive facelift and upgrade. Locally sourced ingredients and the taking of infinite care and trouble are still what underpins cooking of rare quality at this Restaurant of the Year 2007. And you'll kick yourself for ever more if you don't leave room for a pudding – or two.

✚ 196 B3 ✉ Main Street, Blacklion, Co Cavan ☎ 071 9853022; www.macneanrestaurant.com ◎ Jun–Sep Wed–Sat 6:30–9:30, Sun 12:30–3:30, 7–8:30; Oct–May Wed–Sat 6:30–9:30, Sun 12:30–3:30; closed one week over Christmas and all Jan

SLIGO

Cromleach Lodge €€€

Fine views from this modern building on a hill overlooking Lough Arrow are a bonus: Moira and Christy Tighe's genuine hospitality ensures comfort and relaxation for guests, many drawn by Moira's superb food. The best of local ingredients – organically grown vegetables and herbs, goat's cheese, or tender, succulent, local loin of lamb – underlie a light, elegant style with excellent saucing. Simple table settings complement a growing number of mouthwatering house specialities.

✚ 196 A2 ✉ Castlebaldwin, Co Sligo ☎ 071 9165155; www.cromleach.com ◎ Dinner: Mon–Sat 6–9, Sun 6:30–8:30; lunch Sun 12:30–4:30; closed Nov–Jan

Fiddlers Creek €€

Good wholesome food is served in the dining room and cosy bar. Some tables have views over the river. The usual steak and fish dishes are served, with vegetarian options as well. Twists on classics give the menu an interesting slant; Cajun salmon featuring fresh Irish salmon marinated in spices.

✚ 196 A2 ✉ Rockwood Parade, Sligo, Co Sligo ☎ 071 9141866; www.fiddlerscreek.ie ◎ Dinner daily 6–10; lunch Sun only

THE BURREN

Gregans Castle €€€

This remote hotel on the inland road between Ballyvaughan and Lisdoonvarna may seem as stark as the landscape, but appearances are deceptive. In fact, warmth, elegance and tranquillity are the keynotes, both in spacious public rooms and luxurious accommodation. Non-residents are welcome in the restaurant, and also for lunch or afternoon tea in the Corkscrew Room bar. In fine weather you can sit out beside the rose garden.

✚ 199 D5 ✉ Ballyvaughan, Co Clare ☎ 065 7077005; www.gregans.ie ◎ Restaurant: daily 7–8:30 pm, light meals from noon; closed Nov to mid-Feb

Temple Gate Hotel €€–€€€

This hotel right in the centre of Ennis is a clever conversion of a building that formerly served as a gentleman's residence, then a convent. It retains some of its Gothic-style features. The 73 rooms are classic in style but the facilities are modern with neat private bathrooms. There is a restaurant and a traditionally themed pub with music on weekends.

✚ 199 D4 ✉ The Square, Ennis, Co Clare ☎ 065 6823300; www.templegatehotel.com ◎ Closed 25 Dec

Prices

Expect to pay per night for a double room without tax

€   under €70   €€   €70 to €130   €€€   over €130

Ardilaun House Hotel €€–€€€

Set in wooded grounds about 5 minutes' drive from the city centre, Ardilaun House Hotel has elegantly furnished, spacious public rooms, plus a leisure centre with an indoor pool and hydro spa. The bedrooms are well decorated – those with bay views are the most popular, though others are equally attractive. The pleasant dining room overlooks the pretty gardens.

✚ 199 D5 ⊠ Taylor's Hill, Galway ☎ 091 521433; www.theardilaunhotel.ie ⊙ Closed Christmas

Glenlo Abbey €€€

This restored 18th-century abbey, 4km (2 miles) from the centre of Galway City, is set in landscaped grounds and overlooks a beautiful loch. Wooden floors and leather sofas give an exclusive air to the main reception area. The bedrooms are housed in a modern wing, which also has a library, restaurants and bars. Leisure facilities are extensive and include golf, archery, fishing and clay-pigeon shooting. Irish and French cuisine is served in the hotel's restaurant.

✚ 199 D5 ⊠ Bushypark, Galway ☎ 091 526666; www.glenlo.com

Jurys Inn Galway €€

This good-value choice, perfectly set by the river and the bustling Spanish Arch area of Galway City centre, provides a high standard of basic accommodation. Rooms are large and provide every comfort and convenience: neat bathrooms, TV, phone and hospitality tray – but with no room service or other extras. However, there's a pleasant bar, a restaurant/coffee bar, and adjoining parking.

✚ 199 D5 ⊠ Quay Street, Galway ☎ 091 566444; www.galwayhotels.jurysinns.com ⊙ Closed 24–26 Dec

Mallmore House €€

A really delightful country house bed-and-breakfast in lovely gardens, situated a couple of miles outside the Connemara "capital" of Clifden in a beautiful wild part of County Galway. Friendly, approachable and very helpful hosts, turf fires to warm you, and breakfasts that fuel you for a day's exploring.

✚ 194 B1 ⊠ Ballyconneely Road, Clifden, Co Galway ☎ 095 21460; www.mallmore.com

Hodson Bay Hotel €€€

Overlooking Lough Ree, this hotel adjoins Athlone Golf Club and has lovely lake and island views. Amenities include boating, fishing and a leisure centre. Comfortable bedrooms are decorated in a bright contemporary style, and there are well-finished bathrooms, plus all the necessary extras (phone, TV, hospitality tray). The **L'Escale Restaurant** is excellent.

✚ 195 F1 ⊠ Hodson Bay, Athlone, Co Westmeath ☎ 090 6442000; www.hodsonbayhotel.com ⊙ Open all year

Breaffy House €€

A handsome Victorian house in nearly 40ha (100 acres) of landscaped gardens and wooded grounds on the outskirts of Castlebar. Breaffy House is not only a good comfortable hotel, but also a spa with mud- and steam-baths, swimming pools, sauna, dance studio, and all manner of massages and other relaxing and renewing treatments. So if the Mayo weather turns a bit "soft", you can still have a great time here!

✚ 195 D2 ⊠ Castlebar, Co Mayo ☎ 094 902 2033; www.breaffyhousecastlebar.com

Carrabaun €

On the road out towards Galway, a couple of minutes' drive from the traditional music town of Westport, this bed-and-breakfast has great views of the Holy Mountain of Croagh Patrick. It is a first-class stopover, with friendly hosts who'll try their best for you.

Great breakfasts – try the fabulous Carrabaun porridge with a little drop of magic, or sample their salmon with soda bread, a pairing fit for an angel's cookbook.
✚ 194 C2 ✉ Leenane Road, Westport, Co Mayo ☎ 098 26196; www.anu.ie/carrabaunhouse

Markree Castle €€

Home to the Cooper family for 350 years and set in park and farmland, this is a real traditional Irish castle. A huge welcoming log fire always burns brightly in the lofty hall – generosity with heating is one of the castle's most attractive features. There's a very beautiful dining room (non-residents welcome) for more formal dining and a large double drawing room where delicious light food, including afternoon tea, is served. The full Irish Breakfast is not to be missed, and be sure to try the freshly made brown soda bread. Two floors of attractively furnished bedrooms provide guests with all the necessary comforts and amenities and there is the added bonus of pleasant parkland views.
✚ 195 E3 ✉ Collooney, Co Sligo ☎ 071 9167800; www.markreecastle.ie ◷ Closed Dec 24–26

Kee's Hotel €€

Established as a coaching inn in 1845, and in the Kee family since 1892, this comfortable hotel is well placed for touring County Donegal. Rooms at the back of the hotel are quieter and more desirable than those at the front; some have views of the Blue Stack Mountains. There's an excellent leisure centre for guests and a stylish, fine restaurant, **The Looking Glass**, where imaginative Franco-Irish cuisine is served. There is often live music playing on Sunday nights.
✚ 196 B4 ✉ Stranorlar, Ballybofey, Co Donegal ☎ 074 9131018; www.keeshotel.ie

Where to... Shop

A high proportion of the quality goods on sale in western Ireland are locally made. Ennis rewards a leisurely browse in uncrowded streets. **Custy's Music Shop** in Ennis (Francis Street, tel: 065 6821727) is the best place in the west to talk traditional music, to buy instruments, and to pick up news of local sessions. At Doolin, the **Doolin Crafts Gallery** (Ballyvoe, tel: 065 7074309) sells a range of leatherware, ceramics, glassware and clothing, some of which are made on the premises. Go 5km (3 miles) east to the spa town of Lisdoonvarna and you can visit the **Burren Smokehouse Ltd** (tel: 065 7074432) to see how oak-smoking of Atlantic salmon is done (and buy a vacuum-packed side to take back home).

In Galway, a one-stop shop for the best in Irish design is **Judy Greene** (Kirwan's Lane, tel: 091 561753, www.judygreenepottery.com). If you're in the city on a Saturday, the **Galway Market** at St Nicholas Collegiate Church is a must; it sells everything from organic vegetables, cheeses and fresh eggs to flowers, home baking and preserves. The excellent **Kenny's Bookshop and Art Galleries** (High Street, tel: 091 709350, www.kennys.ie) is also worth a visit. It has five floors of Irish-interest books, mainly second-hand and antiquarian, as well as the Kerry Art Gallery. Also a bit different is **Claddagh Jewellers** (Eyre Square, tel: 091 562310), where you'll find a wide selection of attractive traditional Celtic jewellery.

Where to...
Be Entertained

CONNEMARA

Connemara Marble Industries Ltd (Moycullen, tel: 091 555102) sells locally quarried marble items crafted on site, and **Joyce's** of Recess has a range of quality goods. Musicians should head for **Roundstone Musical Instruments** (Roundstone, tel: 095 35808).

Clifden has good gift shops, including **The Celtic Shop and Tara Jewellers** established 1976 (tel: 095 21064) with gifts, clothing, and gold and silver Irish jewellery. At Letterfrack, **Connemara Handcrafts** (tel: 095 41058), a branch of the Wicklow-based Avoca Handweavers, sells fabrics, clothing, crafts and specialist foods. Even better, perhaps, is **Kylemore Abbey** (Kylemore, tel: 095 41146), where there's a good craft shop and an excellent informal restaurant.

Foxford Woollen Mills (Foxford, tel: 094 925 6756) is a good place to buy tweeds and blankets; there's a shop, a restaurant and a Visitor Centre, which recreates the mill in former centuries, with the sights, sounds and smells from a bygone age.

Over at Achill Island, you could take a break at **The Beehive** (Keel, tel: 098 43134), an attractive craft shop and restaurant that serves home-made food all day.

SLIGO AND DONEGAL

The counties of Sligo and Donegal are famous for sweaters, tweeds and parian china (so called after the marble from the Greek island of Paros, which it resembles), all widely available. Useful addresses include the **Donegal Craft Village** (tel: 074 9722225), five minutes' walk from the town centre and **Magee's** (Donegal town, tel: 074 9722660), renowned for tweeds; they also sell quality gifts and have a good self-service restaurant. Tiny, characterful **Ardara** is chock-full of shops selling keenly priced local knits and weaves.

MUSIC

You'll find great pubs in the west of Ireland doing organised and impromptu music sessions. In Ennis, try **Cruise's** (Abbey Street, tel: 065 6841800) and **The Temple Gate** (The Square, tel: 065 6823300); **O'Connors** (tel: 065 7074168) of Doolin is highly regarded, while **Vaughan's** of Kilfenora (tel: 065 7088004) is famous for set dancing and music. Galway is packed with music pubs: **Tigh Neachtain** (Cross Street, tel: 091 568820) is one of the best. In early May, Kinvarra runs a **Cuckoo Fleadh**, with traditional music at **Winkles Hotel** (The Square, tel: 091 637137). Siamsa Company performs traditional music and dance in the summer at Galway's **Claddagh Hall** (tel: 091 755479) and at **Town Hall Theatre** (tel: 091 569777). Westport is noted for its music pubs (► 133). Sligo is another musical hot spot; **Furey's** offers traditional, country, jazz, blue grass and Latino (www.fureys. ie). Look out for the **Ballyshannon International Folk Festival** in Co Donegal (tel: 071 9851088).

OUTDOOR ACTIVITIES

This region offers fine scenic drives, golf, cycling, horseback riding and horse racing. There's surfing on Atlantic beaches such as Strandhill on Sligo Bay (rent boards and suits from **Strandhill Surf School** (tel: 071 9168483). Fishing this area is superb, particularly in County Mayo.

Northern Ireland

Getting Your Bearings

As you explore the cliffs, hills, country lanes and city streets of Northern Ireland, you will find that all the attributes of landscape and people that make the Republic so appealing are here in abundance, along with a remarkably traffic-free road system and a good number of uncrowded visitor attractions.

Northern Ireland remains part of the United Kingdom, and no one coming here can be unaware of the deep divisions between loyalists, those who want to maintain links with Britain, and nationalists, who wish to sever them. As a guest north of the border, it's good to inform yourself about recent history. Violence and hatred flared during the past 30 years or so between small extremist sections of the nationalist and loyalist communities in Northern Ireland, and between hardline nationalists insisting on a united Ireland and the security forces of army and police whom they saw as reinforcing the North's links with Great Britain. This poisonous period in Ulster's history came to be known as "The Troubles". However, the 1998 Good Friday Agreement, signed by all the interested political parties, brought hope and peace, along with the establishment of a devolved Government of Northern Ireland made up of Ulster politicians from both sides of the divide. Optimism has returned to Northern Ireland, and with it a very welcome positive atmosphere of regeneration, and a renewed interest among visitors in all that this great place has to offer.

Belfast has its cheerful black humour, vibrant nightlife and superb Botanical Gardens. The east coast is carved by the Glens of Antrim into beautiful deep valleys, and the Antrim Coast in the north is celebrated for the Giant's Causeway, one volcanic extravaganza among many along this spectacular line of cliffs. Swing across the hair-raising Carrick-a-Rede rope bridge; take a hike over the wild Sperrin or Mourne mountains, watch the geese and wading birds on Strangford Lough, or lazily cruise the great inland waterway of Lough Erne among islands crammed with ancient churches, round towers and enigmatic stone carvings. And spare a day to enjoy welcoming and optimistic Derry.

Page 145: The Giant's Causeway in the evening sun

★ Don't Miss

1 Belfast ➤ 150

2 Antrim Coast, Glens of Antrim, Carrick-a-Rede Rope Bridge and Giant's Causeway, Co Antrim ➤ 154

3 Ulster-American Folk Park, Co Tyrone ➤ 158

4 Lough Erne and Belleek Pottery, Co Fermanagh ➤ 160

At Your Leisure

5 Old Bushmills Distillery, Co Antrim ➤ 163

6 Downhill, Co Derry ➤ 163

7 Londonderry/Derry ➤ 164

8 Sperrin Mountains, Co Derry/Co Tyrone ➤ 164

9 Marble Arch Caves, Co Fermanagh ➤ 165

10 Florence Court, Co Fermanagh ➤ 165

11 Castle Coole, Co Fermanagh ➤ 165

12 Navan Royal Site, Co Armagh ➤ 165

13 Saint Patrick's Trian, Co Armagh ➤ 166

14 Mountains of Mourne, Co Down ➤ 166

In Three Days

If you're not quite sure where to begin your travels, this itinerary recommends a practical and enjoyable short trip in Northern Ireland, taking in some of the best places to see using the Getting Your Bearings map on the previous page. For more information see the main entries.

Day One

Morning

Explore ❶ **Belfast** (➤ 150–153), making sure not to miss the Grand Opera House (right), Botanic Gardens, Ulster Museum and wall paintings along the Shankill and Falls roads.

Afternoon

After an early lunch in the Victorian splendour of the Crown Liquor Saloon (➤ 167), head north around the spectacular Antrim Coast by way of the deep-cut ❷ **Glens of Antrim** (➤ 154). Stick to the minor coast road round Torr Head. Signposted turnings lead to **Carrick-a-Rede rope bridge** (below, ➤ 155), a nerve-tingling crossing above a 24m (79-foot) drop, and the **Giant's Causeway** (➤ 156), from whose slippery basalt promontory there are memorable cliff views. Overnight on the coast at Portstewart or Portrush.

Day Two

Morning
`7` **Derry City** (➤ 164, 181) lies to the west – if you have a little more time, walk around the city walls. To continue the itinerary from Portstewart, head south via Coleraine and Limavady to Dungiven, then on to Feeny (B74). A further 5km (3 miles) south (B44), take the mountain road that crosses the rugged `8` **Sperrin Mountains** (➤ 164) to reach Sperrin village. Head west along the Glenelly Valley for a drink and a snack at Leo McCullagh's pub in Plumbridge, then southeast to Newtonstewart and south to Omagh.

Afternoon
About 5km (3 miles) north of Omagh lies the `3` **Ulster-American Folk Park** (➤ 158–159), well worth an hour's exploration to see the carefully reconstructed houses and the striking emigration exhibition. From Omagh drive southwest (A32) to Irvinestown, then west on A35 or A47 to `4` **Belleek** (➤ 160) and its world-famous pottery. A drive along the south shore of beautiful **Lough Erne** will land you in Enniskillen for the night.

Day Three

Morning
Drive east for 65km (40 miles) to Armagh City, where there is the excellent Armagh Planetarium and nearby historic **Navan** hill fort (➤ 165), then on to Newry and the A2 coast road. At Kilkeel bear left (B27) on side roads through the wilderness of the `14` **Mountains of Mourne** (above, ➤ 166), then head northeast to Downpatrick with its cathedral and St Patrick's Grave.

Afternoon
Take the car ferry from Strangford to Portaferry, and drive north up the Ards Peninsula beside island-dotted and bird-haunted **Strangford Lough** (➤ 184–186); then continue from Newtownards into Belfast.

Belfast

Belfast has had more than its share of bad publicity since the early 1970s. There's no denying that Northern Ireland's chief city has been the setting for some atrocious events, but visitors today need have no qualms about whether they will be welcome here. Belfast humour is black and mordant, but its people are particularly keen to put the bleak past behind them. Every new visitor is a symbol of a return to normal life, and especially welcome because of that. What you will find in Belfast is a fairly old-fashioned looking place, a city of the Industrial Revolution, with red-brick terraces and grandiose public buildings. It doesn't have the instant appeal of Dublin, but well repays a couple of days' exploration.

The Golden Mile

Many of the attractions of city-centre Belfast are within a few minutes' walk of each other. You could start and finish your sightseeing on Great Victoria Street at the **Crown Liquor Saloon** (► 167), now in the care of the National Trust, a splendidly maintained Victorian pub, complete with stained-glass windows, carved-wood booths, an elaborately tiled front, and a fine mosaic of a crown at the front door. The story goes that Patrick Flanagan, the pub's original owner and a passionate Irish nationalist, put the crown in that position so that anyone who wished could wipe their feet on it.

Belfast's ponderously magnificent 19th-century City Hall

Drinking in opulent surroundings at the Crown Liquor Saloon

Across from the Crown is the **Grand Opera House** of 1894, bombed and neglected in the past, but now restored to its overblown best with gilt plaster and woodwork, a ceiling writhing with golden apes, and viewing boxes supported by gilt elephants with immense trunks.

Great Victoria Street forms the west side of a triangle of streets known as the Golden Mile, where chic eateries and nightspots are clustered. At the top of the triangle is Donegall Square, with the remarkable **Linen Hall Library** – a real old-fashioned library with thousands of shelves of well-thumbed books, a splendid curved wooden staircase, an atmosphere of holy hush, and a Members' Room and decent Tea Room tucked away. Over Donegall Square revolves the magnificent **Wheel of Belfast**, a great spoked "bike wheel" with capsules suspended from its rim, from which there are mind-blowing views over the city. Nearby stands the very grand **City Hall** of 1906 under a magnificent dome (reopening 2009). Near here you'll find a fine memorial to the city's crewmen who lost their lives when the Belfast-built *Titanic* sank on 15 April, 1912. There are plans for a massive Titanic attraction by 2012. The interior of the City Hall is baroque, with a handsome central dome seen above a hollow galleried ceiling, and a Council Chamber full of heavily carved wood, stained glass and padded red leather benches. The whole area has recently benefited from a huge makeover, with the smart new retail space, the **Victoria Square** – just what Belfast needs.

EMERALD POET

Poet William Drennan (1754–1820) was born in Belfast. His output is forgotten these days but for one phrase, which has become the most fondly quoted cliché about Ireland – "The Emerald Isle".

The University Area

South of the city centre stands the early Victorian, mock-Tudor pile of **Queen's University**. Just beyond are Belfast's very enjoyable **Botanic Gardens**, a quiet and leafy spot with hundreds of tree species and the splendid Palm House, whose rounded prow and long side wings in cast iron and glass hold tropical vegetation in a hot, steamy atmosphere. Nearby is the 9m (30-foot) deep Tropical Ravine, housed inside a glass-roofed building dating from the 1880s, where fish

Loyalist colours in the lower Newtownards Road

and terrapins swim in the dripping shadows of cinnamon tree, dombeya, loquat and banana. In the **Ulster Museum** (reopening late 2009), alongside, the industrial history of Belfast is illustrated with mighty calendering (pressing) and fulling machines from the textile trade, photos of great ships being launched, tobacco and snuff samples – all reminders of the heavy industry that made this place.

Away from the Centre

Don't leave Belfast without seeing some of the work of the **gable-end artists** thrown up by the Troubles. Out west along the loyalist **Shankill Road** and nationalist **Falls Road** the polemic is fierce: even more so just east of the river in the Short Strand or Lower Newtownards roads. You can buy postcards showing the best examples of this "people's art".

On the eastern outskirts of Belfast stands the imposing mansion of **Stormont**, home of the devolved Government of Northern Ireland. And north of the city centre on the quays of the shipyards stand **Samson and Goliath**, two giant yellow cranes that symbolise the past industrial might and the dogged four-square strength of this most resilient city.

BELFAST: INSIDE INFO

Top tips Avoid the Golden Mile, and particularly Great Victoria Street, in the early hours at weekends if you are likely to get upset by the rowdy behaviour of young clubbers.

Hidden gem Often seen, but seldom noticed with appreciation: the **Marks & Spencer department store** opposite the City Hall, a magnificent Italianate building in red Dumfries sandstone that used to house the Water Office.

One to miss If pushed for time, give **Stormont** a miss – the best thing about it is the long view of the building from way down the drive, and you can see that on any postcard stand in Belfast.

TROUBLES TAXIS

Regular buses were withdrawn in the 1970s due to hijackings, and though some services have been reinstated, black taxis still run what amount to cut-price minibus services to West Belfast. The cab drivers pack their vehicles, and the passengers split the fare.

The splendid Palm House in the Botanic Gardens

FRAGRANT FLATS

Laganside, once a riverside slum area polluted by the smell from the mudflats at low tide, has been redeveloped as high-class residences. Lagan Weir keeps river levels constant and the stink away.

TAKING A BREAK

Stop for lunch at the **Crown Liquor Saloon** (➤ 167) and try the delicious "champ" — mashed potatoes and spring onions. **Roscoff Café** on Fountain Street is also a good place for light lunches.

✚ 197 E3
✉ Belfast Welcome Centre, 47 Donegall Place
☎ 028 9024 6609; www.gotobelfast.com

Crown Liquor Saloon (NT)
✉ 46 Great Victoria Street
☎ 028 9027 9901

Botanic Gardens
✉ Stranmillis Road/Botanic Avenue
☎ 028 9031 4762
🕐 Main garden open without restrictions. Palm House and Tropical Ravine: Apr–Sep Mon–Fri 10–noon, 1–5; Oct–Mar Mon–Fri 10–noon, 1–4, Sat, Sun 1–4 ✋ Free

City Hall
✉ Donegall Square
☎ 028 9027 0456 🕐 Tours Jun–Sep Mon–Fri 11, 2, 3, Sat 2:30; Oct–May Mon–Fri 11, 2:30, Sat 2:30; closed public holidays ✋ Free

Linen Hall Library
✉ 17 Donegall Square North
☎ 028 9032 1707; www.linenhall.com 🕐 Mon–Fri 9:30–5:30, Sat 9:30–1 ✋ Free

Ulster Museum
✉ Botanic Gardens
☎ 028 9038 3000; www. ulstermuseum.org.uk
🕐 Mon–Fri 10–5, Sat 1–5, Sun 2–5 ✋ Free

Wheel of Belfast
✉ Donegall Square East
☎ 028 9031 0607; www.worldtouristattractions.co.uk
🕐 Sun–Thu 10–9, Fri 10–10, Sat 9am–10pm ✋ Moderate

2 The Antrim Coast

The Antrim Coast is Northern Ireland's best-known scenic attraction, with the Giant's Causeway as the plum in the pudding. But don't rush straight to that celebrated piece of volcanic freakery; take your time getting there, and enjoy the beautiful journey north from Belfast through wild glens and along a wonderful coast road.

The Glens of Antrim

Take A2 north from Larne to Carnlough, a pretty little fishing harbour where the cliffs rise in a foretaste of what's in store. The road hugs the shore under steep hillsides for the next 16km (10 miles), curving into Red Bay at Waterfoot with some really striking big hills rearing inland. This is the place to turn aside up **Glenariff**, most spectacular of the series of deep glens carved into the basalt of North Antrim by rivers. Glenariff is bounded by granite cliffs over which waterfalls pour in rainy weather, a dark and rugged cleft. Drive up it and park at the Glenariff Forest Park Visitor Centre, amid mountain scenery. Various waymarked walking trails start from here: short garden and nature trails, a longer scenic trail, and a gorgeous 5km (3-mile) waterfall trail that leads you beside and over some of Glenariff's torrents.

The most spectacular of the Glens of Antrim, Glenariff has dozens of lovely waterfalls

Back on the coast road you go through neat little Cushendall. If you take A2 inland here, you can turn off left shortly and make a back-road loop up **Glenaan** by way of **Ossian's Grave** (► 157), before returning to the coast down quiet and lovely **Glendun**. From Cushendun among its trees there's an exhilarating alternative to A2 – a very rough and bouncy side road in marvellous coastal scenery via Torr Head to Ballycastle.

Carrick-a-Rede Rope Bridge

Carrick-a-Rede rope bridge is well signposted from Ballycastle; but you won't find it if you visit in the winter between October and March, for this clever cat's cradle of rope with a board floor is in position only during the salmon fishing season. It's a good 800m (880-yard) walk from where you park to the bridge, with 161 stone steps, before you arrive at the entrance gate and look down on the nervous visitors swinging across the rope bridge, 25m (82 feet) above the sea. The National Trust has now "improved" the bridge's safety by installing a cage structure.

It's quite safe ...but you'll need some nerve to cross the Carrick-a-Rede rope bridge

The bridge is the only means of crossing the 20m (66-foot) gap between the cliff and the Carrick-a-Rede basalt stack offshore. The name means "rock-in-the-road" – the stack stands in the path of the salmon, who turn aside to pass it and swim into a net stretched out from the stack and anchored in the sea. It's a thrill to cross the bridge (come early or late to avoid the hordes), and a great photo opportunity.

The Giant's Causeway

So to the Giant's Causeway (the only World Heritage Site in Ireland), a short distance along the coast. Here the cliffs are at their most spectacular as they rise almost 100m (330 feet) around a series of rocky bays. The Causeway itself is formed of some 37,000 basalt columns, mostly hexagonal, that slope in a narrowing and declining shelf into the sea. They were made by cooling lava after a volcanic eruption some 60 million years ago. Up in the cliffs of the bay are more formations. The most striking, reached by a footpath, is the Giant's Organ, a cluster of basalt "organ pipes" weathered into vertebra-like rings that rise 12m (40 feet) high. As for the Giant: he was the mythological hero Fionn MacCumhaill (Finn McCool), who, legend has it, laid down the causeway as stepping stones to the island of Staffa.

Dare one say it? The Giant's Causeway, after all the publicity and raised expectations, can strike visitors as rather an anticlimax. Don't expect too much, and do make the footpath circuit if you can, up by the Organ and back along the clifftop footpath, to enjoy one of the best views of the Causeway.

Top: Cooled basalt formed the hexagonal columns of the Giant's Causeway

Right: High cliffs overlook the promontory of stumpy columns that noses out into the sea

TAKING A BREAK

Stop at the **National Trust Tea Room** in the Giant's Causeway Centre (➤ 168).

✉ Tourist Information Centre, Sheskburn House, 7 Mary Street, Ballycastle
☎ 028 2076 2024; www.discovernorthernireland.com

Carrick-a-Rede Rope Bridge and Larrybane Visitor Centre

✚ 197 E5
✉ On B15 between Ballycastle and Ballintoy
☎ 028 2076 9839; www.nationaltrust.org.uk
🕐 Mid-Mar to Sep daily 10–6; Jul–Aug 10–7 ✋ Inexpensive

Giant's Causeway

✚ 197 D5
✉ Giant's Causeway Centre, 3.2km (2 miles) north of Bushmills
☎ Visitor Centre: 028 2073 1582; shop: 028 2073 2972; www.nationaltrust.org.uk
🕐 Giant's Causeway always open for exploration ✋ Donations welcome

SPANISH TREASURE

The Spanish Armada galleon *Girona* was wrecked in Port na Spaniagh ("Spaniard's Bay"), just east of the Giant's Causeway in 1588. Out of 1,300 men, only five were saved. The treasure went to the bottom with the ship, and stayed there until 1968 when much of it was recovered: gold, silver, jewels, implements. The best of what was salvaged is on display in Belfast's Ulster Museum.

THE ANTRIM COAST: INSIDE INFO

Top tips If you want to avoid the 10-minute walk down the road from the Giant's Causeway Visitor Centre to the Causeway itself, **hop on the minibus**.
- Don't take a large shoulder-bag or hold anything in your hands when you cross Carrick-a-Rede rope bridge, as you'll find you need both hands free for the crossing.

Hidden gem Signposted off A2 near the bottom of Glenaan is **Ossian's Grave**. This impressive "horned" cairn (with an entrance courtyard and two inner chambers) lies in a field at the top of a steep, rough lane better walked than driven, and commands a great view. Ossian was a warrior-poet, the son of the great hero Fionn MacCumhaill (Finn McCool).

One to miss The **coast road north** between Belfast and Larne is none too exciting; a better route is M2 to Junction 4, then the pleasant hill-and-valley A8 via Ballynure to Larne.

3 Ulster-American Folk Park

This collection of reconstructed and replica buildings gives a graphic idea of life in 18th- and 19th-century Ireland, of the miseries of emigration, and of the long, hard struggle that emigrants had to face before they could prosper in America.

The collection is split into two halves, Old World and New World.

In the **Old World section** you stroll among buildings brought from their original locations and rebuilt here. Among these are a **weaver's cottage** with a fixed loom, and a **Mass House** where Roman Catholics in the days of the Penal Laws (a collection of laws passed in the 18th century strictly limiting the rights of Catholics in all spheres) were permitted to attend the proscribed Mass. Don't miss **Castletown National School** with its graffiti-scarred desks – though it's a good idea to delay your visit if a school party is swarming there. Also here are the modest **homesteads** of two Irish emigrants who made spectacularly good in America: that of Judge Thomas Mellon (who emigrated in 1818), whose son Andrew Mellon founded the Pittsburgh steel industry, and John Joseph Hughes, Archbishop of New York and founder of St Patrick's Cathedral there. When the Folk Park's Visitor Centre was opened in 1980, the ceremony was attended by the benefactor, Dr Matthew T Mellon. He impressed everyone present by recalling his boyhood conversations with his great-grandfather Judge Thomas Mellon, who would tell tales of the miseries of the three-month Atlantic crossing he had endured way back in 1818.

The **New World section** includes the primitive cabin of a Midwest settler, a smoke house and barn, and a Pennsylvania farmhouse, all built of logs. Both Old and New World collections are brought to life by costumed guides who inform and entertain as they bake and keep sweet-scented turf fires burning.

Particularly poignant is the indoor reconstruction of a 19th-century Ulster street, complete with post office, draper, saddler, ropemaker, pawnbroker and chemist.

Demonstration of cottage handicrafts

The dockside booking office leads to a gangplank into the gloomy hold of an emigrant ship, where the imagination soon re-creates the experience of the passengers, as they pitched westward across the Atlantic in such a dark, cramped, stinking, noisy hellhole.

TAKING A BREAK

There is a restaurant and a coffee shop at the Folk Park.

A log house typical of those built by early Irish-American settlers in the wild Midwest

✚ 196 C4
✉ Mellon Road, Castletown, Omagh, Co Tyrone
☎ 028 8224 3292;
www.folkpark.com
🕘 Apr–Sep Mon–Sat 10:30–6, Sun, public hols 11–6:30; Oct–Mar Mon–Fri 10:30–5 (last admission 90 mins before closing)
✋ Moderate

ULSTER-AMERICAN FOLK PARK: INSIDE INFO

Top tips The Mellon Homestead and the ship and Dockside Gallery are two of the park's most popular sites. For the former, keep ahead as you leave the Information Centre and then bear right; for the latter, bear left from the Centre.
■ Forget your diet, and try any goodies that the guides may offer you: they are all freshly made on site.

Hidden gem Don't overlook the **raised viewpoint** behind the Mellon Homestead. From here you get an excellent view over the whole park, with roofs peeping charmingly out of the trees.

4 Lough Erne and Belleek Pottery

One-third of County Fermanagh is under water. The centre of the county is entirely filled by the island-dotted waters of Upper and Lower Lough Erne. You can follow winding lanes along the shores in a car, on foot or by bicycle. Alternatively, you could rent a cruiser at Belleek, and spend a couple of days drifting lazily among more than 200 islands and their tangled backwaters – a wonderfully relaxing way to see Fermanagh. Now that the Victoria Canal linking Upper Lough Erne with the River Shannon has been reopened, you could actually cruise 480km (300 miles) from Belleek to Killaloe, in sheltered water all the way.

Fine China

Belleek and its celebrated pottery stands at the seaward end of the Lower Lough Erne. They have been making gleaming basket-weave pottery at **Belleek Pottery** since 1857, and in much the same way, with traditional tools made by the workers themselves. Wander around the factory and watch the craftspeople teasing the raw material – Cornish china clay and glass – into long snakes, then painstakingly constructing the delicate bowls and plates of latticework that will be decorated with tiny, handmade china flowers and painted to perfection. Of course you can buy a piece if you want, after the tour.

A craftsman at work at the Belleek Pottery

The calm waters of Lough Erne

The Lough and Its Islands

Once, legend says, Fermanagh was a dry plain, with a fairy well that was always kept covered. Two lovers, hastening to elope, drank at the well and forgot to replace the cover. As the first rays of sun touched the water it overflowed, and went on flowing until it had formed Lough Erne.

The county town of **Enniskillen** sits on an island in the narrow waist between Upper and Lower Lough Erne. This is a great spot to base yourself when you explore the lough and its islands. Apart from their beauty, visitors are attracted by the little islands' extraordinary wealth of relics of the past, Christian and pre-Christian. **Devenish Island** is reached by ferry (Apr–Sep) from Trory Point just downstream of Enniskillen. On Devenish you'll find the ruins of a 13th-century parish church, a fine high cross, the beautiful shell of St Mary's Priory (1449), and a very well preserved round tower dating from about 1160. From the tower's uppermost window, 25m (82 feet) up, you get great views over the lough and islands. A small museum explains the layout and history of this monastic site, founded during the 6th century by St Molaise, "Little Flame the Beautiful from multitudinous Devenish". This island is very peaceful, with its own magic.

A different aura of pre-Christian enchantment hangs round the old cemetery at Caldragh on **Boa Island**, reached by bridge from the north shore of Lower Lough Erne. Here you'll find a much-photographed pagan "Janus figure", dating perhaps from the 5th to the 6th century AD, with two faces looking in opposite directions, and a hollow in the "skull" between them that some have speculated might have been made to hold ceremonial blood.

TOUGH GUY

The story is told that when Belleek Pottery was being built, a construction worker fell from the roof to the ground, miraculously landing on his feet. He swallowed a glass of whiskey and was sent straight back up again to carry on with the job.

On **White Island**, reached by a ferry from Castle Archdale marina, are more enigmatic figures: seven stone statues over a thousand years old, built into a wall side by side. One holds a priest's bell and crosier; one has his hand on his chin; another is a *sheela-na gig* – a cross-legged woman in a sexually blatant attitude. These may signify the Seven Deadly Sins, but no one knows for sure…

TAKING A BREAK

You'll find simple, tasty sustenance such as casseroles with baked potatoes, quiches and salads at the **Belleek Pottery Tea Rooms** (tel: 028 6865 9300). For Enniskillen's best music and hospitality, visit **Blake's Of The Hollow** (tel: 028 6632 2143), a wonderful pub in a dip of the main street.

Belleek Pottery
✚ 196 A3
✉ Belleek Pottery Visitors' Centre, Belleek, Co Fermanagh
☎ 028 6865 9300; www.belleek.ie
🕐 Mar–Jun Mon–Fri 9–6, Sat 10–6, Sun 2–6; Jul–Oct Mon–Fri 9–6, Sat 10–6, Sun noon–6; Nov–Dec Mon–Fri 9–5:30, Sat 10–5:30; Jan–Feb Mon–Fri 9–5:30 ✋ Moderate

Lough Erne
✚ 196 B3
✉ Lough Erne information: Tourist Office, Wellington Road, Enniskillen, Co Fermanagh
☎ 028 6632 3110; www.fermanaghlakelands.com

"JANUS" BY HEANEY
God-eyed, sex-mouthed, its brain
A watery wound…
Nobel Prize-winning poet Seamus Heaney responds to the Janus figure on Boa Island.

LOUGH ERNE: INSIDE INFO

Top tips If you have to select just one of Lough Erne's islands, go for **Devenish Island**: the ecclesiastical remains there are stunning.

Hidden gem Take binoculars to Devenish Island, to see what most visitors miss: the **four stone heads** looking out from under the cap of the round tower.

At Your Leisure

5 Old Bushmills Distillery

Some of Ireland's best malt and blended whiskey is made here in the world's oldest licensed distillery (1608), housed in an attractive huddle of whitewashed buildings in the shadow of two pagoda towers.

The tour takes you around big copper tuns full of steaming mash, swan-shaped pot stills, and a warehouse where wooden kegs give off the smell of the evaporating "angels' share". In the shop you can buy Original or Black Bush blends, or classic malts.

✚ 197 D5 ✉ Bushmills, Co Antrim ☎ 028 2073 3218; www.whiskeytours.ie ⊙ Tours: Mar–Oct Mon–Sat 9:15–5, Sun noon–5; Nov–Feb Mon–Fri 10–4:15, Sat, Sun 12:30–4:15 ✋ Moderate

6 Downhill

This is as eccentric and fascinating a cluster of buildings as you'll find in all of Ireland. Now in the care of the National Trust, and connected by scenic footpaths, they were built on the cliff tops just west of Castlerock by a highly idiosyncratic Bishop of Londonderry.

The **Mussenden Temple** is perched precariously on the cliff edge. It is a classical rotunda, built 1783–85 by Frederick Hervey, 4th Earl of Bristol and Bishop of Londonderry, perhaps to accommodate one of his mistresses. Inland stands the roofless, gaunt ruin of **Downhill House**, the Bishop's country seat, and nearby are a beautiful and sheltered walled garden, a dovecote and an icehouse. The **Lion Gate** is topped with one of Hervey's armorial leopards.

✚ 197 D5 ✉ Mussenden Road, Castlerock, Co Londonderry ☎ 028 2073 1582; www.nationaltrust.org.uk ⊙ Temple: Jul–Aug daily 10–5; Apr–Jun, Sep–Oct Sat, Sun 10–5. Grounds: always open ✋ Inexpensive; parking moderate when Temple open

The Mussenden Temple on the cliff tops at Downhill

The "Hands across the divide" peace statue in Londonderry/Derry

7 Londonderry/Derry

Known as Londonderry to loyalists, and Derry to nationalists, this walled city has been split by politics. Its streets saw major disturbances in the 1970s, but it has emerged as a forward-thinking city. Chief attraction is the walk around the 17th-century city walls (➤ 181–183), but there are plenty of other things to enjoy, including the **Tower Museum**, with exhibitions covering the Armada and The Story of Derry; a looming 19th-century **Guildhall** (➤ 183); **St Columb's Cathedral** with relics of the epic siege of 1688–89, when the Protestant citizens defied the army of Catholic James II (➤ 182); and a **Craft Village** where shops and eateries cluster in the heart of the city.

✠ 196 C4 ✉ Tourist Information Centre, 44 Foyle Street ☎ 028 7126 7284; www.discovernorthernireland.com 🚌 Foyle Street 🚆 Waterside Station, Duke Street

Tower Museum
✉ Union Hall Place ☎ 028 7137 2411; www.derrycity.gov.uk/museums 🕐 Tue–Sat 10–5 ✋ Moderate

Guildhall
☎ 028 7137 7335 to arrange a visit; www.discovernorthernireland.com 🕐 Mon–Fri 9–5 ✋ Free

8 Sperrin Mountains

In the Sperrin Heritage Centre at Cranagh you can learn about geology, local history, wildlife and folklore;

POLITICAL POT

In the Countess's Bedroom at Florence Court the chamber pot is of finest Belleek china. Strategically placed at the bottom is a portrait of 19th-century British prime minister William Gladstone, unpopular with the ruling Anglo-Irish classes because of his support for Home Rule and land reform.

you can even pan for gold in the nearby stream. All good stuff – but it's better still to get out and explore this wild range of hills that straddles the Tyrone/Derry border. Even the highest peak (Sawel, at 683m/2,240 feet) is easily climbed with good walking shoes; golden plover, raven, peregrine and red grouse breed on the moors; and twisting roads soon put you deep into unfrequented back country.

✚ 196 C4 ✉ Sperrin Heritage Centre, 274 Glenelly Road, Cranagh, Co Tyrone ☎ 028 8164 8142; www.strabanedc.org.uk ⊙ Apr–Oct Mon–Fri 11:30–5:30, Sat 11:30–6, Sun 2–6 ✋ Inexpensive

9 Marble Arch Caves

The entrance to this system of semi-flooded caves lies about 8km (5 miles) due west of Florence Court. You can walk much of the system, and boats carry you the rest of the way, through caverns and chambers with glistening mineral walls and plenty of stalactites. Phone before visiting, as the caves can be closed for safety after heavy rain.

✚ 196 B3 ✉ Marlbank Scenic Loop, Florence Court, Enniskillen, Co Fermanagh ☎ 028 6634 8855; www.fermanagh.gov.uk ⊙ Jul–Aug daily 10–5; mid–Mar to Jun, Sep 10–4:30 ✋ Expensive

10 Florence Court

A few kilometres southwest of Enniskillen, the big square central block and arcaded wings of Florence Court look out over immaculate gardens and parkland. This mid-18th-century house belonging to the Earls of Enniskillen was gutted by fire in 1955, but has been superbly restored by the National Trust. Rich plasterwork in the hall, on the dining room ceiling and above the staircase is notable; as are the portraits of the Earls of Enniskillen with

their red hair and imperious eagle noses. There's a fine cutaway scale model of the basement in Florence Court.

✚ 196 B3 ✉ Florence Court, Enniskillen, Co Fermanagh ☎ 028 6634 8249; www.nationaltrust.org.uk ⊙ House: Jun–Aug daily noon–6; rest of year Sat–Sun and public hols noon–6. Grounds: May–Sep daily 10–8; rest of year 10–4 ✋ Moderate

11 Castle Coole

Designed between 1790 and 1798 by James Wyatt, this is Ireland's finest neo-classical mansion. Behind the giant portico of this National Trust property lie superb furnishings, Irish oak floors and silk-hung state rooms. In the library, note the camels' heads on the gilt curtain pole, installed to celebrate Admiral Nelson's victory over Napoleon at the Battle of the Nile in 1798. As you go around, the guide will tell you the sad story of the 1st Earl of Belmore, whose wife ran off and left him desolate and alone in this huge house.

✚ 196 B3 ✉ Enniskillen, Co Fermanagh ☎ 028 6632 2690; www.nationaltrust.org.uk ⊙ House: Jul–Aug daily noon–6; Mar to May, Sep Sat–Sun, public hols noon–6; Jun Wed–Mon noon–6. Grounds: Apr–Sep daily 10–8; Oct–Mar 10–4 ✋ Moderate

12 Navan Royal Site

The Lords of ancient Ulster ruled from the Hill of Navan, just outside Armagh City, from c700 BC to the

4th century AD. Misty figures of legend – bold King Conor's Knights of the Red Branch, the Ulster hero Cuchulainn and his arch-foe Queen Mebh of Connacht, beautiful Deirdre of the Sorrows – walk the domed green hill.

Beneath the turf lies an extraordinary structure built by Iron Age tribespeople: a vast mound of pebbles packed inside a gigantic timber hall, which the builders then deliberately burned down. In the Navan Centre below the hill, a well laid-out exhibition explores the myth and mystery.

✠ 197 D3 ✉ 81 Killylea Road, Armagh
☎ 028 3752 1801; www.visitarmagh.com
🕐 Site: open access; Centre: Jun–Aug Mon–Sat 10–5, Sun noon–5; Apr, May, Sep Sat 10–5, Sun noon–5 ✋ Site: free; Centre: moderate

🄳 Saint Patrick's Trian

This unique visitor complex, in the heart of Armagh, features three major exhibitions: The Armagh Story, a visit to the city's past; Patrick's Testament, The Book of Armagh, featuring one of the greatest treasures to survive from Early Christian Ireland; and the Land of Lilliput, the story of Jonathan Swift's most famous work *Gulliver's Travels*. The adventures are narrated with the help of a 6m (20ft) giant. The word *trian* derives from the ancient division of Armagh into three distinct districts.

✠ 197 D3 ✉ 40 English Street, Armagh
☎ 028 3752 1801; www.visitarmagh.com
🕐 Jul–Aug 10–5:30, Sun 2–5, Sep–Jun Mon–Sat 10–5 ✋ Moderate

🄼 Mountains of Mourne

The beautiful Mountains of Mourne fill Northern Ireland's southeast corner. Their conical profiles give the impression of mountains, but at an average height of just over 600m (1,968 feet), these are really tall fells. They offer wonderful walking and backroad exploring.

The A2 coast road skirts the mountains from Newcastle, the area's main tourist centre, to Rostrevor, and there are numerous side lanes that can lead you up to the reservoir lakes of Silent Valley and over by Spelga Dam in wild scenery.

At the Mourne Heritage Trust in Newcastle, you can buy a pack of ten laminated cards that detail walks ranging from easy to strenuous.

✠ 197 E2 ✉ Mourne Heritage Trust, 87 Central Promenade, Newcastle, Co Down
☎ 028 4372 4059;
www.discovernorthernireland.com
🕐 Mon–Fri 9–5

OFF THE BEATEN TRACK

If you have a little more time to spare, take half a day to drive south of Armagh City through the lanes of South Armagh. This pretty area of tumbled small hills and quiet farming villages was branded "Bandit Country" by the world's media during 25 years of the Troubles. This Republican area of the province has been almost entirely neglected by the tourist industry, but its people are as friendly as anywhere else in Ireland, and steeped in traditions of story-telling and music-making.

Where to...
Eat and Drink

Prices
Expect to pay per person for a meal, excluding drinks and service
£ under £12   ££ £12 to £24   £££ over £24

Crown Liquor Saloon £–££

Belfast's best-known pub (▶ 150), this former Victorian gin palace is now owned by the National Trust. A visit to one of its booths to sample a thirst-quenching pint and half a dozen oysters served on crushed ice, or a bowl of steaming, tasty Irish stew, should be on your schedule. The Britannic Lounge upstairs, built with the timbers from the SS *Britannic* (sister ship to the *Titanic*), is worth a look.

✚ 197 E3 ✉ 46 Great Victoria Street, Belfast BT2 7BA ☎ 028 9027 9901 ◷ Flannigan's Bar and eatery: Mon–Sat 11–9

Deanes ££–£££

An exceptionally well-regarded restaurant where understated elegance belies its sophistication. Exclusive private dining parties enjoy their seclusion upstairs, while down at street level the ambience is stylishly welcoming, with contemporary cooking the keynote.

✚ 197 E3 ✉ 36–40 Howard Street, Belfast BT1 6PF ☎ 028 9033 1134; www.michaeldeane.co.uk ◷ Mon–Sat noon–3; 6–10

The Edge ££

The Bank Gallery Restaurant at the Edge is the River Lagan's hidden jewel, with panoramic views and a great dining experience. On the first floor of the complex, hung with pictures by local artists, the restaurant serves delectable dishes prepared with local produce. The interesting array of starters include seared scallops on a ginger, coriander and noodle salad with peanut sauce. Steaks, sourced from local Northern Irish beef, are deservedly popular. On the ground floor is the Port Bar, perfect for a snack.

✚ 197 E3 ✉ Mays Meadow, Laganbank Road, Belfast BT1 3PH ☎ 028 9032 2000; www.at-the-edge.co.uk ◷ Mon–Sat 11–late

Nick's Warehouse ££

This lively, air-conditioned restaurant makes the most of a clever warehouse conversion. Attentive, friendly service and excellent food are the hallmarks, in both the wine bar and restaurant. Cooking is seasonal and modern, but with a less formal feel than that of many contemporary restaurants (dishes include duck with apple): international influences are certainly discernible, but Irish ingredients and traditional themes are not overlooked. An interesting and fairly priced wine list adds to the appeal. Good vegetarian choice.

✚ 197 E3 ✉ 35–39 Hill Street, Belfast BT1 2LB ☎ 028 9043 9690; www.nickswarehouse.co.uk ◷ Lunch: Mon–Fri noon–3. Dinner: Tue–Sat 6–9:30

Shu ££–£££

South Belfast's most popular brasserie-style restaurant is on the cosmopolitan Lisburn Road. Opened in 2000, it has gone on to receive many accolades for its service and eclectic menu. Salmon, pigeon, hake and much more, all served with divine sauces, plus rich desserts to die for. The set menu (Mon–Thu in the main restaurant) is good value. Downstairs is a cocktail bar and bistro with

DJs entertaining on Fridays and Saturdays.

✠ 197 E3 ✉ 253 Lisburn Road, Belfast BT9 7EN ☎ 028 9038 1655; www.shu-restaurant.com ⊕ Mon–Sat 12–2:30, 6–10 (bar till late)

THE ANTRIM COAST

National Trust Tea Room £

Enjoy simple, tasty food – soup and snacks, good home baking – at the "eighth wonder of the world". There's another National Trust tea room at the harbourside village of Cushendun, open off-season weekends and daily after Easter.

✠ 197 D5 ✉ Giant's Causeway Centre, Co Antrim ☎ 028 2073 2282 ⊕ Daily mid-Mar to mid-Nov; call for opening times

Wysners £–££

After a bracing walk around the nearby Giant's Causeway, you'll enjoy this restaurant on Ballycastle's main street as a good place to refuel. The café has a variety of meals and snacks, and the restaurant offers more sophistication. Here

you can try local salmon from Carrick-a-Rede a mile or two along the coast and dig into a slice of Jackie Wysner's Bushmills malt cheesecake.

✠ 197 E5 ✉ 16 Ann Street, Ballycastle, Co Antrim ☎ 028 2076 2372 ⊕ Mon–Thu 8:30–5:30; Fri–Sat 8:30am–9pm

MOUNTAINS OF MOURNE

The Buck's Head ££

This attractive restaurant/bar has a conservatory at the back and a garden for use in fine weather, with views of Dundrum Bay from the top. Good food and service plus long opening hours make this the place to stop on a tour. Local produce, especially seafood from Dundrum Bay, is prominent and there's always imaginative vegetarian food.

✠ 197 E3 ✉ 77 Main Street, Dundrum, Co Down ☎ 028 4375 1868; www.thebucksheadinn.co.uk ⊕ Lunch: noon–2.30. High tea: 5–6:45. Dinner: 7–9.30 (Sun till 8:30); closed Mon, Oct–Apr and 25 Dec

Where to...
Stay

BELFAST

Malmaison Belfast £££

Fabulous trend-setting hotel in a striking Victorian building in the heart of regenerated Belfast. Posh, slinky rooms with lots of black and white; all 64 rooms are beautifully appointed and well equipped. Other facilities include a brasserie restaurant, stylish bar, fitness room and you can even bring your dog.

✠ 197 E3 ✉ 34–8 Victoria Street, Belfast BT1 3GH ☎ 028 9022 0200; www.malmaison-belfast.com ⊕ Closed 24–27 Dec

Tara Lodge ££

This stylish modern hotel has 18 rooms and a friendly, intimate atmosphere. An advantage is the secure parking – rare so close to the city centre. Each of the comfortable bedrooms has a bathroom, and facilities include satellite TV, Internet access and beverages.

✠ 197 E3 ✉ 36 Cromwell Road, Botanic Avenue, Belfast BT7 1JW ☎ 028 9059 0900; www.taralodge.com

Travelodge Belfast Central Hotel £

The Travelodge organization has cornered the market in decent, no-frills hotels at the price of an inexpensive B&B, and the Belfast Central is no exception – it's well placed, clean, modestly stylish, and friendly. You can hardly ask for more in this price range.

✚ 197 E3 ✉ 15 Brunswick Street, Belfast BT2 7GE ☎ 0870 911 1687; www.travelodge.co.uk

ENNISKILLEN

Abocurragh Farm Guesthouse £–££

This lovely bed-and-breakfast is on a working dairy farm in a very beautiful part of Fermanagh. Spacious bedrooms have wonderful views, and there are facilities for children, such as special meals and a babysitting service.

✚ 196 B3 ✉ Letterbreen, Enniskillen, Co Fermanagh BT74 9AG ☎ 028 6634 8484; www.abocurragh.com

THE ANTRIM COAST

Bushmills Inn ££

Thoughtful development has added to the appeal of this well-run 19th-century coaching inn near the Giant's Causeway. A turf fire and traditional country-style furniture in the hall set the tone, and public rooms are all in keeping with the country theme. Bedrooms are furnished in a comfortable cottage style, and even the new bathrooms seem to belong to an earlier era. There is a Taste of Ulster restaurant and a gas-lit bar.

✚ 197 D5 ✉ 9 Dunluce Road, Bushmills, Co Antrim BT57 8QG ☎ 028 2073 3000; www.bushmillsinn.com

LONDONDERRY/DERRY

Beech Hill Country House Hotel £££

Just outside the city walls, this 18th-century house has retained many of its original details. Bedrooms vary in size and outlook but all have bath or shower rooms and are furnished with antiques. The bar is popular, and good food is served. Gym, Jacuzzi and sauna, massage and aromatherapy steam room.

✚ 196 C4 ✉ 32 Ardmore Road, Londonderry BT47 3QP ☎ 028 7134 9279; www.beech-hill.com ⊘ Closed 25 Dec

Greenhill House £

This Georgian farmhouse nestles in well-tended gardens with splendid views over open countryside. Bedrooms include two large family rooms; the bedrooms are not luxurious, but they have bathrooms and their furnishings make them far more comfortable than one might expect in farmhouse accommodation. Dinner is available for residents by prior arrangement.

✚ 197 D5 ✉ 24 Greenhill Road, Aghadowey, Co Londonderry BT51 4EU ☎ 028 7086 8241; www.greenhill-house.co.uk ⊘ Early Mar–Oct

DUNGANNON

Grange Lodge ££

The comfort and hospitality provided at this lovely Georgian house make this a good base for touring. There are extensive grounds to explore, including one hectare (2.5 acres) of manicured gardens. Bedrooms (and bathrooms) are exceptionally comfortable and the food (residents' dinner and breakfast) is superb.

✚ 197 D3 ✉ 7 Grange Road, Dungannon, Co Tyrone BT71 1EJ ☎ 028 8778 4212; www.grangelodgecountryhouse.com ⊘ Closed 13 Dec–1 Feb

MOUNTAINS OF MOURNE

Hastings Slieve Donard Hotel £££

This prestigious Victorian hotel, part of the Hastings chain, stands in grounds beneath the Mountains of Mourne and beside the Royal County Down Golf Links. Renovated in the late 1990s, the accommodation is furnished to a high standard, and every bathroom sports a yellow Hastings duck! There's a health club, and Tollymore Forest Park provides excellent walking.

✚ 197 E3 ✉ Downs Road, Newcastle, Co Down BT33 0AH ☎ 028 4372 1066; www.hastingshotels.com

Where to...Shop

The North, with its long tradition of craftsmanship, is the best part of Ireland for linen, handmade lace and parian china. Look for beautifully made woollen goods and hand-cut Tyrone crystal.

BELFAST

Belfast's main shopping area is around Donegall Place, High Street and Royal Avenue; **Victoria Square** (between Ann and Chichester streets) is a spanking new shopping arcade. **The Wicker Man** (44–46 High Street, tel: 028 9024 3550) stocks the work of craft workers from all over Ireland. **Smyth's Irish Linens** (65 Royal Avenue, tel: 028 9024 2786) has beautiful linen goods, and **Smyth & Gibson** (Bedford House, Bedford Street, tel: 028 9023 0388) sells its own brand of luxurious linen shirts and accessories. The in-place for up-to-the-minute clothes is **Apache** (60 Wellington Place, tel: 028 9032 9056). Refurbished **St George's Market** (May Street) is a prime venue for crafts and antiques, and the Friday market (6am–1pm) has 250 stalls with everything from bric-a-brac to shark meat.

LONDONDERRY/DERRY

In Derry, **The Donegal Shop** (Shipquay Street, tel: 028 7126 6928) does great linen, tweeds and knitwear, and the **Derry Craft Village** (off Shipquay Street) has demonstrations of craftspeople plying their trade. **Austins** (2 The Diamond, tel: 028 7126 1817) is a department store stocking a wide range of high-quality local goods.

Where to... Be Entertained

The Arts Council of Northern Ireland (tel: 028 9038 5200) produces the monthly *Artslink*. More information is available at tourist information offices and in newspaper listings.

SPORT

In addition to the usual sporting pursuits of greyhound racing, horse racing, soccer, rugby and cricket, the Northern Irish love watching and participating in their native sports, hurling and Gaelic football; in Armagh you might see "bullets" being played, which involves hurling metal balls along country lanes. Other activities include golf, cycling, fishing, walking and riding. Details on all these and other options are available from tourist information offices.

MUSIC

There's plenty of informal music in Northern Ireland. In Belfast, one of the best places to experience traditional music is **Pat's Bar** (Prince's Dock, tel: 028 9074 4524). **The Rotterdam** (54 Pilot Street, tel: 028 9074 6021) has regular folk, jazz and blues, and the **Kitchen Bar** (36–40 Victoria Square, tel: 028 9032 4901) has music on Friday nights. Club fashions move fast, but the Cathedral Quarter of Belfast – an historic area full of media centres and galleries – has characterful examples like **The Network Club** (North Street, tel: 028 9023 7486).

Walks & Tours

1 HILL OF HOWTH

Walk

DISTANCE 11km (7 miles) **TIME** 3 hours (4 if you stop…and you should)
START/END POINT Howth DART railway station (24 minutes from Connolly Station in central Dublin). For information tel: 01 836 6222 ✚ 201 E5

This delightful walk is a favourite weekend stroll of Dubliners. It is easily reached by train, varies between hill slopes and coastal paths, and has tremendous views over the city, Dublin Bay and the coast and hills for 50km (30 miles) around. It makes an ideal change of pace when you are feeling jaded with central Dublin and long to get some fresh sea air into your lungs.

1–2

Turn left out of the DART station in Howth to pass the **harbour**. This was where Erskine Childers, author of the classic spy thriller *The Riddle of the Sands*, landed guns and ammunition from his little yacht *Asgard* in July 1914 to help foment a nationalist uprising.

2–3

In a few hundred metres turn right up Abbey Street. Beside Ye Olde Abbey Tavern climb steps on the right to reach the ruins of the

abbey – a seat of learning famed throughout medieval Europe. There's a great view here over the packed white houses of Howth to the crooked crab-claws of the harbour breakwaters. Howth has long been a favoured

dwelling place for writers, Trinity College dons, poets and artists, and more recently for well-heeled commuters who want to live conveniently close to, but not actually in, Ireland's capital city.

3–4

Turn down Church Street into Abbey Street, and then next right up St Lawrence's Road. In 100m (110 yards) keep going along Grace O'Malley Road, then turn left up Grace O'Malley Drive. At a telephone booth on a bend keep ahead up a path to a road; go ahead for 20m (22 yards), then right up steps.

4–5

Turn right at the top, and ascend a ramp beside house No 53 ("Ballylinn"). Keep ahead up a grassy slope, go through trees, then up a steep bank and on southward up the edge of a rough field, with a golf course and a banked reservoir to your right.

5–6

Bear right around the top edge of the golf course; follow the path into the trees, across the aptly named Bog of Frogs, and on under the crags of Dun Hill. Cross the golf course and climb the steep heathery slope ahead (red-and-white striped poles) on a rough path that leads to the top of Shielmartin.

Take time up here to admire the superb views across Dublin Bay and the city to the Wicklow Hills. Knobby, white quartzite boulders form a ring round the crown of **Shielmartin**. They were placed here 2,000 years ago to mark the burial place of an Irish warrior king, Crimhthan Niadhnair. Helped by his wife, Nar of the Brugh (some say she was a goddess), he became rich beyond dreams of avarice by making frequent raids across the Irish Sea to plunder the Romans who had newly arrived in Britain. Whether his golden treasure is buried on Shielmartin is open to romantic speculation.

6–7

A clear path leads off the summit, steeply down to Carrickbrack Road. Turn left; in 300m (330 yards) cross the road, go through a swing gate ("Dangerous Cliffs" sign – but don't be alarmed!) and take the path down to the shore.

7–8

Here you turn left and follow the narrow but well-defined coastal path for 8km (5 miles), past the Baily Lighthouse on its promontory and on all the way round Howth Head and back to the DART station.

From the ruins of 11th-century Howth Abbey there is a splendid view out across the harbour to the rocky island of Ireland's Eye

Taking a Break

There are many pubs and restaurants in Howth. Try Abbey Tavern in Abbey Street (tel: 01 839 0307) for delicious fish and an excellent pint of stout.

2 BLACKWATER BOG
Tour

DISTANCE 8km (5 miles) **TIME** Around 1 hour
START/END POINT Bord na Mona's Blackwater peat works, 1.6km (1 mile) beyond Shannonbridge on R357, 13km (8 miles) east of Ballinasloe; Bog tour Apr to early Oct daily, on the hour every hour 10–5
Information tel: 090 9674450; www.bnm.ie ✚ 200 A5

At first glance, the great boglands of central Ireland do not look like interesting places. In fact, most visitors hurry past these blankets of brown emptiness, their imaginations fixed on the glorious mountains and coasts of the west. But allow yourself an hour aboard the cranky little green-and-yellow bog workers' train grandiosely named the Clonmacnoise & West Offaly Railway, and you'll have your eyes opened to the rich wildlife and sullen beauty of an environment that very few are privileged to penetrate.

One-seventh of all Ireland is bog – sodden peat moss, laid down thousands of years ago

Sphagnum Sponge
Sphagnum moss, the main building material of a raised bog such as Blackwater, is amazingly absorbent: it can hold up to 20 times its own weight in water, trapped in its myriad pores and cells.

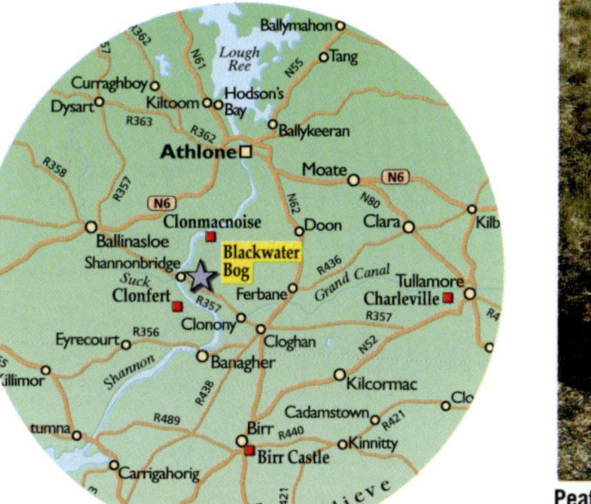

Peat cutter near Castelloe

and hardly touched until the Irish Peat Board, Bord na Mona, was formed in 1946 to harvest the stuff for burning in the electricity-generating stations of Ireland, a country largely without timber and wholly without coal. Bord na Mona, having wreaked havoc across Ireland's bogs, has 20 years to run before peat extraction has to stop, and has now begun to make some conservation moves.

The snail's pace of the little train allows you plenty of time to get down and explore – and even to have a go at cutting turf (the Irish term for peat) by hand with a sharp-edged turf spade called a slane. You can see for yourself how vegetable matter has remained unrotted for thousands of years in the acid environment of the bog. Down in a huge drainage gash, 10m (33 feet) below the

Beautiful Bogland

"On a day of bright sky the bogland is a lovely, far-reaching expanse of purple and rich brown: and the lakelets take on the quite indescribable colour that comes from clear sky reflected in bog-water." – Robert Lloyd Praeger, *The Way That I Went*

surface, lie great trunks and boughs of "bog oak" – twisted, silvery limbs of yew, oak, birch and pine trees that were growing here long

The spotted heath orchid is one of the wildflowers that you might find at Blackwater Bog

before the pharaohs began to build their pyramids in Egypt.

Duckboard trails lead off across the heathery bosom of the bog. Looking closely, you can spot patches of brightly coloured flowers: bog asphodel, heath spotted orchids, bog cotton, lousewort and insect-eating sundew. Birds love the wide spaces of the bog and its scrub trees. It's one of the most peaceful places on earth, something you will appreciate if you come here out of season and have the whole bog to yourself.

Back at the Blackwater works there's a display centre explaining the formation and wildlife of the bog, and a museum of the outlandish machines that have worked it over the years. When harvesting finishes around the year 2030, Ireland's worked bogs are due to become the centrepiece of a wetland landscape with lakes, fens and forests, part recreational, part conservational – not a bad outcome for such a destructive industry.

Taking a Break

There is a pleasant **café** back at the Blackwater works.

3 CROAGH PATRICK
Walk

DISTANCE 7km (4 miles) up and down; ascent of 765m (2,510 feet) **TIME** 4–5 hours. The Pilgrimage Route takes 2 days **START/END POINT** Murrisk, on R355 9km (5 miles) west of Westport, for the ascent of The Reek; Ballintober Abbey, 11km (7 miles) south of Castlebar, off the N84 Ballinrobe road, for the full pilgrimage route ✠ 194 C2

The ascent of Croagh Patrick (or The Reek) is one of Ireland's classic hill climbs. The climb itself is not technically challenging, although the second half forms a stamina-sapping scramble up loose scree. The view from the summit – a huge slice of coastline, hundreds of small islands, Clew Bay, and the Nephin Beg and Connemara mountains – will take your breath away.

Most visitors opt for the short climb from Murrisk, but the 37km (23-mile) pilgrimage route, beginning at Ballintober Abbey, repays the effort.

Maps
If you are following 37km (23-mile) Tochar Phadraig from Ballintober Abbey, you will find these Irish OS 1:50,000 maps useful: 30, 31, 37, 38.

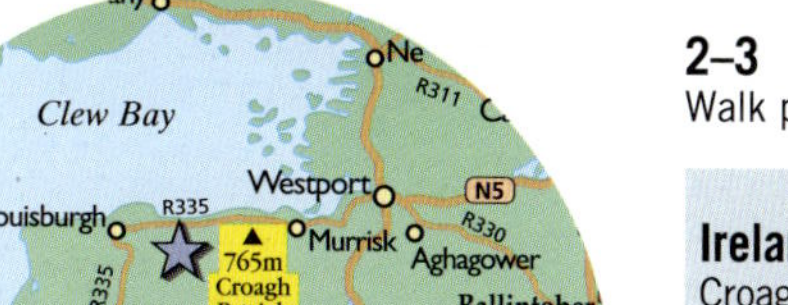

Short Climb

1–2
Leave your car by Owen Campbell's pub in Murrisk and turn up the signposted lane towards Croagh Patrick.

2–3
Walk past the statue of St Patrick and

Ireland's Holy Mountain
Croagh Patrick is a place of pilgrimage and penance. Each year on Garland Sunday, the last Sunday in July, whatever the weather, as many as 50,000 people (many of them barefoot), ranging in age from 8 to 80, climb the mountain and offer prayers to St Patrick in the little church at the summit.

St Patrick (▶ 14) is said to have climbed up Croagh Patrick's steep slopes in AD 441, preaching from the summit and breaking the power of a cloud of demons by hurling his bell through them. He also begged successfully for deliverance of the souls of the Irish people on Doomsday, and banished all snakes from the island.

The distinctive profile of Croagh Patrick dominates the view of pilgrims approaching from Owen Campbell's pub

continue along the well-worn path that leads to the saddle at 500m (1,640 feet).

3–4

Take a deep breath and tackle the very steep slope to the summit. Return on the same path.

Pilgrimage Route

1–2

For this longer route, start at Ballintober Abbey, and follow the marker stones incised with crosses. These will lead you along the field paths and lanes of St Patrick's Causeway, known in Irish as Tochar Phadraig.

2–3

The Tochar, an ancient pilgrim route, runs west for 37km (23 miles), aiming for the cone of Croagh Patrick. *En route* it passes holy wells, standing stones, monastic sites, prehistoric burial mounds and inscribed rocks.

3–4

You can break your journey halfway at the village of Aghagower, or accomplish the whole thing in one go, but take into account the stiff ascent up loose scree that awaits you.

4–5

Once under The Reek itself, follow the track up the south flank to the saddle, then sweat up the rock slide to the summit. You'll be rewarded with spectacular views of Clew Bay and the Nephin Beg and Connemara mountains.

Taking a Break

As you return to Murrisk, refreshed in spirit but leg-weary and footsore, stop at **Owen Campbell's** pub at the foot of the path. The interior of the pub is hung with photographs of Reek pilgrims.

4 YEATS COUNTRY
Tour

DISTANCE 160km (100 miles)
TIME Half-day
START/END POINT Sligo town ✛ 195 E3

William Butler Yeats (1865–1939), winner of the 1923 Nobel Prize for Literature and arguably Ireland's greatest poet, had the flat-topped mountains and sea-beaten shores of County Sligo always in his mind. This beautiful and weathered countryside, where Yeats spent happy childhood months with his grandparents and cousins, inspired many of his best-known poems, and symbolised the mystery, strangeness and strength of his native land.

Most of the ragged circuit of this Yeats Country route is signposted by brown roadsigns showing a quill and inkstand.

1–2

Having first got into the mood by visiting the many W B Yeats sites in Sligo town (▶ 137), leave the town along Castle Street and make your way west towards the distinctive 328m (1,076-foot) mound of Knocknarea.

Just outside Sligo, a brown notice points left for **Carrowmore Tombs**. Sprawling across fields a couple of kilometres down this side road is the largest concentration of megalithic monuments in Ireland – stone circles, dolmens and cairns, most of them now reduced to a few stones but one or two still nearly intact. It is a haunting place, which would be even more impressive were it not for the huge orange-hued riding centre that dominates this ancient site.

Back on the Sligo road, turn left to pass close under Knocknarea; a side road is signposted "Meascán Meadhba", and leads via a 45-minute walk to "**Queen Mebh's tomb**" and a wonderful 80km (50-mile) view. Mebh or Maeve was the 1st-century warrior queen of Connacht who initiated the "Cattle Raid of Cooley". The big green cairn that stands out against the sky on the summit of Knocknarea, said to be her tomb, is in fact a passage grave, filled with 40,000 boulders, that predates Queen Mebh by at least 2,000 years.

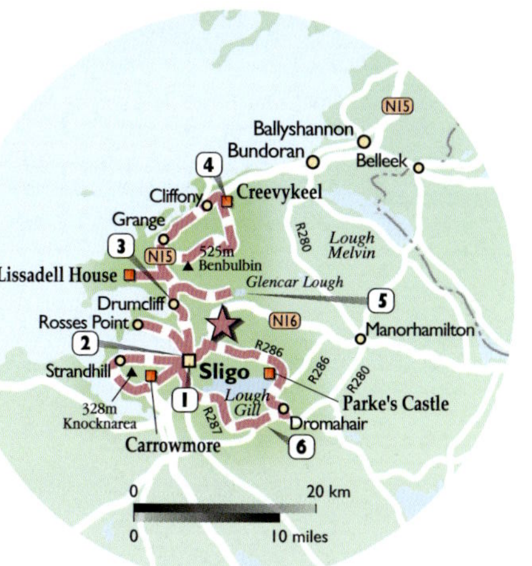

The main road drops to an intersection; turn right here, and beside the Sancta Maria Hotel go left to reach the stony shore, enormous grassy dunes and splendid hill views of Strandhill beach. The cliffs and domed brow of Knocknarea hang behind Strandhill, on whose shore W B Yeats saw and heard the Atlantic waves crash during storms:

"The wind has bundled up the clouds high over
  Knocknarea,
And thrown the thunder on the stones for all that
  Maeve can say."

2–3

Return into Sligo and take the N15 Bundoran–Lifford road north out of town. On the outskirts bear left on R291 to **Rosses Point**, a neat little seaside village with a really beautiful view and some fine sandy beach walks.

Return to N15 and go north to **Drumcliff**. The stump of a round tower stands by the road, and a heavily carved high cross dating from about AD 1000 forms part of the churchyard wall. But the focal point is W B Yeats's grave, next to the northwest corner of the tower. A gravel walk leads to a plain limestone slab which is inscribed with the words:

"Cast a cold Eye
On Life, on Death
Horseman, pass by!"

These are the last lines of the epitaph poem composed by Yeats for himself. It begins:

"Under bare Ben Bulben's head
In Drumcliff Churchyard Yeats is laid..."

And the view is just that: the simple gravestone, a line of trees, and Benbulbin in the distance.

3–4

Continue 8km (5 miles) up N15, then bear left for **Lissadell House**, ancestral home of the Gore-Booth family. Two members of the family befriended Yeats. One was the poet Eva Gore-Booth; the other, her sister Constance, Countess Markievicz, who would win a place in the pantheon of nationalist heroes for her active part in the 1916 Easter Rising. She was subsequently elected to Westminster as the first female Member of Parliament (though she never took her seat).

Horseback riding on a quiet Sligo lane, with the great bulk of Benbulbin as a backdrop

Return to N15 and turn left to run through **Cliffony**, with Benbulbin's profile changing from that of a lion couchant to a perfect flat-topped table. On the right at the far end of the village is a parking place; from here it's just a step to the well-signposted **Creevykeel court tomb**. This complicated cairn was built between 3000 and 2000 BC with a central court and several burial chambers, all approached through massive stone portals. One even has its rugged lintel still in place.

4–5

Turn back along N15, and immediately left (brown "Ballintrillick" sign) on a long, straight country road. Under Ben Wisken, cross a lane and follow "Gleniff Horseshoe" signs. **Gleniff** is a remote upland valley hemmed in by great basalt crags, where sheep graze under huge fellsides rushing with waterfalls.

The great dark rock arch that hangs above the top end of Gleniff is said to be the bed of runaway lovers Diarmuid and Gráinne. Diarmuid had the bad luck to cross swords with the hero Fionn MacCumhaill, a former fiancé of Gráinne, and suffered the posthumous indignity of having his severed head sent to his true love by the implacable Fionn.

Back on the lane, turn left and continue for 8km (5 miles). Turn left on N15 for Sligo. In 3.2km (2 miles) sidetrack left to **Glencar** to view the fine waterfall in its wooded cleft. It is superb after rain, but a beautiful spot in any weather.

5–6

Return to Sligo and take N16 out of town, following R286 for "Dromahair" signs, and also brown "Lough Gill" and "Parke's Castle" signs. You pass Colgagh Lough below, and are soon down on the wooded shore of **Lough Gill**, one of the most attractive stretches of water in County Sligo. Follow the road along the north shore of the lough. You pass the turreted 17th-century stately home of Parke's Castle, a picture of grim impregnability. Boat trips run from the inlet by the castle to the **Lake Isle of Innisfree**, subject of Yeats's most widely known poem, but you can reach the shore much nearer this tiny island by way of Dromahair. On the far edge of the village bear right (following the "Ballintogher/Sligo" sign); then after 1km (0.5 miles) take the first narrow lane on the right to wriggle down to the lake shore. Some 200m (220 yards) out lies the tree-smothered round blob of an islet whose peaceful beauty, pictured in the midst of city bustle, brought great solace to Yeats:

Taking a Break

Hargadon's Bar in O'Connell Street, Sligo, is a traditional pub with old-fashioned wood-panelled bars.

Places to Visit

Carrowmore Tombs

✚ 195 E3 ☎ 071 61534 🕓 Easter–Oct daily 10–5:15 ✋ Inexpensive

Lissadell House

✚ 195 E3 ☎ 071 9163150; www.lissadellhouse.com 🕓 Mid-Mar to end Sep daily 11–6 ✋ Expensive

"I will arise and go now, and go to Innisfree,
And a small cabin build there, of clay and wattles made:
Nine bean-rows will I have there, a hive for the honey-bee,
And live alone in the bee-loud glade…"

Yeats never did build his wattle cabin on Innisfree, of course. But he truly loved this peaceful lake, and you can well appreciate why, as you complete the circuit of Lough Gill before returning to Sligo town on R287.

5 WALLS OF DERRY

Walk

DISTANCE 1.6km (1 mile) **TIME** 2 hours
START/END POINT The Tower Museum, Union Hall Place, near Magazine Gate ✚ 196 C4

This circuit of the city walls of Derry gives insight into the passion that divides society in Northern Ireland. The walk is best known, not so much for the historical interest or beauty of the 17th-century walls themselves as for the bitter emotions stirred up annually through-out the 1950s and 1960s when the Orange Order carried out its ritual Apprentice Boys' Marches around the circuit (▶182).

1–2

Walk into the old city through **Shipquay Gate**, and turn to your right to climb to the top of the walls by the Tower Museum in Union Hall Place. The walls of Derry, 6–8m (19–26 feet) tall and the same thickness, form a belt of solid stone that buckles the city into its high defensive position. They were built during 1613–18 by guilds from London that had taken over the running of the city and were

determined to see it properly protected against all potential enemies – chiefly local clans resistant to the rule of the British Crown. The walls created an enclave based on a cross of streets that ran from a diamond-shaped central marketplace – The Diamond – to four great gates: Shipquay Gate (northwest), Butcher's Gate (northeast), Bishop's Gate (southwest) and Ferryquay Gate (southeast). Three more gates were added later.

2–3

Set off southwest above **Magazine Street**, looking down on the tangled roofs of the walled city. Cross over **Castle Gate**, then **Butcher's Gate**. A little further along, pause on the **Royal Bastion**, a stout outward bulge, and look west across the roofs of the Bogside to the far-off hills of Donegal, a beautiful backdrop.

"No Sectarian Marches" says the house-wall graffiti in the Bogside, and "No Consent, No Parade". Other gable-end paintings put the

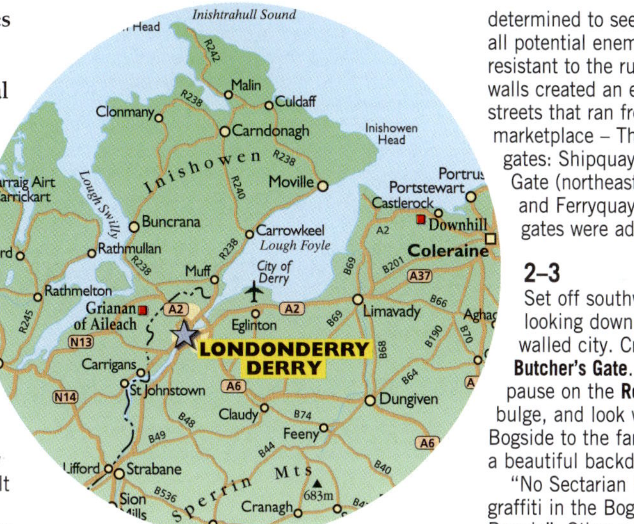

inhabitants' views on the police, army and politicians in graphic if unflattering style. Down on them frown the bastion cannon presented to the city in 1642. Up here stood Walker's Pillar, a great local landmark that offered wonderful wide views from the top until the IRA blew it up in 1973. The Apprentice Boys on their December marches would string up from the pillar an effigy of Robert Lundy, Governor of Derry during the Great Siege of 1688–89.

3–4

Walk on to **Bishop's Gate**, and climb down to admire the gate itself, rebuilt in classical style in 1789. Two local river gods, bearded and crowned with waterweeds, adorn its arch, Foyle looking out and Boyne looking into the city.

It was to Bishop's Gate that Britain's deposed Catholic King James II rode on 18 April, 1689,

Bearded river god, crowned with water weeds, on Bishop's Gate

to demand the surrender of 30,000 Protestants walled up inside Derry. The Great Siege began then; but the citizens of Derry had been locked in since the previous December, when the celebrated 13 Apprentice Boys seized the keys of the four gates and locked them against the Jacobite army.

4–5

Walk down Bishop Street Within, then right up St Columb Court, to reach **St Columb's Cathedral**, a veritable museum to the Great Siege. It was from the tower that the cry of "No Surrender!" was launched in response to King James's demands. Once Governor Robert Lundy had been ejected, the defenders found a champion in the formidable Reverend George Walker.

In the Chapter House are displayed the keys seized by the Apprentice Boys, brick cannon balls, and a portrait of George Walker in armour. In the church is a plaque to Captain Michael Browning, killed on 28 July, 1689, as his ship *Mountjoy* smashed through the boom built by the besiegers across the river, bringing relief supplies into the city. For 7,000 of the 30,000 defenders (who had eaten every dog, cat and rat in the place), it was too late. The cathedral's entrance hall contains a stand

Apprentice Boys' Marches

In the 1950s and 1960s, up to 15,000 Orangemen from all over Northern Ireland would turn up with flutes and lambeg drums to parade on the walls of Derry in full sight of the depressed and decaying Roman Catholic Bogside district below. Provocative triumphalism, said the Bogsiders; a celebration of history, responded the Orangemen. Tensions culminated in a riot in August 1969 that became known as the Battle of the Bogside. To get an idea of just how bad living conditions in the Bogside were for its Catholic residents, take a look at the black-and-white photographs on display in the Tower Museum at the end of your walk. They show barefoot children with rickets, ragged-trousered men and overtired women on slum streets in the shadow of derelict houses. These days, things are different. After a lengthy ban on the Apprentice Boys' parades, a small band of locals now performs the ritual march in August and December, to general indifference among the city's Catholics. Now the dust has settled, you can enjoy this stroll around the 17th-century walls.

holding the "First Air Mail Letter", an iron mortar bomb which was fired into the city with the Jacobites' surrender demands sticking out of its fuse hole.

Don't leave St Columb's without enjoying some of its other treasures: ancient regimental flags, carved pew-ends, the great oak tabernacle over the Bishop's chair, and the beautiful late Victorian "Garden of Gethsemane" window.

5–6

Return to Bishop Street Within and continue down to The Diamond. Turn right along Ferryquay Street to rejoin the walls at Ferryquay Gate. Complete your circuit, to finish at the **Tower Museum**. The museum was built as an act of faith and optimism

Martyrs' Mound

Outside the east end of the cathedral is the Martyrs' Mound, a green burial hump where 4,500 victims of the Great Siege lie. They were interred there a century after the siege, having been exhumed from the city cellars in which they had been hastily buried during the emergency.

Symbol of ancient defiance: 17th-century cannon line Derry's city walls

at the height of the Troubles when over a quarter of the walled city's buildings had been destroyed. It has amply repaid the vision. This is an excellent museum, taking you by way of curving "time tunnels" into various phases of Derry's history. The Troubles are not shirked, but given even-handed treatment.

Taking a Break

The **Dungloe Bar** in Waterloo Street is a good place to stop for a light lunch, and there is sometimes live music.

Places of Interest

Guildhall

Make sure you pop into the splendidly florid Victorian Guildhall. A bombing in 1972 destroyed the stained-glass windows, but by some miracle the original 19th-century watercolour designs had been preserved in London, and the windows were painstakingly reconstructed.

🕓 Mon–Fri 8:30–5

St Columb's Cathedral

☎ 028 7126 7313, www.stcolumbscathedral.org

🕓 Apr–Sep Mon–Sat 9–5; Oct–Mar Mon–Sat 9–1, 2–4

✋ Inexpensive

Tower Museum

☎ 028 7137 2411

🕓 Jul–Aug daily 10–4:30; Mar–Jun Mon–Sat 10–4:30; Sep–Feb Mon–Fri 10–4:30

✋ Moderate

6 STRANGFORD LOUGH

Tour

DISTANCE 160km (100 miles). This includes the 10-minute car ferry ride between Portaferry and Strangford (operates half-hourly)
TIME 1 day
START/END POINT Newtownards (on A20, 10km/6 miles east of Belfast) ✚ 197 F3

The 37km (23-mile) Ards Peninsula hangs down like an elephant's trunk east of Belfast. This narrow outpost of County Down shelters the great tidal inlet of Strangford Lough and all but encloses it. At its southern end, the ferry villages of Portaferry and Strangford face each other across a gap only 500m (550 yards) wide. Strangford Lough is home to millions of geese, ducks and wading birds: brent geese and arctic terns are two species that stop here on their annual migration. The peninsula's east coast, which faces out into the Irish Sea, has a run of huge sandy beaches interspersed with rocky coves. It's a beautiful place, unknown to most visitors to Ireland.

The ferry crosses Strangford Lough

1–2

Starting at **Newtownards** at the northern end of Strangford Lough, take A48 across the shoulder of the peninsula to the fishing village of Donaghadee, whose harbour was extended in the 1820s to cope with a flourishing ferry trade to Portpatrick in southwest Scotland.

Many famous people have stepped ashore or embarked at Donaghadee: among them are the poet John Keats, biographer James Boswell, composer Franz Liszt, writer Daniel Defoe, and Peter the Great, Tsar of Russia, who (locals will tell you) stayed at Grace Neill's pub in the High Street while touring Europe in 1697–98.

Follow A2 down the coast, admiring the fine beaches, to Ballywalter, where you strike inland along B5 to Greyabbey on the shore of Strangford Lough. There's the ruin of 12th-century **Grey Abbey** to explore here; then bear right up the A20 shore road to **Mount Stewart**. This splendid National Trust house, still lived in by a member of the Stewart family, feels warm and domestic notwithstanding the chandeliers and fine inlaid wood floors. Its gardens are among the National Trust's best, developed by Lady Londonderry from 1921 onwards in dashingly idiosyncratic style, and ornamented with weird stone sculptures of freakish beasts.

2–3

Return along A20 through Greyabbey and on south, stopping now and then to get out the binoculars and admire the **bird life** of

Water features are prominent in the beautifully kept gardens at Mount Stewart

Strangford Lough – godwit, redshank, curlew and plover, and in winter huge flocks of pale-bellied brent geese all the way from Greenland. At Kircubbin, weave your way back across the peninsula and continue your coast drive south through small fishing villages such as Ballyhalbert and Portavogie.

When you reach Cloghy, you can either carry on south to the rugged tip of the peninsula at Ballyquintin Point, or cut back again inland to Dorn on Strangford Lough, a national nature reserve and another excellent birdwatching spot. Either way, aim to end up at the pretty little port of **Portaferry**, where you catch the car ferry over the narrows to Strangford.

Crossing the mouth of Strangford Lough, you enter what is known as "St Patrick's Country". Here Ireland's patron saint is said to have landed in AD 432 on his great mission to convert the heathen Irish; and here in the abbey at the monastery of Saul he died in AD 461. It's worth spending a couple of hours cruising around the back roads of this quiet green landscape.

3–4

Follow A25 from Strangford to pass **Castle Ward**. The house, now a National Trust property, was built in 1762–68 by Bernard

Ward and his wife, Anne. He liked the Palladian style, she romanticism; and both wanted their own way. So Castle Ward has a graceful Palladian front and some tastefully furnished classical rooms, while around the back are Moorish windows, pinnacles, and rooms with extravagant pointed door arches and elaborate plasterwork fan vaulting. As for the ill-matched couple, they eventually separated.

Continue along A25 into **Downpatrick**. On a mound outside the cathedral lies a giant slab inscribed "PATRIC". Does St Patrick lie under this stone together with Ireland's other two major-league saints, Brigid and Columb? Historians say no: folklorists and others say yes, and strew the slab with daffodils on St Patrick's Day. It's a lovely spot, whatever the truth.

4–5

Two or three kilometres (2 miles) southeast of Downpatrick, signposted off the Ardglass road, you'll find **Struell Wells**, a curious and peaceful spot where ancient stone bathhouses conceal ice-cold springs in which Patrick is said to have immersed himself.

Return to Downpatrick, from where A22 takes you back north to Newtownards up the west shore of Strangford Lough. Spare time for a stroll along the waterside track at **Quoile Pondage National Nature Reserve** just outside Downpatrick, and be sure to detour out across the causeways to lonely little **Mahee Island**. Here you'll find a broken round tower, grave slabs of monks, ancient walls and hut foundations – relics of the 5th-century monastery of Nendrum, one of Ireland's earliest Christian foundations, where St Patrick is said to have preached.

A massive grave slab, which many people believe marks St Patrick's burial place, lies just outside Downpatrick Cathedral

Places to visit

Grey Abbey
✚ 197 F3 ☎ 028 4278 8585 🕙 Apr–Sep Tue–Sat 10–7, Sun 2–7; Oct–Mar Sat 10–4, Sun 2–4 ✋ Free

Mount Stewart
✚ 197 F3 ☎ 028 4278 8387; www.nationaltrust.org.uk 🕙 House: Jul–Aug daily noon–6; Jun daily 1–6; May and Sep Wed–Mon 1–6; early Mar–Apr and Oct Sat–Sun noon–6. Formal gardens: May–Sep daily 10–8; Apr and Oct daily 10–6; Mar daily 10–4. Lakeside gardens and walks: Daily 10–dusk. Temple of the Winds: Apr–Oct Sun 2–5 ✋ Moderate

Castle Ward
✚ 197 F3 ☎ 028 4488 1204; www.nationaltrust.org.uk 🕙 House: Jul–Aug daily 1–6; Apr–Jun and Sep Sat, Sun 1–6. Grounds: Apr–Sep daily 10–8; Oct–Mar 10–4 ✋ Moderate

Quoile Countryside Centre
✚ 197 F3 ☎ 028 4461 5520; www.ehsni.gov.uk/quoile 🕙 Apr–Aug daily 11–5; Sep–Mar Sat–Sun 1–5 ✋ Free

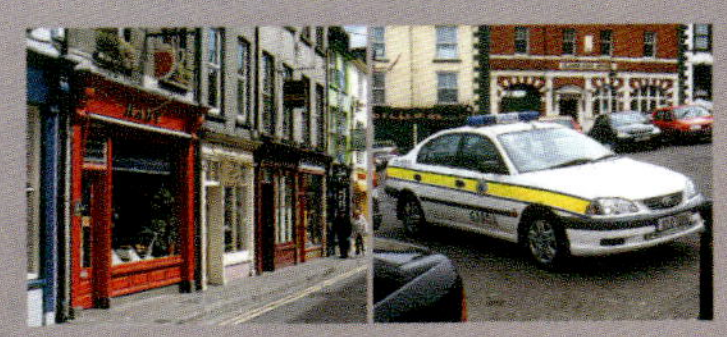

Practicalities

BEFORE YOU GO

WHAT YOU NEED

- ● Required
- ○ Suggested
- ▲ Not required

Some countries require a passport to remain valid for a minimum period (usually at least six months) beyond the date of entry – check before booking.

	UK	Germany	USA	Canada	Australia	Ireland	Netherlands	Spain
Passport/National Identity Card	▲	●	●	●	●	▲	●	●
Visa (regulations can change, please check)	▲	▲	▲	▲	▲	▲	▲	▲
Onward or Return Ticket	○	○	○	○	○	▲	○	○
Health Inoculations (tetanus and polio)	▲	▲	▲	▲	▲	▲	▲	▲
Health Documentation (► 192, Health)	●	●	●	●	●	▲	●	●
Travel Insurance	○	○	○	○	○	○	○	○
Driving Licence (national)	●	●	●	●	●	●	●	●
Car Insurance Certificate	●	●	n/a	n/a	n/a	●	●	●
Car Registration Document	●	●	n/a	n/a	n/a	●	●	●

WHEN TO GO

Dublin

High season   Low season

JAN	FEB	MAR	APR	MAY	JUN	JUL	AUG	SEP	OCT	NOV	DEC
46°F	46°F	50°F	55°F	59°F	64°F	68°F	66°F	63°F	57°F	50°F	46°F
8°C	8°C	10°C	13°C	15°C	18°C	20°C	19°C	17°C	14°C	10°C	8°C
Wet	Wet	Wet	Sun	Sun	Sun	Wet	Cloud	Cloud	Cloud	Wet	Wet

☀ Sun   ☁ Cloud   ☁ Wet

Temperatures are the **average daily maximum** for each month.

The best weather is in spring and early summer (April and June) when the countryside looks its best. Winter (November to March) can be dark, wet and dreary, especially in the mountainous west, but good-weather days can be magical. In high summer (July and August) the weather is changeable and often cloudy. Autumn (September and October) generally sees good weather. The cities are great places to visit at any time, regardless of the weather, and Christmas and New Year are particularly popular.

It will almost certainly rain at some time during your stay, no matter when you visit. Be prepared, but try to accept the rain as the Irish do, as a "wet blessing".

GETTING ADVANCE INFORMATION

Websites
- ● Tourism Ireland: www.discoverireland.com
- ● Northern Ireland Tourist Board: www.nitb.com

In the Irish Republic
Dublin: ☎ 1 850 230330; www.visitdublin.com
Tourism Ireland: ☎ 0800 039 7000

In Northern Ireland
Belfast: ☎ 02890 231221; www.gotobelfast.com
Tourism Ireland ☎ 0800 039 7000

GETTING THERE

By Air Scheduled flights operate from Britain, mainland Europe and North America to Dublin, Cork, Knock, Shannon and Belfast. **Aer Lingus** (tel: 0870 876 5000; www.aerlingus.com) operates services from London and regional UK airports, many European countries and the US. **Ryanair** (tel: 0871 246 0000; www.ryanair.com) flies to Dublin from all over Britain and **British Midlands Airways (bmi)** (tel: 0870 60 70 555; www.flybmi.com) from Heathrow to Dublin and Belfast. Check with your travel agent, the airlines or the Internet for details of other carriers. **Flying time to Dublin:** from mainland UK (1–2 hours), from Europe (2–4 hours), from USA/Canada (8–11 hours), from Australia/New Zealand (24-plus hours). **Flying time to Belfast:** from mainland UK (1–2 hours), from Europe (2–3 hours), from USA/Canada (8–11 hours), from Australia/New Zealand via London (24-plus hours).

By Sea Most ferry services **from Britain** arrive at Dun Laoghaire and Belfast. **Crossing times:** Holyhead–Dun Laoghaire (99 minutes by HSS); Holyhead–Dublin (3 hours 45 minutes, or under 2 hours by fast ferry); Fishguard–Rosslare (3 hours 30 minutes); Swansea–Cork (10 hours); Stranraer–Belfast (3 hours 30 minutes, or 1 hour by SeaCat, 1 hour 45 minutes by HSS); Cairnryan–Larne (2 hours 15 minutes, or 1 hour by Jetliner); Campbelltown–Ballycastle (3 hours). There are also services **from France** to the Republic: Roscoff–Cork (15 hours); Cherbourg–Rosslare (18 hours). **Ferry companies** operating services to Ireland are **Irish Ferries** (tel: 0870 5171717), **Stena Lines** (tel: 0870 5707070) and **Brittany Ferries** (tel: 08703 665333).

TIME

Ireland is on Greenwich Mean Time (GMT) in winter, but one hour ahead of GMT from late March until late October.

CURRENCY AND FOREIGN EXCHANGE

Currency The monetary units are (in the Republic) the Euro (€), and (in Northern Ireland) the pound sterling (£).

Euro: notes are issued in denominations of 5, 10, 20, 50, 100, 200 and 500 Euros, and **coins** in denominations of 1 and 2 Euros, and 1, 2, 5, 10, 20 and 50 Euro cents.

Pounds sterling: notes are issued in £5, £10, £20 and £50 denominations and **coins** in 1p, 2p, 5p, 10p, 20p, 50p, £1 and £2 denominations by the Bank of England, and in notes of £5, £10, £20 and £50 by the provincial banks. Provincial bank notes are not accepted in other parts of the UK. There are 100 pence in each pound.

Sterling or US dollar **travellers' cheques** are the most convenient way to carry money. All major **credit cards** are recognised.

Exchange Currency exchange bureaux are common in Dublin, Belfast, at airports, sea ports and some rail stations. They often operate longer hours but offer poorer rates of exchange than banks. Many banks have ATMs for cash withdrawals; check with your bank for details.

In mainland UK
☎ 0800 039 7000

In the USA and Canada
☎ 1-800-223-6470

In Australia and New Zealand
☎ 02 9299 6177 (Sydney)
☎ 09 977 2255 (Auckland)

WHEN YOU ARE THERE

CLOTHING SIZES

Australia/UK	Rest of Europe	USA	
36	46	36	Suits
38	48	38	
40	50	40	
42	52	42	
44	54	44	
46	56	46	
74	1	8	Shoes
7.5	42	8.5	
8.5	43	9.5	
9.5	44	10.5	
10.5	45	11.5	
11	46	12	
14.5	37	14.5	Shirts
1538	15		
15.5	39/40	15.5	
1641	16		
16.5	42	16.5	
1743	17		
834	6		Dresses
1036	8		
1238	10		
1440	12		
1642	14		
1844	16		
4.5	38	6	Shoes
53	8	6.5	
5.5	39	7	
63	9	7.5	
6.5	40	8	
74	1	8.5	

NATIONAL HOLIDAYS

1 Jan	New Year's Day
17 Mar	St Patrick's Day
Mar/Apr	Good Friday (RI)
Mar/Apr	Easter Monday/Easter Tuesday (NI)
First Mon May	May Holiday
Last Mon May	Spring Holiday (NI)
First Mon Jun	June Holiday (RI)
12 Jul	Orangeman's Day (NI)
First Mon Aug	August Holiday (RI)
Last Mon Aug	Late Summer Holiday (NI)
Last Mon Oct	October Holiday (RI)
25 Dec	Christmas Day
26 Dec	Boxing Day/St Stephen's Day

OPENING HOURS

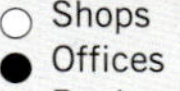
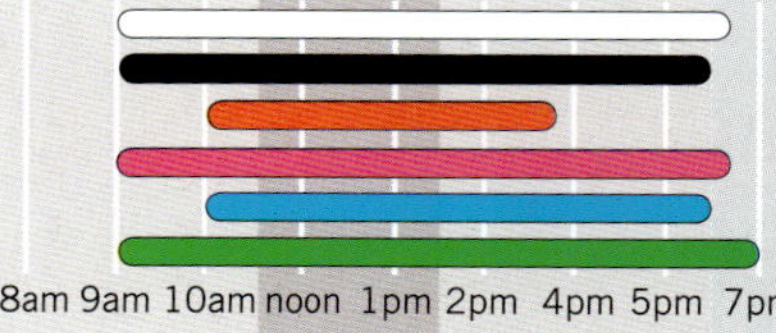

- ○ Shops
- ● Offices
- ● Banks
- ● Post Offices
- ● Museums/Monuments
- ● Pharmacies

8am 9am 10am noon 1pm 2pm 4pm 5pm 7pm

□ Day   ■ Midday   □ Evening

Shops Some open until 8 or 9pm on Thursday and Friday. Smaller towns and rural areas have an early closing day (1pm) on one day a week.
Banks Nearly all banks are closed on Saturday. In smaller towns they may close for lunch (12:30–1:30).
Post Offices In rural areas post offices may close for lunch (1–2).
Museums/Tourist Sites Hours vary. Many smaller places close Oct–Mar or have limited opening.

TIME DIFFERENCES

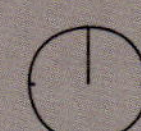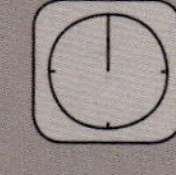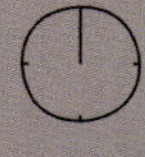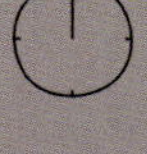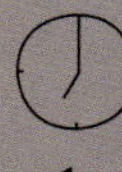

GMT	Ireland	London	USA (NY)	USA (West Coast)	Sydney
12 noon	12 noon	12 noon	7am	4am	10pm

PERSONAL SAFETY

The national police forces are:
RI – Garda Siochána
(pronounced *sheekawnah*) in black-and-blue uniforms.
NI – Police Service of Northern Ireland (PSNI) in dark green uniforms.

- Belfast is as safe as any modern city: observe your usual personal security precautions.
- Take care of personal property in Dublin.
- Avoid leaving property visible in cars.

Police assistance:
☎ **999** from any phone

TELEPHONES

Telephone boxes are: (RI) cream, or green-and-white; (NI) red,

or Perspex-and-metal booths. Payphones accept: (RI) 10, 20 and 50 cents and €1 coins; (NI) 10p, 20p, 50p and £1 coins. Callcards (RI) or phonecards (NI) are widely accepted, sold at post offices and newsstands. For the domestic operator, dial: (RI) 10; (NI) 100. For the international operator, dial: (RI) 114; (NI) 155.

International Dialling Codes
Dial 00 followed by

UK:	**44**
(from RI only; no code from NI)	
USA/Canada:	**1**
Australia:	**61**
Germany:	**49**
Spain:	**34**

POST

In the Republic, mail boxes and vans are painted green. You can buy stamps from post offices, machines or some newsstands. In the North, mail boxes and vans are red; British stamps are used and British postal rates apply.

ELECTRICITY

The power supply is: 230 volts (RI); 240 volts (NI).

Type of socket: 3-square-pin (UK type). Parts of the Republic also have 2-round-pin (continental type). Overseas visitors should bring an adaptor.

TIPS/GRATUITIES

Yes ✓ No ✗

Restaurants (service not included)	✓	10%
Bar service	✗	
Tour guides	✓	(RI) €3; (NI) £1
Hairdressers	✓	(RI) €3; (NI) £1
Taxis	✓	10%
Chambermaids	✓	discretion
Porters	✓	discretion
Lavatories	✗	

POLICE 999

FIRE 999

AMBULANCE 999

COASTAL RESCUE 999

HEALTH

Insurance
Citizens of EU countries receive free or reduced-cost emergency medical treatment with relevant documentation (European Health Insurance Card), although private medical insurance is still advised, and is essential for all other visitors.

Dental Services
EU nationals, or nationals of other countries with which Ireland has a reciprocal agreement, can get reduced dental treatment within the Irish health service with an EHIC card (not needed for UK nationals). Others should take out private medical insurance.

Weather
The sunniest months are May and June (average 5–7 hours of sun a day in the southeast), although July and August are the hottest. During these months you should "cover up", use a good sunscreen and drink plenty of fluids.

Drugs and Medicines
Prescription and non-prescription drugs are available from pharmacies. Pharmacists can advise on medication for common ailments. When closed, most pharmacies display notices giving details of the nearest one that is open.

Safe Water
Tap water is safe to drink. Mineral water is widely available but is often expensive, particularly in restaurants.

CONCESSIONS

Students Holders of an International Student Identity Card can buy a Travelsave Stamp which entitles them to travel discounts including a 50 per cent reduction on Bus Éireann, Iarnród Éireann and Irish Ferries (between Britain and Ireland). Contact a student travel agency for further details. The Travelsave Stamp can be purchased from USIT, 19–21 Aston Quay, O'Connell Bridge, Dublin 2 (tel: 01 602 1904).

Senior Citizens Discounts on transport and admission fees are usually available on proof of age.

TRAVELLING WITH A DISABILITY

Increasing numbers of hotels and other public buildings are being adapted or specially built to cater for travellers with disabilities. For information on travelling with a disability useful contacts are: National Disability Authority, 25 Clyde Road, Dublin 4 ☎ 01 608 0400; www.nda.ie. For Northern Ireland: Disability Action ☎ 028 9029 7880; www.disabilityaction.org.

CHILDREN

Well-behaved children are generally made welcome everywhere. Public houses operate individual admittance policies. In the North there are designated areas for children in most pubs. Concessions on transport and entrance fees are available.

LAVATORIES

Public lavatories are usually clean and safe. Some are coin-entry, others are free.

WILDLIFE SOUVENIRS

Importing wildlife souvenirs sourced from rare or endangered species may be illegal or require a special permit. Before purchase, you should check your home country's customs regulations.

EMBASSIES AND CONSULATES

UK	**USA**	**Australia**	**Canada**	**Germany**
01 205 3700 (RI)	01 668 8777 (RI)	01 664 5300 (RI)	01 417 4100 (RI)	01 269 3011 (RI)
	028 9032 8239 (NI)	020 7379 4334 (NI)	020 7258 6600 (NI)	020 7824 1300 (NI)

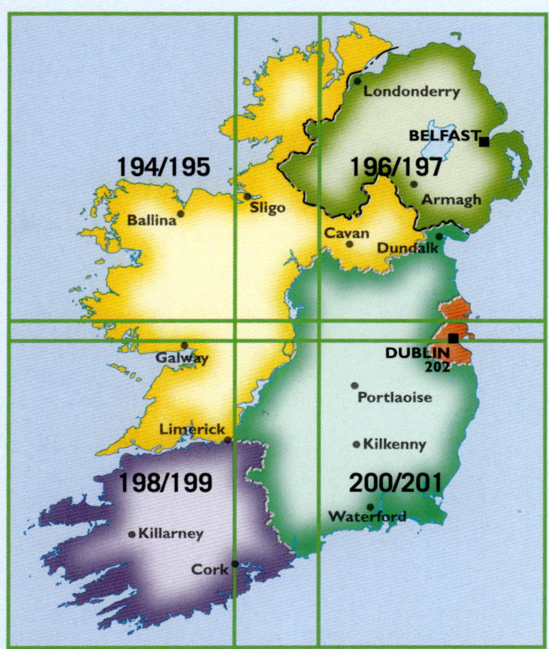

To identify the regions see the map on the inside of the front cover

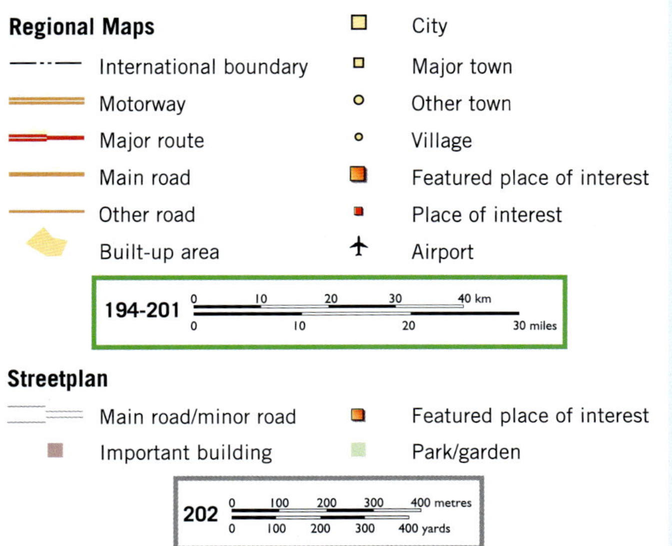

194
198
A
B
C
5
4
3
2
1
Barre na Binne Buí
Benwee Head
Ceann Iorrais
Erris Head
Beal an Mhuirthead
Belmullet
R314
Céide Fields
R313
Carrowmore Lake
Inis Gé Thuaidh
Inishkea North
Bun na hAbhna
Bunnahowen
Bangor Erris
Inis Gé Theas
Inishkea South
N59
Bellacorick
Cuan an Fhóid Dhuibh
Blacksod Bay
722m
Nephin Beg Mts
R312
672m
Slieve More
Achill Head
Keel
R319
N59
Lough Feeagh
R317
R312
Achill Island
8
Mulrany
Newport
R311
Clare Island
Clew Bay
Westport
N5
Louisburgh
R335
R330
R335
765m
Croagh Patrick
Murrisk
Aghagower
Inishturk
Caher Island
Killary Harbour
820m
Mweelrea
Inishbofin
Inishshark
Connemara Nat Park
Kylemore Abbey
N59
Leenane
673m
Loch Measca
Lough Mask
Letterfrack
Sléibhte Mhám Toirc
An Mám
Maum
An Fhairche
Clonbur
Omey Island
R344
Maumturk Mts
Connemara
Mannin Bay
Clifden
Na Beanna Bola
The Twelve Pins
Corr na Mona
Cornamóna
Ballyconneely
R341
R342
R340
N59
Oughterard
Roundstone
Glinsce
Glinsk
R340
Pearse's Cottage
An Más
Mace Head
Cill Chieráin
Kilkieran
Casla

D
E
F
195
Toraigh
Tory Island
Corrán Binne
Horn Head
Dunfanaghy
5
Cnoc Fola
Bloody Foreland
R257
R256
Creeslough
Milfo
Gabhla
Gola Island
R251
Kilmacrenan
Donegal
International
Croithlí
Crolly
Glenveagh
National Park
R251
Letterkenny
Árainn Mhór
Aran Island
R252
N11
An Clochán Liath
Dunglow
196
R250
N15
Béal an Bheara
Gweebarra Bay
R250
N56
R253
676m
Ballybofey
N15
4
Ardara
Glenties
R261
N56
Lough
Eask
Cas
Gleann Cholm Cille
Glencolumbkille
Folk Village
Mount
Charles
Donegal
Lough
Derg
Málainn Mhóir
Malin More
An Charraig
Carrick
N56
Killybegs
Dunkineely
R232
595m
Sliabh Liag
Slieve League
Ballintra
St John's Point
N15
Pettigo
Belleek
Pottery
Castle
Caldwell
AA7
Donegal Bay
Ballyshannon
Belleek
Lough
Erne
Wh
Figu
Inishmurray
Bundoran
A46
Cliffony
Kinlough
Creevykeel
Rosscor
Tully
Ca
Are
Grange
525m
Benbulbin
Garrison
B52
Lissadell House
N15
Lough
Melvin
B81
Derrygonnelly
Monea
3
Downpatrick Head
Drumcliff
Glencar
Waterfall
R280
R282
R281
B52
Enniskiller
Ballycastle
Easky
Rosses Point
Parke's
Castle
Manorhamilton
Belcoo
R314
Killala
Bay
Dromore
West
Sligo Bay
R291
Sligo
N16
Blacklion
A32
R315
Killala
Enniscrone
Strandhill
R292
Carrowmore
Lough
Gill
Dromahair
R286
R280
Marble Arch Caves
Moyne
Abbey
Ballysadare
R207
Florence Court
N59
Mts
Col
looney
R290
Drumkeeran
Dowra
Swanlinbar
Ballina
Bunnyconnellan
N4
R284
R280
R200
Crossmolina
Ox
R294
Ballymote
Castle
Baldwin
Lough
Allen
R207
R202
Lough
Conn
N26
R310
Tobercurry
N17
R296
Carrowkeel
Lough
Arrow
Ballyfarnan
R208
Ballinamore
Kil
807m
Foxford
N58
R315
Curry
R293
R295
Ballinafad
Keadue
Lough Key
Drumshanbo
N209
Fenagh
R201
Charlestown
Carracastle
Lough
Gara
Boyle
Leitrim
Lough
Cullin
Swinford
N5
Knock
International
N5
Ballaghaderreen
R361
Carrick-on-
Shannon
Lough
Boderg
Drumsna
Mohill
Turlough
Museum of Ireland -
Country Life
R325
Frenchpark
N61
N4
R202
Lough Rynn
House
Castlebar
Kiltimagh
R320
Kilkelly
N83
Loughglinn
R369
Dromod
Farnaght
Lo
Go
Balla
R324
Strokestown
Park House
Roosky
Ballyhean
N60
Knock
R323
R293
R325
R361
Drumlish
Ballintober
Abbey
Clonalis
House
Castlerea
Tulsk
R371
Newtown
Forbes
N5
Lough
Carra
Claremorris
Ballyhaunis
Ballinlough
N60
Castleplunket
Strokestown
Scramoge
R393
Partry
R331
R327
Ballymoe
Ballintober
Cloondara
Longford
N4
Ballindine
R328
R360
N60
196
Killashee
Ballinrobe
R362
Roscommon
R392
Ra
Kilmaine
R332
Dunmore
Glenamaddy
N17
R328
R362
Knockcroghery
Ballymahon
R345
R334
Shrule
Athleague
R362
Ballygar
R257
Lough
Ree
Tang
Tuam
N63
Ballykeeran
I
Headford
Curraghboy
R362
Kiltoom
Hodson's
Bay
Lough
Corrib
N84
R347
Mount
Bellew
R363
Dysart
R363
Aughnanure
Caltra
R358
Athlone
Moate
N6
Maigh
Cuilinn
N59
N17
199
R357
N6
N80
N6
R339
N62
N61
2
1

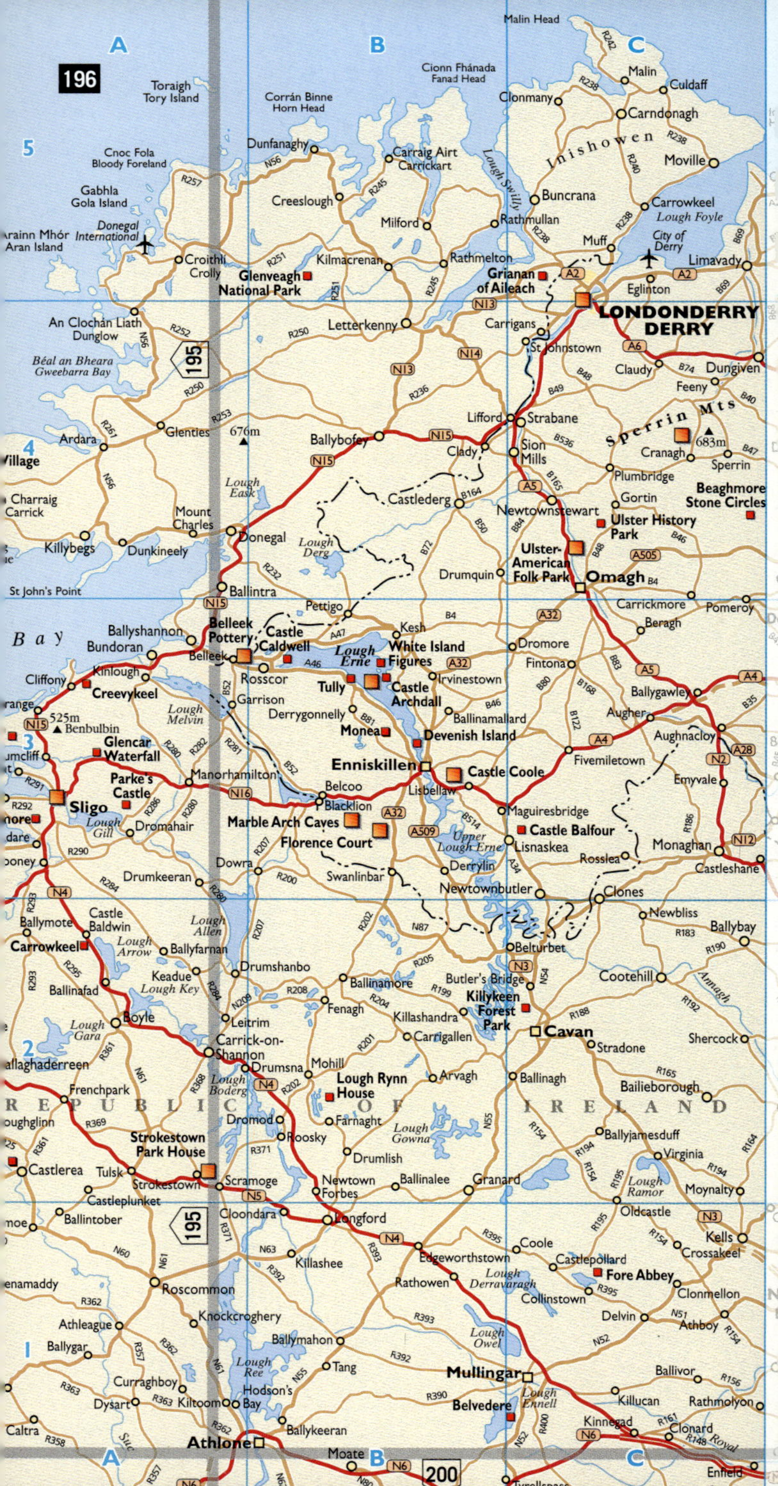
196
A
B
C
5
Malin Head
Toraigh / Tory Island
Corrán Binne / Horn Head
Cionn Fhánada / Fanad Head
Clonmany
Malin
Culdaff
Carndonagh
Inishowen
R242
R238
R238
R240
Moville
Cnoc Fola / Bloody Foreland
Dunfanaghy
Carraig Airt / Carrickart
Lough Swilly
Buncrana
Carrowkeel
Lough Foyle
Gabhla / Gola Island
Creeslough
Milford
Rathmullan
N56
Muff
City of Derry
B69
Árainn Mhór / Aran Island
Donegal International
Croithlí / Crolly
Kilmacrenan
Rathmelton
A2
Limavady
Eglinton
A2
B69
An Clochán Liath / Dunglow
Glenveagh National Park
R251
Grianan of Aileach
N13
LONDONDERRY DERRY
Letterkenny
Carrigans
R250
195
R252
N14
St Johnstown
A6
Claudy
B74
Dungiven
Béal an Bheara / Gweebarra Bay
R236
N13
Lifford
Strabane
Feeny
B40
Ardara
Glenties
676m
Ballybofey
N15
Clady
Sion Mills
B536
Sperrin Mts
683m
Cranagh
Sperrin
B47
Village
R253
N15
Castlederg
B164
B50
A5
B165
Plumbridge
Gortin
Beaghmore Stone Circles
Charraig / Carrick
Lough Eask
Lough Derg
B72
Newtownstewart
Ulster History Park
B46
Killybegs
Mount Charles
Donegal
Drumquin
Ulster-American Folk Park
A505
Omagh
B4
Dunkineely
R232
Lough Derg
Omagh
St John's Point
Ballintra
Pettigo
B4
Carrickmore
Pomeroy
Bay
N15
Kesh
Beragh
Ballyshannon
Belleek Pottery
Castle Caldwell
White Island Figures
Dromore
A32
Fintona
A5
Bundoran
Belleek
AA7
Lough Erne
A32
Rosscor
B83
Ballygawley
B35
Cliffony
Kinlough
Tully
Castle Archdall
Irvinestown
B80
B168
Augher
Creevykeel
B52
Garrison
Derrygonnelly
B81
Monea
B46
Devenish Island
B122
A4
Aughnacloy
A28
N15
525m
Lough Melvin
Enniskillen
Emyvale
N2
Benbulbin
Glencar Waterfall
R282
R281
B52
Belcoo
Lisbellaw
Castle Coole
Fivemiletown
R291
Manorhamilton
N16
Blacklion
A32
A509
Castle Balfour
R186
N12
Parke's Castle
Marble Arch Caves
Upper Lough Erne
Lisnaskea
Sligo
Lough Gill
Dromahair
Florence Court
B514
Maguiresbridge
Rosslea
Monaghan
Castleshane
R292
R290
Drumkeeran
Dowra
R207
R200
Swanlinbar
Derrylin
Newtownbutler
Clones
Newbliss
Ballybote
Castle Baldwin
Lough Allen
R207
N87
Belturbet
R183
Ballybay
Carrowkeel
Lough Arrow
Ballyfarnan
R205
Butler's Bridge
N3
R190
Ballinafad
Keadue
Lough Key
Drumshanbo
Ballinamore
R199
Killykeen Forest Park
Cootehill
R192
Boyle
R209
R208
R204
Killashandra
Cavan
Shercock
Leitrim
Fenagh
R201
Carrigallen
Stradone
Frenchpark
Carrick-on-Shannon
Drumsna
Mohill
Arvagh
Ballinagh
R165
Bailieborough
allaghaderreen
N61
R368
Lough Boderg
N4
R202
Lough Rynn House
N55
Ballyjamesduff
Virginia
R164
oughglinn
R369
Dromod
Farnaght
Lough Gowna
R154
Ballinalee
R194
Strokestown Park House
Roosky
Drumlish
R195
Lough Ramor
Moynalty
Castlerea
Tulsk
Strokestown
Scramoge
Newtown Forbes
Granard
R154
Oldcastle
N3
Castleplunket
195
R371
Cloondara
Longford
N5
R395
Coole
Kells
Ballintober
N63
Killashee
N4
Edgeworthstown
Castlepollard
Crossakeel
N60
N61
Fore Abbey
Roscommon
R392
Rathowen
Lough Derravaragh
R395
Clonmellon
enamaddy
R362
Knockcroghery
R393
Collinstown
Delvin
N51
Athboy
Athleague
R257
R362
Ballymahon
Lough Owel
R156
Ballygar
N61
Tang
Ballivor
Curraghboy
Lough Ree
Mullingar
Killucan
Rathmolyon
Dysart
R363
Kiltoom
Hodson's Bay
Belvedere
Lough Ennell
Kinnegad
R161
Clonard
Caltra
R358
R362
Ballykeeran
N52
R400
N6
Royal
Athlone
Moate
200
N6
Enfield
N80
Tyrrellspass

197
201
D
E
F
Rathlin Island
Inishowen Head
Giant's Causeway
White Park Bay
Carrick-a-Rede
Fair Head
Torr Head
Ballycastle
Portrush
Portstewart
Castlerock
Bushmills
Old Bushmills Distillery
B15
B67
B15
Downhill
Armoy
Glendun
Cushendun
Coleraine
A37
A2
B201
B66
B190
B64
B17
A29
A26
B15
Red Bay
Cushendall
Glenariff (Waterfoot)
Garron Point
Aghadowey
Ballymoney
Dunloy
B14
A44
Glenariff
Garvagh
Kilrea
Rasharkin
A26
Carnlough
Glenarm
Maghera
Draperstown
Portglenone
Culleybackey
Ahoghill
Ballymena
438m
Ballygalley
Ballygalley Head
Gulladuff
Bellaghy
Moorfields
A42
A36
Larne
Island Magee
Stranraer
NORTHERN IRELAND
Magherafelt
Randalstown
Kells
B59
B94
A8
B100
B149
Ballycarry
Troon (summer only)
Cairnryan (summer only)
Fleetwood
Moneymore
A31
Ballyronan
Antrim
Ballynure
Ballyclare
B58
Whitehead
Liverpool Douglas (summer only)
Springhill
Coagh
M22
A6
M2
Carrickfergus
Cookstown
A29
B520
B161
Ardboe Cross
Belfast International
Crumlin
Lough Neagh
Glenavy
A52
Holywood
Newtownabbey
Bangor
A2
Donaghadee
Donaghmore Cross
Stewartstown
Mountjoy
BELFAST
Belfast City
M5
A55
Newtownards
Mount Stewart
Comber
Greyabbey
Ballywalter
Coalisland
Dungannon
B12
A26
Lisburn
Mazetown
M1
B39
B23
Carryduff
A24
A21
Ballygowan
Strangford Lough
Grey Abbey
Kircubbin
The Argory
Ardress House
Portadown
Craigavon
Lurgan
Hillsborough
Saintfield
A7
Killyleagh
Portavogie
Benburb
Caledon
Armagh
Moy
A3
Gilford
A1
Dromore
B177
A49
Ballynahinch
Quoile Pondage
Portaferry
Navan Royal Site
St Patrick's Trian
Tandragee
Banbridge
B7
Inch Abbey
Castle Ward
Strangford
Middletown
Markethill
B3
Loughbrickland
B10
A50
Clough
A25
Downpatrick
Keady
Poyntzpass
A27
A25
Ardglass
Killough
Newtownhamilton
A28
A1
Rathfriland
Castlewellan
Dundrum
St John's Point
N2
R181
Hilltown
Drumena Cashel
Newcastle
Newry
B8
Mourne Mts
852m Slieve Donard
Castleblayney
Narrow Water
Warrenpoint
Annalong
Crossmaglen
A29
Omeath
Rostrevor
B27
Kilcurry
N53
Carlingford
Kilkeel
Dundalk
Greencastle
Carrickmacross
Dundalk Bay
Dún a' Ri Forest Park
Kingscourt
N2
Castlebellingham
Drumconrath
Ardee
R165
M1
Dunany Point
Monasterboice
Carlanstown
Collon
Termonfeckin
Mellifont Abbey
Slane
R166
Knowth
Dowth
Drogheda
Navan
Newgrange
Laytown
Bective Abbey
Duleek
Hill of Tara
Balbriggan
Trim
Boyne
Garristown
Naul
Skerries
Dunshaughlin
N3
Ballyboghil
Lusk
Rush
Summerhill
Fairyhouse
Newbridge
Dublin
Lambay Island
Kilcock
Dunboyne
Malahide
Portmarnock
Maynooth
M4

194
198
A
B
C
5
4
3
2
1
Glinsce
Glinsk
Cottage
An Más
Mace Head
Cill Chiaráin
Kilkieran
Leitir Móir
Lettermore
Casla
Costelloe
Leitir Mealláin
Lettermullan
Garumna
Gorumna Island
An Spidéal
Spiddal
R336
An Sunda ó Thuaidh
North Sound
Inis Mór
Inishmore
Galway
Black
Dún Aonghasa
Dunaengus
Cill Rónáin
Kilronan
Newtown
Oileáin Árann
Aran Islands
Inis Óirr
Inisheer
Inis Meáin
Inishmaan
R477
Lisdoonvarna
R478
The
Doolin
Cliffs of Moher
Liscanor
Ennistymon
Hags Head
N67
Mal Bay
Milltown Malbay
R460
Mutton
Island
Doo Lough
Doonbeg
Donegal Point
Cooraclare
N68
Kilkee
R483
Kilrush
N67
R466
R487
N67
Loghil
Loop Head
Tarbert
Mouth of the
Shannon
Ballylongford
R551
Glin
Ballybunion
Glin
Castle
R553
Ballyduff
Listowel
Kerry Head
Causeway
Feal
R555
Ballyheige
R551
N69
Abbeyfeale
N21
Ballyheige
Bay
Kilkinlea
Mulla
M
Rough
Point
Ardfert
357m
R576
Brandon
Bay
Tralee
Bay
Tralee
Stacks Mts
Ceann Baile Dháith
Ballydavid Head
An Clochán
Cloghane
R560
N21
Castleisland
953m
Brandon Mtn
828m
Beenoskee
Camp
852m
N22
R571
Scartaglen
R578
Gallarus
Oratory
Kilmalkedar
Church
Slieve Mish Mts
N70
N23
Dún Chaoin
Dunquin
R559
Anascaul
N86
Farranfore
R561
Ballydesmond
An Blascaod Mór
Great Blasket
Island
An Daingean
Dingle
Castlemaine
R561
Kerry County
R582
Ceann Trá
Ventry
Milltown
Ceann
Sléibh
Slea Head
Killorglin
N72
Rathmore
Glenbeigh
N70
Laune
Killarney
N72
Dingle Bay
Lough
Caragh
Lough
Leane
Muckross
Doulus Head
1041m
Carrauntoohil
Killarney
National
Park
Muckross
House
Poulgorm
Bridge
Valencia
Island
774m
Mullaghanattin
Cahersiveen
Derrynasaggart
Mts
Portmagee
R565
Macgillycuddy's Reeks
R568
N71
Kilgarvan
R569
An Coireán
Waterville
Staigue
Fort
Sneem
RING OF KERRY
Kenmare
Béal Átha an
Ghaorthaidh
Ballingeary
N70
Tahilla
R571
N71
Sceilg Mhichíl
Skellig Michael
Ceann Bhólais
Bolus Head
Cathair Dónall
Caherdaniel
R573
707m
Knockboy
R584
Lee
Castlecove
Kenmare River
Lauragh
R585
Derrynane
An Scairbh
Scariff Island
Ardgroom
R571
Glengarriff
Caha Mts
R574
Garinish
Island
Bandon
Cod's
Head
Adrigole
R572
Bantry
Dunmanway
R586
Dursey
Island
Allihies
R575
686m
Castletown
Bearhaven
R572
Durrus
N71
Drimoleague
Bear Island
Bantry Bay
R593
Leap
N71
Muntervary or
Sheep's Head
Dunmanus Bay
Ballydehob
Castle
Mizen Head
Signal Station
Schull
R591
Skibbereen
Glandore
Goleen
Toormore
R592
R595
Mizen Head
Crookhaven
Roaringwater Bay
Baltimore
Toe Head
Sherkin Island
Cape
Clear
Oileán Cléire
Clear Island
Fastnet
Lighthouse

195
199
200
D
E
F
Caltra
R339
R358
Suc
Ballykeeran
Athlone
R362
Moate
N6
N62
N80
Doon
Clara
Maigh Cuilinn
Moycullen
Bushypark
N59
N17
Ballybric
N6
Galway
GALWAY
N6
Oranmore
Athenry
Turoe Stone
N6
Ballinasloe
N6
Clonmacnoise
Shannonbridge
Blackwater Bog
Clonfert
Ferbane
Charlevi
Grand Canal
Clonony
Cloghan
Banagher
Kilcormac
Cadamstown
Kinnitty
Birr
R440
Birr Castle
Bay
Clarinbridge
Kilcolgan
Craughwell
R349
N18
Loughrea
N66
N65
Killimor
Eyrecourt
R356
Clonony
R357
R357
R138
R489
Head
Dungory Castle
Kinvarra
Thoor Ballylee
▲368m
R353
Portumna
Carrigahorig
Castle
Ballyvaughan
Aillwee Caves
Coole Park
Gort
Lough Cutra
Carrigahorig
N52
N62
R421
Slieve Mt
Mount
Castleto
Burren
N67
R480
Slieve Aughty Mts
R352
Borrisokane
N65
200
N62
R421
Kilfenora
R460
Lough Graney
R493
Roscrea
N7
Borris-in-Ossory
R435
Corofin
N18
R461
Crusheen
Mountshannon
Scarriff
Lough Derg
Portroe
Borrisokane
Moneygall
R490
N7
O'Dea's Castle
R476
N85
R532
Tulla
533m▲
▲462m
Nenagh
Toomyvara
Rathdowney
Ennis
R474
R462
Craggaunowen Project
Killaloe
N7
R497
R499
Templemore
R501
R502
Johnstown
R435
Clarecastle
R469
Knappogue
Ballina
694m
Borrisoleigh
R503
Thurles
R690
Urli
Newmarket-on-Fergus
Sixmilebridge
Cloonlara
Newport
R503
R498
N62
R690
Killadysert
N18
N19
Bunratty Castle & Folk Park
Shannon
River Shannon
LIMERICK
N7
Holycross
Foynes
N69
N20
Patrickswell
R512
R506
R661
N8
Ballingarry
Askeaton
R518
Adare
Lough Gur
N24
R497
R661
R505
Rock of Cashel
Killenaule
Rathkeale
Croagh
Croom
Herbertstown
Pallas Green
Golden
Cashel
R689
R523
N21
R520
R518
R512
R513
Tipperary
N74
Bansha
Fethard
Newcastle West
R515
Galbally
918m▲
N24
3 721m
Slievenama
R515
Kilmallock
R513
Galty Mts
Cahir
N76
hareirk
ts
▲409m
Charleville
R515
R517
Swiss Cottage
Clonmel
Kilsheelan
Dromcolliher
N20
517m▲
Ballyhoura Hills
Mitchelstown
Ballyporeen
R665
Comeragh Mts
Ca
o
Newmarket
R576
R522
Buttevant
R522
N73
Kildorrery
R665
Cloghleen
Knockmealdown Mts
792m▲
R577
Kanturk
R576
Annes Grove
653m
Bally-macarbry
Banteer
N72
Castletownroche
Ballyduff
N72
Mount Melleray Abbey
727m▲
Lemybrien
R583
Blackwater
Mallow
429m▲
Fermoy
R668
Millstreet
Boggeragh Mts
646m▲
R579
Rathcormack
Tallow
Tallowbridge
Dungarvan
N72
R582
N20
Watergrasshill
R626
R627
Blackwater
Clashmore
An Rinn Ring
N22
Macroom
R618
Blarney Castle
Blarney
N8
Old Midleton Distillery
Killeagh
Youghal
2 Mionn Ard
Mine Head
Kilmichael
Crookstown
CORK
Passage West
Carrigtohill
N25
Midleton
Castlemartyr
Youghal Bay
R584
N22
Douglas
Cork
Fota Island
Cloyne
Shanagarry
Ballinhassig
N28
Cobh
Whitegate
Ballycotton
Cross Barry
R613
Ringaskiddy
R587
R585
Bandon
N71
Inishannon
Crosshaven
200
R586
R589
Dunderrow
R611
Belgooly
Kinsale
Swansea (not winter)
R602
R599
Timoleague
R600
Ballinspittle
Roscoff (summer only)
Clonakilty
R600
Courtmacsherry
Rosscarbery
Butlerstown
Old Head of Kinsale
Drombeg
Clonakilty Bay
ownshend
Galley Head
D
E
F

Caltra
R358
Suc
Athlone
Ballykeeran
R362
196
Moate
N6
Enfield
Clonard Royal
R148
N6
N6
200
Ballinasloe
N6
Doon
Clara
Kilbeggan
Tyrellspass
Edenderry
Donadea
Forest Park
R400
R401
R402
Clonmacnoise
Blackwater
Bog
Shannonbridge
Grand Canal
Ferbane
R436
Tullamore
Charleville
Daingean
Grand
R402
Robertstown
R403
Clonfert
R357
R357
Clonony
Cloghan
N52
Killeigh
N80
Bracknagh
Rathangan
R419
R414
Kilmeage
Eyrecourt
R356
Banagher
Kilcormac
Clonaslee
Portlaoise
Portarlington
R423
Monasterevin
R422
Curragh
Kildare
Killimor
N65
N52
Shannon
199
R438
Cadamstown
R421
R422
Mountmellick
R422
M7
Irish National Stud/
Japanese Gardens
N78
Portumna
R489
Birr
R440
Kinnitty
Fontstown
Carrigahorig
Birr Castle
Slieve Bloom Mts
Portlaoise
Stradbally
R417
Athy
Moone
Borrisokane
R493
R65
Mountrath
Castletown
R440
N8
Timahoe
Ballylynan
R418
N9
Kilkea
Lough Derg
Roscrea
N7
Borris-in-Ossory
Ballyroan
Abbeyleix
Ballinakill
N78
N80
Castledermot
Arless
Portroe
R490
Moneygall
R435
Newtown
R430
462m
Nenagh
Toomyvara
Rathdowney
Durrow
R432
Carlow
Brownshill
Dolmen
N7
Templemore
N7
Ballyragget
Castlecomer
N9
Leighlinbridge
Newport
R497
R499
R501
Johnstown
R693
Oldleighlin
R724
R503
Borrisoleigh
R498
Urlingford
R690
Dunmore
Caves
Bagenalstown
Myshall
Thurles
R690
Kilkenny
Paulstown
R705
Holycross
R661
N62
R689
N10
Gowran
Barrow
R506
N8
R660
Ballingarry
R691
Bennettsbridge
Borris
Gur
N24
R691
Killenaule
Callan
Kells
Abbey
N10
Dungarvan
Blackstairs Mt
732m
Pallas Green
R497
R505
Golden
Rock of Cashel
Cashel
R689
R690
Stonyford
N9
Graiguenamanagh
Tipperary
N74
Bansha
Fethard
Knocktopher
Thomastown
Inistioge
St Mullin's
R515
N24
R688
Slievenaman
721m
Ballyhale
Jerpoint
Abbey
R700
R705
N30
Galbally
918m
Cahir
N76
Ormond
Castle
Mullinavat
Glenmore
R704
New Ross
R513
Galty Mts
Swiss Cottage
Clonmel
Kilsheelan
N24
N9
N25
R733
John F Kennedy
Arboretum
N8
Ballyporeen
Clogheen
R671
792m
Carrick-
on-Suir
R680
WATERFORD
Dunbrody
Abbey
Kildorrery
R665
Knockmealdown
Mts
Bally-
macarbry
653m
Kilmeadan
Passage
East
Ballyhack
Fermoy
R659
Mount Melleray
Abbey
727m
Kilmacthomas
Waterford
Crystal
Waterford
R684
Duncannon
Fethard
Ballyduff
N72
Lemybrien
Kill
Tramore
R685
Dunmore East
Tallowbridge
N72
Bunmahon
Slade
Tallow
Dungarvan
Hook Head
R626
R627
R634
Clashmore
An Rinn
Ring
Mionn Ard
Mine Head
Old
Midleton
Distillery
Killeagh
Youghal
N25
Carrigtohill
N25
Midleton
Castlemartyr
Youghal
Bay
Fota Island
Cloyne
Shanagarry
Cobh
Whitegate
Ballycotton
Crosshaven
199
Swansea (not winter)
Roscoff
(summer only)

197
201
D
E
F
5
4
3
2
1
Summerhill
Canal
R156
Fairyhouse
Newbridge
Dublin
Lambay Island
Kilcock
Dunboyne
M1
Malahide
Portmarnock
M4
Maynooth
Howth
Castletown House
Lucan
Howth Castle
Celbridge
M50
St Anne's Park
DUBLIN
Clondalkin
Clane
R407
Rathcoole
N7
Dun Laoghaire
Sallins
Tallaght
James Joyce Tower
Brittas
R114
Leopardstown
Dalkey
Killiney
M7
Punchestown
Naas
M11
Newbridge
R81
Enniskerry
Bray
Ballymore
Blessington
Powerscourt
M9
Eustace
Poulaphouca Reservoir
Kilmacanoge
Kilcullen
Russborough House
R759
Greystones
Hollywood
R758
848m
R755
N11
Newtownmountkennedy
Mullaghcleevaun
818m
Tonelagee
R756
Roundwood
R764
R761
Ballitore
R412
Wicklow
N81
Glendalough
Laragh
Mount Usher
927m
Ashford
Rathnew
Lugnaquillia
Mts
R752
Wicklow
Baltinglass
Rathdrum
Wicklow Head
R747
Rathvilly
Hacketstown
R755
Avondale
Brittas Bay
R727
Aughrim
R753
R754
R750
Avoca
Tullow
Woodenbridge
Mizen Head
R747
Tinahely
R747
Arklow
Ballon
R725
Shillelagh
R748
N11
Kildavin
Carnew
Kilmichael Point
R746
Gorey
Bunclody
R725
Courtown Harbour
R746
Ferns
Ballycanew
Kiltealy
Cahore Point
R702
Enniscorthy
R741
R744
R742
Clonroche
Blackwater
R730
N11
Oilgate
Wexford or North Bay
Slaney
Irish National Heritage Park
Castlebridge
N25
Ferrycarrig
Wexford Wildfowl Reserve
Johnstown Castle
Wexford
R733
N25
Rosslare
Waddingtown
Killinick
Duncormick
Rosslare Harbour
R736
Bridgetown
Lady's Island Lake
Fishguard
Pembroke
Ballyteige Bay
R739
Tacumshane
Kilmore Quay
Carnsore Point
Roscoff (summer only)
Cherbourg
Saltee Islands
Douglas (not winter)
Liverpool
Holyhead

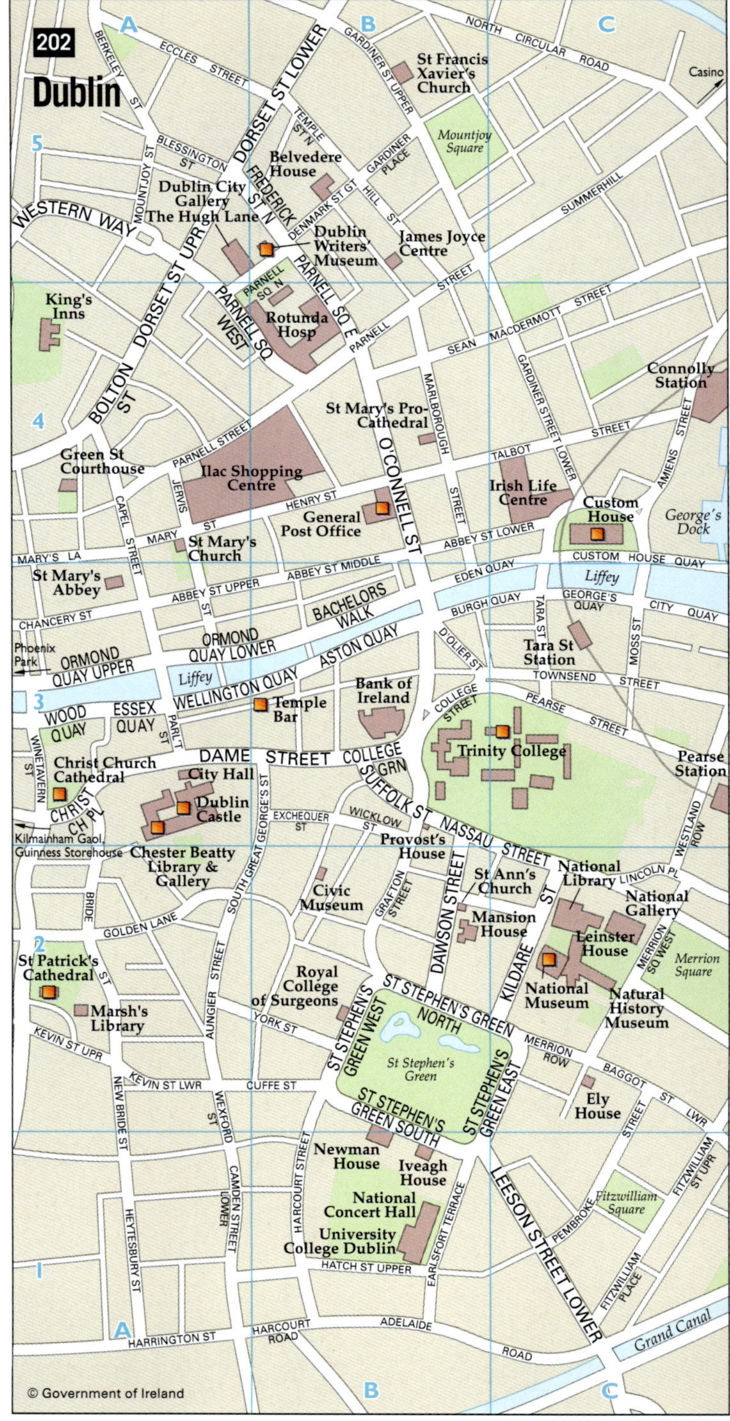

202
Dublin
Berkeley St
Eccles Street
Blessington St
Mountjoy St
Western Way
Dorset St Upr
Dorset St Lower
Frederick St N
Temple St N
Gardiner St Upper
Gardiner Place
North Circular Road
Casino
St Francis Xavier's Church
Mountjoy Square
Summerhill
Belvedere House
Dublin City Gallery The Hugh Lane
Denmark St Gt
Hill St
Dublin Writers' Museum
James Joyce Centre
Parnell Sq N
Parnell Sq E
Gardiner Street Lower
King's Inns
Bolton St
Parnell Sq West
Rotunda Hosp
Parnell Street
Sean MacDermott Street
Connolly Station
Green St Courthouse
Parnell Street
Ilac Shopping Centre
Jervis St
Capel Street
St Mary's Church
Mary St
Mary's La
Henry St
General Post Office
O'Connell St
St Mary's Pro-Cathedral
Marlborough Street
Gardiner Street Lower
Talbot Street
Irish Life Centre
Amiens Street
Custom House
George's Dock
St Mary's Abbey
Chancery St
Abbey St Upper
Abbey St Middle
Abbey St Lower
Custom House Quay
Liffey
Ormond Quay Lower
Bachelors Walk
Eden Quay
Burgh Quay
George's Quay
City Quay
Moss St
Phoenix Park
Ormond Quay Upper
Liffey
Wellington Quay
Aston Quay
D'Olier St
Tara St
Tara St Station
Townsend Street
Wood Quay
Essex Quay
Winetavern St
Temple Bar
Bank of Ireland
College Street
Pearse Street
Pearse Station
Christ Church Cathedral
Christ Ch Pl
Dame Street
City Hall
College Grn
Suffolk St
Nassau Street
Trinity College
Kilmainham Gaol, Guinness Storehouse
Dublin Castle
South Great George's St
Exchequer St
Wicklow St
Provost's House
Westland Row
Lincoln Pl
Chester Beatty Library & Gallery
Bride St
Golden Lane
Civic Museum
Grafton Street
St Ann's Church
Dawson Street
Kildare St
National Library
National Gallery
Merrion Sq West
St Patrick's Cathedral
Marsh's Library
Aungier Street
York St
Mansion House
Leinster House
National Museum
Natural History Museum
Merrion Square
Kevin St Upr
Kevin St Lwr
Cuffe St
Royal College of Surgeons
St Stephen's Green West
St Stephen's Green North
St Stephen's Green
St Stephen's Green East
Merrion Row
Ely House
Baggot Street Lwr
New Bride St
Wexford Street
Harcourt Street
St Stephen's Green South
Newman House
Iveagh House
National Concert Hall
University College Dublin
Earlsfort Terrace
Leeson Street Lower
Pembroke Street
Fitzwilliam Square
Fitzwilliam St Upr
Heytesbury St
Camden Street Lower
Hatch St Upper
Fitzwilliam Place
Harrington St
Harcourt Road
Adelaide Road
Grand Canal
© Government of Ireland

Picture credits

Abbreviations for terms appearing below: (t) top; (b) bottom; (l) left; (r) right; (c) centre.

The Automobile Association wishes to thank the following photographers, libraries and associations for their assistance in the preparation of this book.

2t AA/S McBride; 2c AA/C Jones; 2c AA/S Day; 2b AA/M Short; 3t AA/D Forss; 3c AA/C Coe; 3c AA/C Coe; 3b AA/L Blake; 5l AA/S McBride; 5c AA/S Day; 5r AA/C Jones; 6-7 Chris Hill/Scenic Ireland; 7c AA/S Day; 8-9 Michael Cooper/Getty Images; 9 Julian Herbert/Getty Images; 10 Chris Hill/Scenic Ireland; 11 Chris Hill/Scenic Ireland; 12 AA/S Day; 13 Joe Fox/Alamy; 15t Mary Evans Picture Library; 15c Mary Evans Picture Library; 15b Mary Evans Picture Library/Mary Evans ILN Pictures; 17t Niall Carson/PA Archive/PA Photos; 17c Rui Vieira/PA Archive/PA Photos; 17b AA/C Coe; 18 The Print Collector/HIP/TopFoto; 19 Topical Press Agency/Getty Images; 20 AA/C Jones; 21 Paul Faith/AFP/Getty Images; 22-23 AA/L Blake; 24 Leon Farrell/Photocall Ireland; 26 Sergio Pitamitz/Corbis; 27 OSD Photo Agency/Rex Features; 28 Tony Kyriacou/Rex Features; 29 David Sanger Photography/Alamy; 31 David Lyons/Alamy; 32 Chris Hill/Scenic Ireland; 33l AA/C Jones; 33c AA/C Jones; 33r AA/C Jones; 45l AA/S Day; 45c AA/S Day; 45r AA/S McBride; 46 AA/S Whitehorne; 48cr AA/S Day; 48b AA/S Day; 49 AA/S Day; 51 The Board of Trinity College, Dublin, Ireland/The Bridgeman Art Library; 52t AA/S McBride; 52b Illustrated London News; 53 AA/S McBride; 54 National Museum of Ireland, Dublin, Ireland/Boltin Picture Library/The Bridgeman Art Library; 55 AA/S Day; 56 National Museum of Ireland, Dublin, Ireland/Boltin Picture Library/The Bridgeman Art Library; 57 AA/S Whitehorne; 58/59 AA/S Whitehorne; 60 AA/S Day; 62 Slide File; 63 AA/S Day; 64 AA/S Day; 71l AA/M Short; 71c AA/C Jones; 71r AA/M Short; 74c AA/M Short; 74b AA/C Coe; 75 Arco Images GmbH/Alamy; 76 Chris Hill/Scenic Ireland; 78 Waterford Crystal Ltd; 80 AA/C Jones; 81 AA/P Zollier; 82 AA/C Jones; 82/83 AA/C Jones; 83 AA/C Jones; 84 AA/C Coe; 85 Irish National Heritage Park; 86 AA/S McBride; 87 AA/D Forss; 88 AA/C Jones; 93l AA/D Forss; 93c AA/S Hill; 93r AA/J Blandford; 96 AA/C Jones; 97 AA/C Jones; 98c AA/C Jones; 98b AA/C Jones; 99 AA/C Jones; 100 AA/S McBride; 101 AA/S McBride; 102/103 AA/S McBride; 102 AA/S Hill; 104/105 AA/C Jones; 105 AA/C Jones; 106 AA/C Jones; 107 AA/C Jones; 108 David Kilpatrick/Alamy; 109 AA/S Hill; 110 David Noton Photography/Alamy; 111 AA/P Zollier; 112 AA/D Forss; 119l AA/C Coe; 119c AA/S Hill; 119r Paul Lindsay/Scenic Ireland; 121t AA/C Coe; 121b AA/S Day; 122c AA/M Diggin; 122b AA/S Hill; 123t AA/C Coe; 123b AA/C Hill; 124 AA/S Hill; 125 David Woodfall/NHPA; 126 AA/S McBride; 127 Robert Thompson/NHPA; 128 AA/S Hill; 129 AA/S Hill; 130 AA/L Blake; 131 AA/C Jones; 132 AA/C Coe; 133 AA/L Blake; 134 AA/P Zollier; 135 AA/S McBride; 136 AA/M Diggin; 137 AA/I Dawson; 138 AA/C Coe; 145l AA/C Coe; 145c AA/C Coe; 145r AA; 148c Chris Hill/Scenic Ireland; 148b AA/G Munday; 149 Chris Hill/Scenic Ireland; 150 AA/C Coe; 151 AA/C Coe; 152 AA/C Coe; 153 Joe Fox/Alamy; 154 AA/C Coe; 155 National Trust NI/John Lennon; 156 AA/C Coe; 157 AA/C Coe; 158 AA/C Coe; 159 AA; 160 AA/J Johnson; 161 AA/C Coe; 162 AA/G Munday; 163 AA/G Munday; 164 AA/C Coe; 171l AA/L Blake; 171c AA/C Coe; 171r AA/M Short; 173 AA/S Whitehorne; 174 AA/C Jones; 175 Ross Hoddinott/Nature Picture Library; 177 AA/L Blake; 179c AA/C Coe; 179r AA/C Hill; 182 AA/C Coe; 183 David Lyons/Alamy; 184 AA/I Dawson; 185 AA/G Munday; 186 AA/G Munday; 187l AA/C Jones; 187c AA/C Jones; 187r AA/I Dawson; 191t AA/C Jones; 191cl AA/C Jones; 191c AA/C Jones.

Acknowledgements

The author would like to thank John Lahiffe and Katrina Doherty of the Irish Tourist Board for their help during the research of this book.
Extract from *Decline and Fall* by Evelyn Waugh (Copyright © Evelyn Waugh 1928) on page 32 reproduced with kind permission of Peters, Fraser & Dunlop on behalf of the Evelyn Waugh Trust Extract on page 32 from *An Evil Cradling* by Brian Keenan, published by Hutchinson. Reprinted by permission of The Random House Group Ltd.

SPIRALGUIDE
Questionnaire

Dear Traveller

Your comments, opinions and recommendations are very important to us. Please help us to improve our travel guides by taking a few minutes to complete this simple questionnaire.

You do not need a stamp (unless posted outside the UK). If you do not want to remove this page from your guide, then photocopy it or write your answers on a plain sheet of paper.

Send to: The Editor, Spiral Guides, AA World Travel Guides, FREEPOST SCE 4598, Basingstoke RG21 4GY.

Your recommendations...

We always encourage readers' recommendations for restaurants, night-life or shopping – if your recommendation is used in the next edition of the guide, we will send you a FREE AA Spiral Guide of your choice. Please state below the establishment name, location and your reasons for recommending it.

____

____

____

____

____

Please send me AA Spiral _______________________

(see list of titles inside the back cover)

About this guide...

Which title did you buy?

____ **AA Spiral**

Where did you buy it? _______________________________

When? m m / y y

Why did you choose an AA Spiral Guide? ________________

____

____

____

Did this guide meet your expectations?

Exceeded ☐   Met all ☐   Met most ☐   Fell below ☐

Please give your reasons _____________________________

____

____

____

continued on next page...

Were there any aspects of this guide that you particularly liked?

____

____

____

____

____

Is there anything we could have done better?

____

____

____

____

About you...

Name (Mr/Mrs/Ms) ____

Address ____

____

____ **Postcode** _______________

Daytime tel no ___________________________ **email** _______________

Please *only* give us your email address and mobile phone number if you wish to hear from us about other products and services from the AA and partners by email or text or mms.

Which age group are you in?

Under 25 ☐   25–34 ☐   35–44 ☐   45–54 ☐   55–64 ☐   65+ ☐

How many trips do you make a year?

Less than one ☐   One ☐   Two ☐   Three or more ☐

Are you an AA member? Yes ☐   No ☐

About your trip...

When did you book? mm/ y y   When did you travel? mm/ y y

How long did you stay? ____

Was it for business or leisure? _______________________________________

Did you buy any other travel guides for your trip?   ☐ Yes   ☐ No

If yes, which ones? ____

____

Thank you for taking the time to complete this questionnaire. Please send it to us as soon as possible, and remember, you do not need a stamp (unless posted outside the UK).